W9-DFK-886

HELPING THE AGING FAMILY

A Guide for Professionals

Victoria E. Bumagin
Kathryn F. Hirn

SPRINGER PUBLISHING COMPANY
New York

WARNER MEMORIAL LIBRARY
EASTERN COLLEGE
ST. DAVIDS, PA. 19087

2-6-97

Copyright © 1990 Victoria E. Bumagin and Kathryn F. Hirn.

All rights reserved.

Published by Springer Publishing Co.

1 2 3 4 5 / 94 93 92 91 90

Library of Congress Cataloging-in-Publication Data

Bumagin, Victoria E.
   Helping the aging family: a guide for professionals/Victoria E. Bumagin
and Kathryn F. Hirn.
     p.   cm.
   Includes bibliographical references.
   ISBN 0-8261-7530-9
   1. Social work with the aged—United States.   2. Family social work—
United States.   3. Aged—United States—Family relationships.
   1. Hirn, Kathryn F.   II. Title.
HV1461.B85   1990b
362.6'0973—dc20   90-44784
                                                CIP
Printed in the United States of America.

HV 1461 .B85 1990b
Bumagin, Victoria E.
Helping the aging family

Preface

In recent years the field of aging has discovered the importance of families, and the field of family treatment has begun to discover aging as a fact of life. We can no longer speak of "the aged" as one entity and "families" as another. Old people continue to be members of families, and families span many generations. The old, the middle-aged, and the young are involved with each other in mutual concern and, sometimes, mutual confusion and dismay. Longer life for more people means that relationships, with their gratifications and conflicts, continue over a long span of years and are likely to be affected by the frailties to which the aged are often vulnerable. What is experienced by one generation has repercussions on all the others.

Emergence of the Multigeneration Family

The longevity revolution has changed the face of the American family. Three- and four-generation families have become commonplace rather than a rarity, but multigeneration families do not usually live under one roof. They may, in fact, live at great distances from one another. However, most old people who have living children are in frequent contact with at least one of them, and more than 80 percent of the assistance elders receive comes from their families, sometimes augmented by help from friends and neighbors.

Individuals grow and change in the course of their life span as they encounter and attempt to master various life tasks. One of the complications of family life is that different individuals are dealing with different developmental tasks simultaneously, and these tasks impact on each other. The parental nurturing role, for instance, takes a different form with infants, schoolchildren, teenagers preparing to leave home, or young adults starting their own families. Later, the parents may struggle with the need to accept help from these same children, now perhaps middle-aged or retired. Illness may shift critically the balance of a marriage or the relationship of grandparents to grandchildren. The meanings of change, to individuals and within the family, have great influence on the coping strategies used in dealing with change. Individuals carry within themselves the lessons learned as they grew up as family members; therefore, the family context remains relevant, whether they are dealing with individual persons or groups inside or outside the family circle. The family is still there, perhaps invisible but real. Thus, even when we are discussing interventions with individuals, it must be remembered that we assume a family context.

As the interplay of roles and life tasks affects family development, so the interplay of biological, psychological, and social factors affects individual development. The course of development throughout the life span is another name for the aging process.

An Interdisciplinary Approach to the Helping Process

When aging families seek help, or when individuals seek help with problems of aging, they may turn to a variety of potential helpers. Doctors, nurses, social workers, the clergy, service organizations, or recreational centers may be approached, depending on the focus and definition of the problem for which help is sought. This is a natural result of the fact that aging is a physio-psycho-social process with many interrelated manifestations. If, for instance, Aunt Mary is feeling lonely because she wanted to join her friends for an inexpensive lunch followed by a bingo game at their senior nutrition site, but she can't get there because her arthritis prevents her from taking the bus, is her problem physical, emotional, social, nutritional, or financial? It is, of course, all of them in combination. None can be effectively addressed without taking the others into account.

The physio-psycho-social nature of human development and aging means that those who study and intervene with its various aspects must work together if they are to be effective. An interdisciplinary, collaborative approach is needed rather than a multidisciplinary, parallel process.

This book is meant to be useful to members of all the helping professions who work with the aging. We have used various designations and titles for these helpers. Some of them are generic, such as professional, practitioner, or human service worker. Others are specific to particular disciplines or functions, such as physician, social worker, nurse, counselor, case manager, or therapist. We have usually referred to the persons being served as "clients," because this is a more inclusive term than "patients." However, we do use "patient" in the context of health problems or health care settings. In referring to clients past the age of sixty or sixty-five, we call them "aged," "elders," "older persons," "elderly," and "old" more or less interchangeably.

A Dynamic Approach to Assessment and Intervention

To understand the needs of an aging individual or an aging family, practitioners need a comprehensive physio-psycho-social assessment. People are in constant interaction with their physical and social environments, and this includes the professionals who work with them. Assessment and intervention are, therefore, interactive processes. They include relationships between clients and professionals and what the professionals as well as the clients bring to them. However, living persons are not static figures to be examined at leisure. To borrow a metaphor from the arts, professionals must view their clients not as still life paintings but as video portraits. We refer to this approach as "dynamic assessment," a process that continues throughout the course of intervention.

Skillful interviewing is essential to dynamic assessment and intervention. For this reason we have devoted much attention to the interviewing process with individuals and families and, to a lesser extent, with groups. Part One discusses the early stages of intervention: the interactive approach; the dynamics of interviewing with individuals, families, and groups; assessment guidelines; and the principles of counseling. Part Two discusses ongoing work with specific problems: physical decline, socially distressing behavior, cognitive loss, bereavement, and depression. Part Three discusses the problems of termination and various means of evaluating the success of interventions, both completed and in process.

Throughout the book there is an emphasis on the importance of hope, both in the client and in the professional. Without hope the client can have no motivation for improvement. Discouraged clients can, however, develop hope through experiencing realistic hopefulness in their professional helpers. The degree of hopefulness in the professional is therefore often the critical factor in successful intervention.

We have used many vignettes and case examples to illustrate the intervention process. They were drawn from actual practice but have, of course, been disguised to protect the privacy of the originals. We have given these people names rather than initials in order to make their experiences more real to the reader.

The intervention process is carried on by real people—both clients and professionals. We hope this book will prove to be a useful guide to those engaged in it.

Acknowledgments

The path that led to the writing of this, as well as our previous book, began when we worked together in the then newly developing field of gerontology. We responded to the excitement of discovery—and the lack of time to talk about it during work hours—by sharing in writing the ideas, diagnostic impressions, insights, and anecdotes that filled our thoughts and sent us in hungry pursuit of new knowledge and new applications of what we knew.

This search gave us the opportunity to read and listen to innumerable colleagues who were breaking new ground in research and practice. We are now proud to number among our friends those who have most directly influenced our thinking and enriched our understanding. Although we did not involve them in the writing of our book, we were prompted by the respect, admiration, and affection which we have for them, and we thank David Gutmann, Donna Cohen, and Carl Eisdorfer for stimulating, challenging, and unknowingly driving us on.

Sheldon Tobin has been a facilitator and source of support for many years. He and Lisa Gwyther honored us with their thoughtful reviews of the manuscript, which strengthened both the book and our appreciation of the richness of our collegial resources.

We are especially grateful to A. Jean Lesher, Executive Editor at Scott, Foresman and Company, for her vision and enthusiasm in developing the Series on Aging which inspired us to complete the manuscript in record time.

V.E.B.
K.F.H.

This book is dedicated to our clients, colleagues, and loved ones, who have taught us most of what we know about family life and aging.

Contents

PART ONE

Initial Encounters between Clients and Professional Helpers

CHAPTER 1

The Old Person in Interaction with the Environment: Practice Implications

Two eighty-year-old women live next door to each other in very similar apartments. Both are widows; both have frequent contact with their children; both have fairly serious physical disabilities; both live on their Social Security income with few other assets. But there the similarity ends. One apartment is full of family pictures and the handiwork of its occupant; the other is virtually bare of all but basic furniture. One woman has an extensive telephone network and a smile for all visitors; the other stares out the window all day and has little good to say of her neighbors. In Eriksonian terms one seems to personify "ego integrity"; the other, "despair" (Erikson, 1963).

Why? What determines success or the lack of it in the accomplishment of developmental tasks in early or late life?

To what extent do the vicissitudes of early development persist in old age?

Do late-life losses cause personality change?

Can changing the environment compensate for social or physical losses and/or personality deficits?

Can "successful aging" be predicted and/or arranged for?

If personality deficits interfere with ability to cope, to what extent can coping skills be restored or newly developed in middle age or later?

3

What constitutes "treatability" in old age?

These are the questions that concern human service practitioners as they struggle to devise effective interventions with elderly people and their families.

As the numbers of people over sixty-five increase, their diversity becomes more obvious. They include the very wealthy and the desperately poor, the gregarious and the isolated, the healthy and the frail, the generous and the selfish, those who find life fascinating and those who are bored and bitter. Many older Americans, especially those over eighty, have physical or mental disabilities that cause them to need help with some aspects of daily living. Contrary to the prevalent belief that the old are abandoned and ignored, most of the help they receive is provided by their families, friends, and neighbors. Some have such severe disabilities or such a meager social network that they can be cared for only in institutions. However, the majority of older persons, even those in their eighties or nineties or above, live in the community and are as likely to be care providers as care receivers (American Association of Retired Persons, 1984).

It is important for human service practitioners, who are apt to see people in crisis, to be aware of the diversity and strength of the older population. Otherwise, they will not be able to assess the extent of support and adaptive capacity that exists or can be drawn upon in working with those who are facing serious problems. Before we can determine what interventions are appropriate, we need to look at the nature of human personality: how it develops, what factors promote or retard growth, and how the individual interacts with his or her social and physical environment.

Personality Development

It is an axiom of developmental psychology that the infant becomes a human being (that is, socialized) by living in a nurturing environment that includes both adequate, consistent care for its physical needs and the loving interest of those who provide the care. In other words, those babies thrive who are held, cuddled, and smiled at by their mothers and mother surrogates (Bowlby, 1969, 1973, 1980; Mahler, Pine, and Bergman, 1975; Winnicott, 1965). In the progression from infancy through childhood and adolescence, a person will thrive in an environment that changes to meet his or her changing needs. The expectation is that the person whose needs have been adequately met will then be able to provide nurture to the next generation and contribute to the environment through productive work, and that these accomplishments will give personal satisfaction.

DEVELOPMENT IN CHILDHOOD

Studies of child and adolescent development have attempted to gain a more precise understanding of how the social and physical environment facilitates growth in order to define the optimum environment and to determine how a less-than-optimum environment can be modified. Such studies have taken into account the fact that many children whose environments as a whole were far from ideal were nevertheless able to use whatever opportunities were provided and to achieve far more than their childhood experiences would have led anyone to predict. On the other hand, there are some children whose early environments appear quite benign but who are unable to make much use of them. These discrepancies fuel the ongoing controversy about whether inborn characteristics or environmental factors are more important in the outcome of human development. Nevertheless, most observers would agree that neither operates unilaterally. Therefore, clinical interventions with children who are deprived, disabled, or disturbed generally include both environmental modifications and efforts to help the child use these modifications. Yet it is impossible to say with certainty which children will respond to intervention and which will not.

ADULT DEVELOPMENT

Studies of adult development are more recent and less extensive than those of childhood development. A great deal of research in aging has focused on "life satisfaction"—what it is and how it can be predicted. Yet as more than one researcher has pointed out, these studies, even in combination, are not very conclusive. In general, they find that people who are healthy, are married, have good incomes, and are engaged in many activities tend to report higher life satisfaction than those who are not. This is hardly surprising. Yet even in this fortunate population more variances are unexplained than are accounted for (Cutler, 1979; Ryff, 1982; George, 1986).

Another source of information about what it is that enables a person to enjoy his or her life lies in previous history. How have earlier experiences affected the ability to deal with present events? As with the two women described at the beginning of this chapter, circumstances do not seem to account fully for the elusive quality of "life satisfaction."

One question that has been raised and to some extent explored is whether any particular kind of loss or trauma makes a person especially vulnerable to other losses. Colin Murray Parkes's studies of bereavement indicate that there is a high correlation between the first year of widowhood and illness (Parkes, 1972; Parkes and Weiss, 1983). He believes that the emotional stress of losing a spouse makes one more vulnerable to illness, accidents, and even premature death. Other students of aging have hypothesized that physical illness itself is what makes coping with other losses most difficult (Busse, 1980; Busse and Blazer, 1980). Still others caution against considering the external factors of loss as sole explanations for inadequate or unhappy functioning, and they suggest that psychological development and societal norms determine the timing and success of growth and adaptation to change (Gutmann, 1987). Nonetheless, many of the changes affecting the old are experienced as losses.

Perhaps the most dreaded of all the possible deficits that may accompany aging is cognitive loss, often followed by change in personality. When memory fails, how can one continue to be the same person one has been throughout life? Can one be a person at all? The nightmare of the death of the personality, while the body it inhabited lives on, haunts those who contemplate old age. This includes not only the old persons but their families as well. Reassuring statistics on the relative infrequency of cognitive loss or personality change are little comfort to the person who wonders, "But what if it happens to me?" The possibility of becoming totally unaware of one's surroundings, unable to recognize even one's closest associates, and uncertain of how to cope can make even minor forgetfulness terrifying. How can one cope with other stresses if the coping mechanism itself is out of commission? Paradoxically, the fear of total disability often generates refusal to recognize the existence of any deficits whatsoever and may lead families and even physicians to believe that pathological personality change has in fact occurred.

Research on life satisfaction in old age has attempted to define what is typical, normal, or desirable in the hope of establishing norms for what can be expected in the later years. Yet even if this is accomplished, it does not assure anyone of a "normal" old age or provide guidelines on what can be done if one's life does not go according to plan.

Nevertheless, there is increasing recognition that in the old as in the young personality and environment do not exist independently but in dynamic interaction (Wendley and Schiedt, 1980). In reacting to the physical and social environment, a person modifies it and is affected by it. For instance, a shy person may not respond to the conversation of others. When that happens, the others stop trying to talk to her, and she retreats even further into her shell of isolation. Another person may provoke withdrawal in others by being abrasive and disagreeable in his dealings with them or by manifesting bizarre behavior. In its extreme form such behavior may be regarded as antisocial or "crazy." As D. W. Winnicott (1965, p. 218) put it so succinctly, "Mental illness consists in not being able to find anyone who can stand you." Or he might have added, it consists of not being able to find anyone you can stand.

Services as Compensation for Loss

In recent years attempts to compensate for some of the most commonly anticipated deficits of aging have been made by establishing a varied scope of services for the aged, which are considered to be a form of treatment. Subsidized housing, meals on wheels, home health care, and day care for the physically or mentally impaired are a sample from a long list. Yet those who administer such services are well aware that many old people in need of help do not make use of it even when it is available. Even more confusing, they may accept service from one source but not from another, although the services offered appear comparable. And service providers, if they are honest, will readily admit that some people are much easier to help than others. The degree of ease or difficulty depends not so much on the extent of need as on the nature of the interaction between provider and client.

In order for the service to be effective, therefore, the user must be able to accept what the provider has to offer. The analogy of a hook and eye may be useful here. Both the hook and the eye are equally essential; neither can function alone. In the same way, no matter how abundant the resources may be, the individual must be able to "hook" into them in order to get any benefit.

Making use of the formal service network is only one example of such ability. Again, we may recall the next-door neighbors described at the beginning if this chapter. Although both women had about the same kinds of resources available, one made fuller use of them. We could say that she had more "hooks" in her environment than her neighbor did.

But why do some people have more "hooks" than others? Furthermore, if the ability to make use of one's environment is or has become deficient, can it be developed or restored in later life? The issues of growth potential and life satisfaction are thus closely linked to the question of treatability.

The Past in the Present

One method commonly used to predict the course of future growth is the study of the individual's past. Interaction with those in one's environment occurs not only in the here and now but also on a time continuum. Today's reactions are conditioned by the cumulative effect of repeated experience in similar or apparently similar situations. Although the tasks that typically confront the members of each age group vary as they progress through the stages of life, each individual's basic coping style tends to persist over time. It is this combination of unfolding development throughout the life course and the durability of the individual's unique style that makes for the infinite variety of human personality.

To understand these unique characteristics and the problems with which the aged are wrestling, professionals must view each individual in terms of previous history, present coping skills, and the effect environmental influences have had on them. It is important to remember that the helpers themselves, whether they are family, professionals or paraprofessionals, are a part of the environment with which the client is interacting; and as such they become potential facilitators of the client's growth and adaptation. It is no less important, however, to remember that they, too, are reacting and interacting. Practitioners are not unmoved movers or unaffected observers. In other words, it is as true in human ecology as it is in physics that the measurement of phenomena affects the phenomena measured (Capra, 1975; Mahoney and Arnoff, 1978).

Estimating Treatability

It has been frequently documented that the elderly receive fewer mental health services than other segments of the population (Butler and Lewis, 1982; German, Shapiro, and Skinner, 1983; Buckwalter, 1988). They are less likely to have emotional problems identified during medical examinations and less likely to be referred to psychiatrists or other mental health professionals even when such problems are identified. The tendencies of current cohorts of elderly to see emotional problems as a stigma or sign of weakness or to be unable to get to the settings where treatment is offered probably account for some of this underutilization. However, mental health professionals themselves have tended to see the elderly as unpromising candidates for treatment (Wilensky and Barmack, 1966; Garfinkel, 1975; Greene, 1986).

It is often supposed that personalities become more rigid with advancing years—less open to new experiences, less able to adapt to change of any sort. While this is true of some individuals, it is more a factor of personality than of chronology. Yet the stereotype of old age being equivalent to rigidity is so built into the language that those who exhibit openness are called "young at heart"; younger people who are extremely resistant to any variation may be called "old before their time."

Sigmund Freud, the founder of psychoanalysis, believed that people beyond the age of fifty would be unlikely to benefit from his method of treatment (Kahana, 1978). Ironically, Freud himself continued to teach and write for thirty years after passing his fiftieth birthday. Although he modified many of his other ideas, his belief in the rigidity of the older personality was unaffected. And although psychoanalysis as a treatment of choice has fallen out of favor in recent years, Freud's attitude toward the aged as intractable patients has persisted among many of the followers as well as the opponents of Freudian theories and methods.

Along with expectations of rigidity, there is often the assumption that the emotional problems encountered in old age are biologically based and therefore irreversible, or that the deficits of aging have left the personality so depleted that the only possible intervention is that of changing the structure of the external environment. The old person is not seen as capable of interacting with or affecting his or her environment—only as someone to be rescued. Therefore, intervention may be seen as doing something *to* the environment rather than engaging *with* the person to help him or her make fuller use of all available resources, both internal and external. But it is precisely such enabling efforts that comprise the most valued help for aged persons: a realistic set of responses to the physical conditions in the client's situation and a focused examination and counsel to ease internal stress and facilitate adaptation.

In recent years the ability of older people to respond to counseling and psychotherapy has been well documented (Sandler, 1978; Herr and Weakland, 1979; Butler and Lewis, 1982; Gwyther, 1986; Thompson and Gallegher, 1986). Psychosocial and environmental interventions need not be mutually exclusive. On the contrary, they are often most effective in combination and in conjunction with appropriate medical intervention. Nevertheless, the effectiveness of any intervention varies from person to person.

What, then, does determine treatability? Who is the most likely to benefit from intervention, and of what kind? Or to return to our original question, what factors make for the realization of the individual's potential for growth and change?

FACTORS IN TREATABILITY

The Ripple research study done at the University of Chicago in 1956 attempted to address the question of treatability by studying a sample of people who actually continued in treatment and a sample who dropped out after fewer than five interviews (Ripple, Alexander, and Polemis, 1964). By analyzing the content of initial social work interviews in three agencies, they concluded that what governs treatability (as measured by continuation in treatment) is a combination of three factors: motivation, capacity and opportunity.

Motivation is a mixture of discomfort over one's situation and hope that something can be done about it.

Capacity refers to the individual's current coping skills as well as the personal history of how earlier life situations were dealt with.

Opportunity refers to the range of resources available to the person, particularly to those offered by the helping organization to which he or she has applied.

Motivation and capacity, therefore, are what the individual brings; opportunity is what the helping agent provides. Together they constitute a special instance of the hook-and-eye type of interaction that has the potential for facilitating growth.

The Element of Hope. The Ripple study further concluded that an important aspect of opportunity was the amount of confidence demonstrated by (in this case) the social worker who conducted the interview. If the worker felt strongly that the problem was workable and that agency service could contribute to its resolution, the client was much more likely to continue in treatment. That seems almost too obvious to be worth stating. We all know that confidence generates confidence and that nothing succeeds like success. The question might have been stated in another way: Why did some workers have a strong sense of hopefulness but others did not? Was it confidence in their own abilities? In the efficacy of agency service? In the client's potential? Hope is not generated in a vacuum; it is always based on something. We might hypothesize that those workers who demonstrated optimism perceived a good match between their own skills, the clients' needs, and the appropriateness of their agency's services for that particular situation. The worker's perception then influenced the clients' self-perception and enabled them to acquire new ways of making use of available resources, external or internal, and perhaps even to advance beyond their previously achieved levels of development.

In older persons, the level of hope may be affected not only by the individual's personality and situation but also by societal expectations that old age is a time of inevitable losses and little reason to hope for improvement. Professionals need to be sensitive to this, remembering that their task is to reinforce hope, not to quench it. As long as anything can be changed for the better, there is always a basis for realistic hope. However, professionals must also beware of automatically discounting elders' expressed feelings of hopelessness. To do so will only convince potential clients that their true plight has not been understood.

The Professional as Facilitator of Growth. This extended discussion of the importance of realistic hope in the professional practitioner should not lead anyone to infer that professionals are the only or the chief facilitators of growth in the elderly or in anyone else. Growth begins in the mother-infant dyad and expands through the multiple interactions and changing tasks of childhood, adolescence, adulthood, and old age. It is only when something goes wrong that the professional is called in.

Mr. Bracey, sixty-six, was a professional man; Mrs. Bracey worked part-time as a bookkeeper. They had a comfortable income, owned their home, had many friends and activities. Their only son was married and living in another state but maintained close contact by telephone and by visits several times a year. Despite some problems Mr. and Mrs. Bracey were both basically in good health. Then, both were severely injured in an automobile accident. Mr. Bracey's injuries were more serious and required extensive hospitalization and several surgeries. When he was finally able to return home, he was confined to a walker and needed both physical therapy and assistance with most tasks of daily living. Mrs. Bracey, although her injuries had been less extensive, was depleted in energy and felt overwhelmed by the responsibility for her husband's care. Their Medicare benefits were exhausted and huge medical bills had eaten into their assets.

Mrs. Bracey was quite resourceful in locating services. One of the agencies she turned to provided physical therapy in a day-care center and offered some household help at home. When the social worker visited to discuss these services, Mrs. Bracey confided that she was feeling terribly inadequate and fearful of having a nervous breakdown. She had always been a rather timid, fearful person who had felt that her husband was the stronger one. Now that she needed to be in charge, she was terrified.

The social worker acknowledged the validity of these feelings and pointed out what a good job Mrs. Bracey was doing in spite of them. She then asked if Mrs. Bracey might like to have some additional discussions of this kind on a regular basis. At first, Mrs. Bracey acknowledged that that might give her some relief, but then she hesitated. Wouldn't that just be a sign of further weakness on her part?

The worker pointed out that, on the contrary, if Mrs. Bracey could use the comfort of confiding in someone to tide her over until she could develop more confidence, it would be a sign of strength and further evidence of her resourcefulness. Mrs. Bracey seemed reassured, but as the worker was getting ready to leave, she said, "But you didn't answer my question. Am I having a nervous breakdown?" The worker replied that she saw no evidence of it. Mrs. Bracey persisted, "Would you tell me if you did?" "Certainly, I would," the worker replied. "I'd be pulling out all stops trying to get you to a hospital." Mrs. Bracey breathed a sigh of relief.

The point of this illustration is that the professional must take account of both service needs and feelings in order to help someone to remobilize his or her resources. Giving Mrs. Bracey an opportunity to discuss her fears without giving any practical assistance would not enable her to cope more effectively and might even reinforce her feelings of inadequacy. On the other hand, the provision of services would not, in itself, relieve her fears. In combination, she could use both the services and the counseling to help her move toward a new and more realistic perception of her abilities.

In this instance the worker was able to identify and support the client's strengths while acting as an ally against the feelings of weakness and helplessness that threatened to overwhelm her. The client had had a lifetime of experiences through which she had grown to be the person she was. The worker's task was not to undo these experiences but to build on them, thus adding another opportunity for growth. What distinguished that particular interaction from others was the conscious and intentional use of self by both worker and client. Unlike friendships that arise spontaneously and last as long as they are mutually satisfactory, the declared intention of the professional-client relationship is to help the client deal with certain identified obstacles that interfere with the business of living. Such obstacles may be presented by the external situation or may be internal in origin, but usually both external events and intrapsychic structure play a part.

Uses and Hazards of Diagnostic Categories. It is the nature of the intrapsychic structure that really determines the course of growth. But the web of interrelationships between one individual and others in the environment is so complex that change may reveal unexpected weaknesses or unsuspected strengths. Mrs. Bracey, for instance, had appeared to be very competent but internally had seen herself as dependent on her husband. When his disability deprived her of his support, she felt as helpless as an abandoned child. Sometimes, the reverse happens, and one who has always appeared to be a clinging vine displays unexpected strength when given permission to exercise it.

For this reason professionals should be very cautious about applying psychological labels to behavior or using past behavior as a sure predictor of what must follow. We can observe events; what we may not see is the individual's interpretation of those events. Our view of another person is thus always partial and incomplete. "The map is not the territory," is how Korzybski (1941) defined this concept.

A great deal of thought and effort has gone into devising a consistent set of psychiatric diagnostic terms, such as the several editions of the *Diagnostic and Statistical Manual* published by the American Psychiatric Association. The intent is to use words that refer to the same phenomena in a standardized fashion and thus to approach the exactness of mathematics. As a protection against the sloppy use of terminology, diagnostic labels serve a useful purpose. However, there are risks inherent in their use. As we noted earlier, we never see an individual in such totality as to make any diagnostic category an adequate summary. A more subtle danger is that the label creates an illusion of certainty. Holding firmly to the map, we think we know the territory. Furthermore, such labels, once applied, are likely to stick and to be regarded as fact.

Another hazard in the use of diagnostic categories is that they often provide an excuse for doing nothing. If the patient is believed to have an untreatable condition, the professional cannot be faulted for failing to treat.

The conditions defined as "untreatable" vary from generation to generation. Some years ago, one such was schizophrenia, and many persons who exhibited unpleasant or frightening behavior were labeled as being schizophrenic. Today, they might be called manipulative or narcissistic or impulse-ridden but still with the implication of being beyond treatment.

Alzheimer's Disease as the New Focus of Hopelessness. The current "untreatable" condition, especially among the elderly, appears to be Alzheimer's disease. This is a neurological degenerative disease of great interest to researchers. Biology, chemistry, genetics, immunology, and neurology are being explored to determine their possible contribution to the identification, prevention, and treatment of the condition. At present, however, the disease process is irreversible. It results in memory loss and progressive inability to manage self-care. Eventually, even physical functions may be beyond the person's control. Not surprisingly, the very name evokes feelings of terror and helplessness, as the word *polio* did before the advent of the Salk vaccine.

Confusion and forgetfulness in the elderly (and others) have many possible causes, including infection, malnutrition, mismedication, depression, and stress. Because of the current concern with Alzheimer's disease, those who exhibit some degree of memory loss might be labeled as victims of Alzheimer's, whether or not the disease has been diagnosed. What complicates such situations is that at present the only conclusive diagnosis of the disease can be made by autopsy, although medical and neurological work-ups can rule out other conditions and indicate the most promising approach for treatment and management. Nevertheless, if these meticulous procedures are not used, many persons exhibiting memory loss are likely to be assumed to be suffering from Alzheimer's disease. This not only prevents exploration of the actual cause of the symptoms but also conveys the implication of hopelessness.

Memory loss in the elderly used to be called senility. When it was recognized that "senility" was an inaccurate catchall term, the same symptoms were referred to as "organic brain syndrome"(OBS). The intent was to achieve a more scientific exactness of description, but the precision was more apparent than real. Now, the scientific terminology is "senile dementia," in which are included Alzheimer's disease and related disorders; but the aura of medical authority the word evokes is still somewhat spurious. Alzheimer's is the most common form of senile dementia, but the range of dementing conditions is wide. In the interest of research and eventual control of disease, it is certainly appropriate for medical and scientific personnel to pursue neuropathological diagnoses and pinpoint specific characteristics of each dementing illness, as far as these can be ascertained. However, families of persons suffering from dementia and the practitioners who try to assist them are not particularly helped by the specificity of a disease name; they can be helped much more by specific suggestions on how to maintain the patient's dignity and the functioning capacities that still remain.

It cannot be stated too often or too emphatically that words are not facts. Words are only approximate descriptions of experience. The human experience of the loss of memory and autonomous functioning, however labeled, is one of fear, loneliness, and frustration. But it is not outside the scope of human response.

Such human response is called for in all the professions serving the aged and is essential when dealing with patients who suffer from cognitive impairment or show irrational behavior. Even in cases of advanced dementia irrational behavior may be purposeful and attempt to convey a message. It is the responsibility of the caregiving professional to decipher the message, sometimes in a manner that resembles detective work (Edelson, 1976).

A charge nurse in a care facility noticed that a patient with severe memory loss was screaming bawdy songs as the attendants tried to bathe her. The woman was very heavy, and two male orderlies were needed to lift her in and out of the bathtub.

The charge nurse knew that the patient was very religious, and the bawdy songs were thus out of character. She speculated that the patient was ashamed of being naked in front of the orderlies. When she asked the woman, "Are you ashamed?" the patient said, "Yes." The nurse then assured her that from now on she would always be covered when the orderlies were present, and the screaming stopped.

The current concern with strategies for communicating with the mentally impaired shows that there are, indeed, effective interventions with the impaired when the emphasis is shifted from the disease itself to the person who is experiencing it. Similarly, focus on the repercussions of impairment in the elderly and resulting family stress is evidenced by a growing volume of research and practice observations.

Multiple Pathologies. The elderly who are most in need of help and often least likely to get it are those who are suffering from multiple deficits — cognitive, sensory, physical, social, and characterological. Yet there is still a personality underlying all these deficits, and communication remains a key to effective intervention.

Mr. Rose, age seventy-eight, lived alone in a dilapidated apartment in a run-down urban neighborhood. His physical ailments included severe arthritis, ulcerated legs, and chronic digestive difficulties whose etiology was unclear. Mr. Rose was in pain and frightened. He was also extremely hard of hearing, and this deficit increased when he became anxious. Anxiety was his most frequently expressed emotion. He

was fearful of the consequences of any decision and constantly berated himself for having made "wrong" choices in the past.

Mr. Rose had never married. He had lived with and cared for his mother until her death, but he labored under a tremendous burden of guilt for his inadequacies as a caregiver. In spite of his unattractive demeanor Mr. Rose had a few friends of very long standing and a network of relationships within his religious community. Although he described himself as incompetent, he took care of himself and his apartment, met his financial obligations, and carried on his modest social life. As his physical condition deteriorated, however, he felt the need of some assistance in self-care and apartment maintenance. He became involved with a social agency that provided such services, and this involvement continued for a number of years.

Mr. Rose presented himself as inadequate, and most of the service providers took him at his word. His social worker, however, did not. She disregarded the cover of incompetence and admired Mr. Rose's toughness and ability to survive the many vicissitudes of life. She refused to regard him as fragile and consistently advocated, both with him and with those who worried about him, for his ability to maintain his independence, make his own decisions, and live with the conse-quences thereof.

Eventually, his health declined to the point where he decided he would be better off in a nursing home. Although he suffered many anxieties and second thoughts, he was able to carry out this decision with the worker's consistent confidence in his ability to do so. He did very well in the new setting and even allowed himself to enjoy it—when no one was looking.

Mr. Rose's ability to cope with his many deficits was rein-forced by his worker's consistent support of his strengths. He was thus enabled to make and carry out decisions that fostered his well-being despite his generally low self-esteem and numerous physical ailments.

Dynamic Assessment as a Model of Therapeutic Interaction

Mr. Rose's story is an example of the use of an interactive rather than a static model of intervention. This concept owes its origin to Alfred Flarsheim's (1972) description of therapeutic diag-nosis, which he contrasted to medical diagnosis. The difference, in his view, was that therapeutic diagnosis takes into account not only the client's history and behavior but also the therapist's perceptions and reactions and the client's responses to them. Therapist and client thus form a dyad, which becomes the frame of reference for the work to be done. Both parties share ownership in the work and its outcome. It is interactive rather than hierarchical, mutual rather than authoritarian.

Flarsheim's model of therapeutic diagnosis was developed in the context of psychotherapy. We have expanded the concept to encompass the interaction of clients and professionals in many disciplines and settings. To indicate its generic applicability, we are referring to it as *dynamic assessment*. A basic tenet of our model is that assessment and intervention are ongoing, intertwined processes. They are not done by the professional to the client but are accomplished through the interaction of client and professional helper.

In the case of Mr. Rose, for instance, the core of the dynamic assessment was the worker's perception that her client was not as fragile as he said he was and—no less important—the client's response to that perception. A dynamic assessment is not a once-and-for-all session but a continuing exploration, a dynamic interchange, that utilizes both the worker's reactions evoked by the client's material and the client's response to the worker's interventions.

The effectiveness of dynamic assessment depends on the professional's awareness of his or her own part in the interaction with the client. The cultivation of such self-awareness is part of the discipline of professional education, and its mastery, like that of any other skill, requires continuing practice. Nevertheless, it provides a more flexible and versatile tool for both assessment and intervention than does a diagnosis based only on history, symptomatology, or observed functioning capacity in the client.

THE INTERACTIVE APPROACH

Throughout the life course human development is facilitated by interaction with the social and physical environment.

It is impossible to predict the course of individual personality development except in very general terms. Personality is the sum of the experiences of a lifetime as perceived by the self. No one ever knows the totality of another person's experience, for descriptions are one-dimensional and linear, whereas experience is multiple and simultaneous. Nevertheless, awareness of the meaning of one's experience is expanded by sharing it with others.

The individual impacts his or her environment as well as being influenced by it. This applies to interaction with helping professionals as well as with family, friends, and other associates. The professional is not an unmoved mover but a participant in a process. The professional's awareness of this process makes possible a dynamic assessment that provides a frame of reference for helping a particular individual deal with a particular situation.

Dynamic assessment as a means of clarifying personality development is fundamental to our concept of intervention with the elderly. Whatever the individual's physical, social, cognitive, and emotional assets and liabilities, it is the responsibility of the professional to seek and to help the client find — internally and in the environment — that which, in Eriksonian terms, promotes growth rather than stagnation, integrity rather than despair (Erikson, 1963).

CHAPTER 2

Initial Encounters between Client and Professional Helper: Interviewing Strategies

Interviewing is an essential ingredient in the helping process and a basic skill for many professions in which one person elicits information from another. For some it is the primary tool of their trade and a major area of their professional training. For others it is an adjunct to knowledge and technical expertise and not something routinely taught. In gerontological practice interviewing consists of the ability to engage a help-seeking older person and/or his or her family members in a discussion that states and clarifies a problem or need and stimulates the understanding and cooperation needed to achieve an effective response and plan of action.

Our focus in this chapter is on the use of interviewing techniques essential to the helping professions as they are used in work with the aged and their families. The goal of a gerontological interviewer is to obtain sufficient information to assist with the need for counsel, services, and interpretation of aging issues in order to arrive at short-term and long-range approaches to solving difficulties, whether current or anticipated. In essence, the gerontological worker as interviewer is part historian, part diagnostician, part planner, and part counselor. Too often, when older clients seeking help are described as poor historians, the real problem may lie in the interviewer's difficulty in conducting the interview. It is the purpose of this chapter to anticipate and address such difficulties, close the gap that may have been created in the interviewer's formal training, and help practitioners apply preexisting skills to more effective and gratifying use in gerontological work.

Interviews usually take place under the auspices of an agency or organization and may be held either in person or by telephone. Each setting and method has its own characteristics, advantages, and disadvantages, and these will also be addressed here.

Purposes of the Helping Interview

There are many reasons why an interview may be held; each interview may have several purposes. Both the interviewer and interviewee play a role, and they both have their own expectations. Usually, the reason a client or potential client is willing to undergo an interview is that it is accepted as a procedure that will lead to the solution of a current (often pressing) problem and holds the promise of some helpful action for the applicant or for someone about whom the applicant is concerned. Overtly, this appears to the client/applicant to be a single purpose. On the other hand, although the helping professional may also have one primary purpose in mind (for example, obtaining information), the interview is likely to serve several purposes, and some of them may even be outside the conscious intentions of the interviewer. Overall, the multiple purposes are as follows:

- Obtaining and providing information
- Clarifying expectations and roles
- Identifying and solving the problem
- Establishing rapport
- Understanding feelings
- Providing emotional relief
- Targeting need for practical help

OBTAINING AND PROVIDING INFORMATION

Often, the chief purpose of an initial interview is to gain information about the situation of the person who is seeking help.

This information may be of several kinds. It usually includes identifying information such as name and address and demographic information such as age, marital status, and (in rare instances, when there is a specific rationale for needing them) race and religion. Beyond these issues the information sought may serve such diverse purposes as establishing a medical or psychiatric diagnosis, determining eligibility for a particular program or service, or directing the person to a more appropriate agency or facility. Initial interviews generally seek to match the applicants' needs to the purposes and capabilities of the organization or individual from whom help is being sought. In addition to providing an understanding of the applicants, such interviews also clarify the nature of the help to be offered in order to facilitate its use.

It is important to remember that interviewing is always a two-way process. The applicant who is providing information is also seeking it and drawing conclusions about the situation, the helping person, and the helping organization. The applicant thus perceives the situation not only from what is said but also from what is not said. The impression he or she gains may not be what the potential helper intended to convey, and the reverse is equally true. Therefore, the interviewer must beware of making assumptions, should be very explicit with both questions and responses, and should explore what the applicant may have in mind even when it has not been openly stated. It is always safer to hazard a guess or an interpretation than to remain with a speculative and perhaps erroneous conclusion.

If the interviewee is seeking help for someone else, such as an older relative, an important aspect of his or her information gathering is to clarify the nature of the involvement of the applicant (the person present at the interview), the needs of the potential client as perceived by the applicant, whether the potential client is aware of the applicant's concern and the interview, and how the client is to be included in the help-seeking process.

CLARIFYING EXPECTATIONS AND ROLES

The scenarios, the behaviors, the personality profiles, and the ways in which people ask for help are as varied as their numbers. It is the task of the interviewer to make sense out of chaos and to form relationships with those who come for help willingly, as well as with those who do so reluctantly. Part of this task involves teaching interviewees how to participate in an interview—in fact, how to become effective clients (Kadushin, 1983). For the potential client or the person making inquiries on behalf of the potential client, the major prerequisite is a willingness to cooperate with the interviewer in responding to questions and exploring the problem and its precipitants. For the interviewee the principal task is to examine, with the interviewer's help, how the problem or situation is perceived by those involved or affected by it. Frequently, older clients are most welcoming and conversational, but this may be more the result of loneliness and a desire for socialization than of motivation to become engaged in the process of problem solving. On the other hand, family members seeking help for their aged relatives may appear to be very open in describing their elders' problems, when in actuality this may be camouflage for their own underlying discomfort and anxiety, which may be compounded by their unfamiliarity with the client role.

The interviewer helps them master the role through cues and responses to the material presented, as well as through the personal attributes that helping persons almost intuitively bring to every interview—namely, warmth, empathic understanding, desire to help, compassion, respect, and availability. Acknowledging that the situation is an unfamiliar one and explaining in simple language why certain information is being requested provide guidance to the client. People function better when they know what is expected of them and when their own expectations are recognized and responded to.

Persons seeking help come with the expectation that the information they provide will be used to help solve the problems they present. Indeed, the expectation may be that the more information provided and the more involved and complex the process of application, the more certain is the entitlement to help. If help—the kind of help expected—is not forthcoming, the applicants are likely to feel not only disappointed but also deceived. Interviewers can help clients avoid such feelings of letdown by relating, as the interview progresses, the material presented to the solution hoped for, rather than getting so caught up in the story that the original purpose is forgotten. Another expectation of applicants is likely to be that the solution they are expecting will arrive magically, without effort on their part. This notion may in part be the result of the proliferation of "instant" products and advertising on the theme that "faster is better." Whatever its origin, the idea is a pernicious one. Ready-made solutions are seldom possible outside a television script; and, even when available, they are usually not satisfactory. If persons seeking help have no hand in developing the solutions to their problems, they are not likely to feel much ownership in them. The applicant who says to an organization and the older person who tells the family "Do whatever you think best" are both creating a setup that will allow them to say later "I wouldn't be in this mess if I hadn't followed your advice." This perception may not be conscious, but it is nonetheless powerful.

Interviewers can help both themselves and their clients avoid this trap by frequent reminders that decisions about life-style are the prerogative of the client and family, not that of the helping organization, and that the organization needs their input in order to provide effective help.

IDENTIFYING AND SOLVING THE PROBLEM

If interviewers cannot and should not provide the instant solutions for which the applicants may be asking, what then should be their role?

The interviewer's essential task is to identify the problem that the client wants to work on. As we noted earlier, the client may be so eager to talk about everything, or so hesitant to disclose anything, that it becomes difficult to determine what action, if any, is desired. Questions such as "Is there anything in your life that you would like to change?" or a brief comment such as "That must have been a disappointment" may help focus the flow or elicit some indication of need. The change desired may or may not be feasible and may have no apparent connection with a service. (Examples: "I wish my daughter would visit more often"; "I wish I didn't have arthritis.") However, the underlying loneliness or restriction of activity indicated by such wishes may help identify an issue that the client would like to address.

The interviewer may see many more problems than the client is willing to acknowledge or attempt to act on. Nevertheless, it is better not to overwhelm the client with too many recommendations. If one problem can be resolved or ameliorated, the experience of success may increase the client's willingness to tackle other problems. Pressure to attempt too much too soon is likely to result in discouragement and withdrawal. The interviewer's frame of mind must be that the client knows the problem and kind of help desired, is emotionally healthy, and can provide the necessary factual picture. If the interviewer proceeds with this premise as a foundation and listens attentively, discrepancies and gaps will emerge and can then be systematically addressed.

Techniques in Problem Identification

In the problem-solving phase of an interview the role of the interviewer is to help interviewees examine their perception of the problems and their ideas about available options. One may begin by asking what has been done so far, or in the past, about this or a similar problem. If whatever is being tried now is not satisfactory, why not? The interviewer can then begin to describe other possibilities. However, this must be done with an acute sense of appropriate timing. A potential pitfall is that if the interviewer responds too quickly to the interviewee's sense of urgency and makes a premature or inappropriate recommendation, the applicant may become overwhelmed. For instance, giving an applicant six telephone numbers to call may not expand choices but only compound confusion. It is more helpful to discuss what is known about the various services or options in terms of cost, availability, convenience, reliability, or whatever other factors may be relevant. The likelihood is that none of the available options will provide an exact match for the needs of the applicant, nor can it be assumed that all needs can be met by available resources. Clients must be advised that this is the case and that a "perfect" solution will probably not be achieved. This should be done without implying that clients are somehow unappreciative if they seek additional solutions outside the agency.

REFRAMING REQUESTS DISGUISED AS SOLUTIONS

When the applicant is an older person, the focus is more likely to be on practical solutions that ease a specific situation resulting from a change of circumstances, health, or social supports. Most often, the tendency is to adjust current upheavals by reaching for some tangible, visible, and socially acceptable help. Furthermore, when concrete responses to the applicant's requests fail, it is usually because the real problem or issue has not been expressed but, rather, has been submerged or buried under an apparently more benign or more socially acceptable face-saving request.

 Mr. Muñoz called a social service agency to request home-delivered meals. He said he lived alone and did not know how to cook. When the telephone interviewer asked how he had managed in the past, he offered a number of not very convincing reasons, which the worker did not accept at face value. Again, she asked Mr. Muñoz why he decided to call at this time. Finally, he said: "Well, my wife did all the cooking, but she died last week."

Obviously, it is easier for a person in Mr. Muñoz's position to ask for a practical service that is reasonable for a single, older man than to admit to his need to be taken care of or to express the fear, the loneliness, and the grief that resulted from his wife's death. However, having understood the underlying as well as the overt need, the human service worker offered Mr. Muñoz an in-person interview, reflecting that the meals as well as other adjustments to his loss could be explored. In the subsequent interview, grateful that his real issue had been heard, Mr. Muñoz agreed to engage in a series of counseling sessions. These meetings helped him get through the early stages of his widowhood, after which he came up with a number of creative responses to his lack of cooking ability and canceled the meal service.

RECOGNIZING THE PAIN OF ASKING FOR HELP

It must be remembered that asking for help is a difficult, sometimes impossible task for older persons. They are accustomed to having made decisions on their own throughout their lives and are loath to relinquish their autonomy, even when recognizing their own vulnerability. Furthermore, asking for help is an admission that needs to be hidden not only from oneself but also from others who may want to say something about possible solutions or actions. The underlying fear of losing one's independence or control often prompts older persons to hide their symptoms or distress from their loved ones, sometimes under the pretext that "they wouldn't understand" or because "I don't want them to worry." The anger at one's condition is often fraught with a great deal of ambivalence, and an interviewer will spot inconsistencies between what is said and what is meant. To solve problems as they are presented therefore requires probing into underlying motives or concerns and listening hard for the music that accompanies the words.

DECIDING WHOSE PROBLEM IT IS

As we indicated earlier, problem solving in gerontological work is not undertaken exclusively by interviewers and their elderly clients. It often happens that an initial request for assistance comes not from the person who will actually use their service but from a family member, a neighbor, a friend, or a health or human service agency. In such cases the interviewer has an additional set of tasks to add to the process of problem solving. It must first be established whether the person requesting help on behalf of an older person has consulted and obtained agreement to pursue the matter from the potential service recipient. Are the older person's preferences clearly known and accurately interpreted? The interviewer must be able to ascertain, particularly when dealing with relatives, whether it is the older person who truly requires outside intervention or whether the presenting problem is rooted in the dynamics of the family. "Whose problem is it?" is as important a question as "Why is this request being made now?" and "How would we like to see this problem solved?"

If there are several persons who are involved in the presentation of the problem or will be affected by whatever decisions are arrived at, even if they are not present at the interview, they must be included soon thereafter so that they are not taken by surprise. This is to enable them, if indicated, to make necessary adjustments, reconcile differences, or, at the very least, have an opportunity to be heard and to participate in the process of planning for the older family member.

Problem solving—whether with individuals, small or extended family groups, or those who will eventually provide or are already providing practical services—is not so much a matter of listing or even describing services as it is a process of weighing what the professional practitioner concludes and recommends against what the potential service user will accept and what the family or significant others can handle.

ESTABLISHING RAPPORT

To enable an interviewee to become engaged in the process that will result in obtaining the desired help or services, the interviewer must be attentive and indicate interest and availability. This is established by the interviewer's words and manner of speech, which are direct and clearly and simply stated. It is also communicated by intense, active listening, a bodily position that is intent on the interviewee, the ability to maintain eye contact (balanced by a shift in attention to other objects so as not to appear to be staring), lack of unwarranted interruptions, and responding appropriately to what the interviewee is introducing. These techniques convey to the interviewee that this is the place where one is heard and this interviewer is the person with whom one can share one's problems. The beginnings of a relationship based on client trust and interviewer acceptance are thus established, to grow into ongoing rapport as the work together continues.

UNDERSTANDING FEELINGS

The feelings of both the interviewer and the interviewee have great impact on the ability to solve problems and carry the interview to a productive conclusion. Even if the primary purpose of the interview is not to explore feelings as such, they are part of the data pertinent to the case and must be taken into account.

Some interviews, such as those of clearly psychiatric or psychotherapeutic nature, have as their stated purpose eliciting and discussing feelings. Then the interviewer's task is to make sure the interviewee understands that this is the purpose and why. The interviewer's understanding is conveyed not only by an explanatory statement but also by acknowledgement of and responsiveness to the feelings that are being displayed and expressed.

Not all therapists believe that feelings of the old should be explored in depth. For instance, Goldfarb and Sheps (1954) and Turner (1961) suggest that exploring feelings is an approach to be used with the young, but that interviews with the old should differ appreciably from those with younger persons. With older clients they advocate a directive, authoritarian role, on the premise that this responds to the helplessness of the aged and enables them to have their dependency needs met.

This philosophy has the flaw of assuming that all elderly people are helpless and dependent. This assumption may have been made because the researchers studied only an institutional population. Other researchers have been successful in engaging older people in discussion of feelings and have found such discussions productive. Silverstone and Burack-Weiss (1983) suggest that older people, especially if frail, respond more readily to "what" questions than to "why" questions. For instance, "Why are you upset?" or "How do you feel about growing old?" may elicit only a denial or a shrug, but "What happened when your daughter visited?" will probably result in a story from which feelings may be deduced. Comments on the material, such as "You look very sad" or "I imagine that was disappointing," can be used to encourage further communication. Feelings do not occur in a vacuum; they are connected to people, events, and objects. Talking about people, events, and objects that are of concern to the client will bring out feelings in a way that is natural rather than forced. It is possible, even in a brief interview, to convey understanding not only by offering explanatory statements and interpretations but also by acknowledging and reflecting on the feelings actually being expressed.

PROVIDING EMOTIONAL RELIEF

Whether an interview is specifically focused on understanding feelings or on solving problems of a practical and tangible nature, emotional relief is often the unintended result of a discussion held for some other reason. Nevertheless, it is the emotional relief that may be critical to the client's use of the experience and that may facilitate the problem-solving process.

Mrs. Green, an elderly, black public aid recipient, received regular visits from a young student in a social work practicum. The student became fascinated by Mrs. Green's stories of her childhood in Jamaica and her creative solutions to unemployment and poverty during the Great Depression. Concurrently with these visits, Mrs. Green, who was legally blind and diabetic, learned to use a white cane, modified diabetic recipes in order to improve her diet, and completed a move to a better apartment. When the student asked Mrs. Green how she had been able to accomplish all these things in such a short time, Mrs. Green smiled and patted the student's hand. "When you've been here I feel so consoled," she answered simply.

Emotional release (known as catharsis in the psychological literature), which is experienced in the interested presence of another, may thus free a person to accelerate problem solving. However, it may also have the effect of making the solution to a real problem seem unnecessary, because the interviewee feels so much better already. That is a risk of which the interviewer must be aware.

Another risk is that the interviewee may be so embarrassed by having indulged in an outburst or sharing of feelings that he or she will recoil and avoid further contact with the interviewer or the setting in which the interview took place. Thus, emotional catharsis is an experience that can either facilitate or impede a person's ability to work on his or her problem. Rather than shunning catharsis altogether, the interviewer should try to cap it within optimum limits. One way to do so is by not permitting extensive or excessive disclosures in an initial interview, indicating that there will be future opportunities to readdress these important issues. It is essential to be very careful with persons who have the need to spill in one session all that has accumulated for them over a lifetime. They need to come away assured that the interviewer is interested, available, and not put off or overwhelmed by the person or the situation, and that postponing parts of the exploration is not a rejection but an attempt to deal systematically with everything that is causing the current concern.

TARGETING THE NEED FOR PRACTICAL HELP

The nature and extent of an interviewer's activity is usually dictated by the setting in which the practitioner works and, as we indicated above, by the purpose of the interview. Settings that are geared to provide psychological treatment and solace currently still appear to be less familiar and less sought after by older persons whose orientation and rules of behavior have prepared them to be emotionally self-sufficient. They are, therefore, more likely to accept concrete help of an instrumental (that is, practical) nature. There is less shame in being physically ill and thus requiring assistance than in being unable to cope emotionally or admitting to cognitive deficits or failure.

It is not surprising, therefore, that the most prevalent interviews held with older persons or on their behalf address the extent and quality of required care and consist of extensive exploration of available resources, costs, implementation, and management of service plans.

The daughter of an eighty-seven-year-old man telephoned a service-providing agency with a request for a housekeeper. The telephone interview was brief and sharply to the point. Father needed a woman twice a week to clean and do the laundry, shop for groceries, and prepare some simple meals, in bulk, so that some food could be kept for future meals. Father had a heart condition and could not exert himself. When asked why the request was being made, the daughter explained that her husband was being transferred and she and her family were moving to another state. The daughter suggested that her father hire a full-time companion, but he only grudgingly agreed to a two-day "cleaning lady."

This request could certainly be met easily, pending an in-person interview with the father and other assessment steps. However, the interviewer also understood that the man might be too distressed by his daughter's imminent departure to focus his energy on his practical needs, and that his agreement to the least intrusive solution would allow him the privacy to mourn his loss and maintain his dignity as a functioning adult. The daughter, on the other hand, saw the protection a full-time person would offer as a replacement for her own presence and a way of dealing with her feelings of separation and guilt. In other words, the service had quite different meanings to the father and the daughter but could partially meet the needs of both.

Techniques of Interviewing

Techniques are devices to accomplish stated purposes in the execution of professional responsibility. They serve to clarify what needs to be done in a given situation and how these challenges can be met. Knowing what to do, how to react, how to phrase a question, when to speak and when to remain silent—in short, to trust one's knowledge—is to be freed to choose the most appropriate responses from many available choices instead of worrying about what to ask or to say next.

PUTTING THE CLIENT AT EASE

The first step is putting the potential client at ease. Most prospective clients approach asking for help with a great deal of discomfort and anxiety. In order to demonstrate that the helping process is not as uncomfortable as clients might imagine, interviewers must prove that they are ready to help, have something of value to offer, and are themselves reliable, trustworthy, and caring. Whether by telephone or in person, they convey this by showing an interest in the interviewee's comfort, communicating respect, and giving the client undivided attention.

INITIAL TELEPHONE INTERVIEWS

The following pointers are useful in putting clients at ease in telephone contacts:

- Assurance of ability to help
- Following the client's lead
- Nonintrusive use of forms and procedures

Initially, the interviewer should confirm that the caller has reached an organization and person that could indeed be of help (even if this help might consist of referring the caller to a more appropriate source). This is then followed by uninterrupted listening, asking only for clarification and for related bits of information. Only when the caller indicates a willingness to go further and the interviewer senses the beginnings of the client's becoming engaged can the process of the information gathering begin—after the interviewer explains the reason for needing it. Starting with an exploration of what the client perceives to be the problem, the interviewer establishes the reason for the call. "Why now?"—that is, what in the caller's current situation has prompted this call?—usually provides a comfortable lead-in for getting further detail and offers an opportunity to ask for concrete information, such as dates, names and marital status.

 Mrs. Francioni called a mental health clinic, sobbing uncontrollably, stating that she needed to talk to someone. The professional interviewer who took the call reflected that something serious must have happened

to get Mrs. Francioni so upset. "Yes," the woman answered, "my dog just died." She began to sob again. The interviewer then commented that this must be a very painful loss, and Mrs. Francioni agreed. But she continued, saying that she lived in a dangerous neighborhood, and the dog was her protector. This allowed the interviewer to ask where she lived and whether she lived alone. "I do now," said Mrs. Francioni, "because my husband died two years ago."

Trusting the normal evolution of this interview, the interviewer was able to ascertain some basic facts about the client without bombarding her with questions. More important, however, was the unstated explanation for the enormity of Mrs. Francioni's grief: Not only had she lost the companionship and security her dog had provided, but she was also still grieving for her husband and all the losses that accompanied and followed his death.

Most agencies and organizations have forms that their interviewers are required to fill out while on the telephone and that ask for detailed demographic and personal data. There is a strong temptation to walk a client through the form, question by question. This, however, is fraught with hazards; instead of putting clients at ease, it may put them on guard, and an opportunity to demonstrate the professional worker's interest and caring is lost. It is better, although somewhat more demanding, to listen for the information volunteered spontaneously by the clients, take notes, and ask questions to fill in gaps when the client appears to be more relaxed. Also, as interviewers become more familiar with the necessary forms, they can skip around to fill in the needed slots as they listen and thus meet both agency and client requirements.

Advantages and disadvantages of initial telephone interviews. With certain older persons, as well as some family members, having an initial interview by telephone may have certain advantages. People who are uncomfortable about asking for help are offered a certain anonymity by not being seen. If they are anxious, they can express themselves more easily to someone unseen; and the interviewer, sensing the discomfort, may be able to postpone requesting some identifying information until the client is ready to provide it or a further contact materializes.

In work with the aged the telephone interview is both an important tool and a source of potential frustration. Especially for homebound persons, the telephone offers contact with the outside world and access to sources of help and support. However, resistant clients may try to use telephone interviews in order to avoid the more demanding or costly in-person interviews, and those who tend to have dependent personalities may use the telephone to excess by calling constantly.

Despite the psychological advantage of having ready access to service providers, older persons who have speech or hearing difficulties may require, and prefer, a home or office visit. Interviewers also may find dealing with such deficits by telephone unproductive and wearing, in which case face-to-face communication is advisable. How to work with persons whose conditions present barriers to communication will be addressed later in this chapter.

IN-PERSON INTERVIEWS

If the first contact takes place in the professional's office, a few minutes can be spent on "breaking the ice," to put the client at ease. While the client is getting settled, some neutral remark about the weather, offering to hang up his or her coat, or expressing an interest in whether the trip to the agency was smooth are all means of easing the client's reactions to the unfamiliar, perhaps threatening or anxiety-provoking situation. Such benign introductions are especially reassuring for older persons who may indeed find it difficult to overcome obstacles posed by inclement weather or inadequate transportation facilities, not to mention having to ask for help from an agency. By the choice of "small talk" comments, the professional is communicating awareness of the client's effort to keep the appointment, as well as empathy and appreciation.

Such casual inquiries may also prove to be of diagnostic value. The interviewer may learn, for example, that the client has physical problems affected by weather conditions, has little access to transportation or other resources but has neighbors who can be asked for rides, is resourceful in seeking help but won't request it of family, and so forth.

How a question is phrased is as important as what is being asked. For instance, "I hope it was easy for you to get here" shows concern, whereas "Did you have a hard time getting here?" anticipates a problem upon which a nervous client may seize to express this and other complaints or which may give a resistant client the opportunity to say, "Sure did. I don't think I can come again."

It should be remembered that even if a question evokes this kind of undesired response, it offers the opportunity to explore the question further. The interviewer can now address the feeling the client is expressing by answering: "It must be hard for you to get around from where you live" or "Is there a better way for us to meet so that we can talk about your concerns?"

Avoiding unclear terms and jargon. Choice of words plays an important role. The actual words used to communicate with the clients must be carefully selected to ensure that their meaning is as clear to the client as it is to the professional. To someone for whom time moves slowly, promising to make another appointment "soon" may mean "tomorrow," whereas for a busy professional "soon" may mean "next week" or even a month from now. Especially in the beginning phases of working with the elderly, for whom this process may be totally unfamiliar, it is necessary to clarify what the agency can offer and what procedures are followed to provide the requested service. Nothing can be more confusing than to say to a prospective client: "Now that we know that you want housekeeping services, you will have to have an assessment before we can arrive at a service plan. You will also need to speak to our fiscal coordinator so that we can determine your eligibility for Title XX subsidy, which is provided by the local AAA. And if you have some problems with that, I would recommend a few counseling sessions and can have the counselor call you to set up an appointment."

Use of unfamiliar terminology, reliance on professional jargon, and use of acronyms that have no meaning to laypersons are disturbing and bewildering and are strong barriers to comfort and motivation to accept help.

TECHNIQUES OF ENGAGING THE CLIENT

In order to persuade potential clients to involve themselves in the helping process, human service workers must prove that they respect their clients as individuals, that they themselves are reliable and trustworthy. They accomplish this by the following practices:

- Using names and titles properly
- Making and keeping appointments reliably
- Listening actively
- Obtaining feedback
- Framing and testing hypotheses
- Encouraging and focusing communication
- Thinking actively
- Identifying what the client wants to address

Proper use of names and titles. One of the earliest means of assuring clients that professionals respect their dignity is through the use of correct names and titles. The automatic use of first names, common among younger people, may be offensive to those who were reared in a more formal age. If the client's name is Muriel Sands, she should be addressed as Mrs. (or Miss) Sands, not as Muriel. If she prefers to be called Muriel, it is her option to say so. Even more demeaning is the practice, common in some settings, of addressing all older women as "Mother" or "Granny" and all older men as "Pop" or "Gramps." Such familial terms of endearment are not in the public domain, nor are such terms as "Dearie" or "Honey."

A very dignified eighty-five-year-old was offended when a young nurse greeted her breezily: "And how is Mother today? Shall we have our bath now?"

"I am not your mother," snapped the old lady, "and I bathe alone."

A more poignant story was told by a daughter whose eighty-year-old-mother tried in vain to get hospital personnel to call her "Mrs. Simon" instead of "Grandma." Depriving her of her customary title also made it easy for staff to ignore her requests, as if she were a nonperson whose wishes were unimportant. Individualizing the client begins with taking the trouble to use correct names and to find out how the person wishes to be addressed.

Making and keeping appointments. Another method for setting the stage for good communication is the way appointments are made. Calling in advance, setting a specific time, and answering any questions about the purpose of the interview help to set a professional tone. If it is an office visit, the interviewer should make sure the client knows how to get there. If it is a home visit, information on how the interviewer can be identified should be included. Staff members should carry identification and encourage clients to verify the credentials offered. It must be remembered that there are plenty of scam artists, confidence tricksters, and others who exploit the elderly. Caution about admitting a stranger to one's home is not only justifiable but also a sign of healthy functioning in the client.

Professionals should also take care to be on time for appointments. If delay is unavoidable, it is courteous to call ahead and apologize for the inconvenience. This is another way of demonstrating respect.

Another, less direct, means of showing respect is communicated by how human service workers handle their own behavior. If they are so convinced that they know what is best for their clients that they take charge and become directive, they may be responding more to their own needs than to those of their clients. Sharing their recommendations is perfectly valid, but insisting that these are ideal for the clients is not. It therefore behooves professionals to strive for a balance between empathic interest in their clients while being self-aware and maintaining an emotional objectivity that supports the clients without becoming enmeshed in or overwhelmed by their problems.

Active listening. Once the interview begins, the first task of interviewers is to demonstrate to clients that their communications are heard and that the professional wants to understand and is willing to work at it. This is accomplished through *active listening*. Active listening means attending to what the client says, with a view to grasping its meaning *to the client*. Sometimes, interviewers — because of anxiety or a sense of time pressure — simply wait for a break in the flow so that they can describe the agency's services or the application process. This usually results in talking at cross-purposes or in missing vital clues that would make the explanation more relevant.

Example of inattentive listening:

MRS. SMITH: *I want to order your home-delivered meals for my mother. I'm so tired, I don't know what else to do.*

INTERVIEWER: *Well, we can send her one or two meals a day, beginning next week. The cost is $3.50 per meal. You will have to get a diet order from her doctor.*

MRS. S.: *Well, I don't know why she needs a diet order. Dr. North never told me about any restrictions. But maybe she wouldn't like the meals anyhow. She's an awfully fussy eater.*

INT.: *Getting a diet order is agency policy.*

MRS. S.: *Oh. . . . Well, I'll have to think about it.*

INT.: *OK. Call me if you decide to use the service.*

Example of active listening:

MRS. S.: *I want to order your home-delivered meals for my mother. I'm so tired, I don't know what else to do.*

INT.: *Have you been preparing her meals then?*

MRS. S.: *Yes, and everything else too—shopping, laundry, cleaning, taking her to the doctor. Her glasses need changing, too.*

INT.: *Your mother lives with you?*

MRS. S.: *It might be easier if she did! She's lived alone in that big apartment ever since my father died last winter. I have to manage my own house and then run every day to take care of her. My husband says something's got to be done—he never sees me any more.*

INT.: *It does sound like you're handling an awfully big job. Maybe if you and your husband and your mother came into the office, we could help you find ways to make it more manageable.*

MRS. S.: *Well, I'd never want to hurt my mother's feelings. But I really do need some help. I just can't take care of everybody!*

INT.: *Let's make an appointment to talk about it. You and your husband could come by yourselves first, if you'd rather. Of course, it's important for us to understand your mother's point of view too. We could plan to have her join you at a second meeting. How would that be?*

MRS. S.: *I'd rather like that. Would it be OK if I talk to my husband first and let you know when he could come?*

INT.: *That would be fine. I'll expect your call.*

Obtaining feedback. Active listening means encouraging the client to clarify the request or concern he or she is presenting. Another aspect of active listening is *obtaining feedback.* An interview may be furthered by rephrasing the client's words, asking for feedback, or making *brief* comments. (Example: "You have a big job on your hands.") In the early stages of a relationship with the client, the interviewer should beware of making extended comments and interpretations. In the interview with Mrs. Smith described above, the professional might have assumed that Mrs. Smith and her mother lived together, which was not the case. By asking, the interviewer helped Mrs. Smith open up another dimension of the problem — the conflict between her roles in relationship to her mother and her husband.

Framing and testing hypotheses. Feedback is needed not only about the external facts in a case but also about their meaning to the various people involved. For instance, the interviewer might hypothesize that Mrs. Smith's mother is very frail, dependent, and demanding; that Mr. Smith resents his wife's involvement with her mother; and that Mrs. Smith wants to extricate herself from the situation. We have no way of knowing whether any of these suppositions is true, *except by asking.* Another interviewer might hypothesize that Mrs. Smith is lavishing attention on her mother in an attempt to win her approval; that the mother is aloof and critical of her daughter's efforts; and that Mr. Smith is worried about his wife's health. This scenario could also be true, but we can only verify it (or any of a dozen others) through further exploration — that is, by asking.

Answers to questions of meaning can often be gained through historical context. Rather than asking Mrs. Smith if she resents her mother's dependency, one might ask how the mother managed before her husband's death, how the mother and daughter spent time together before that happened, and if Mrs. Smith has brothers and sisters. If so, where do they live and how are they involved with their mother? One might also ask what else is going on in the Smith household. Perhaps Mr. Smith is planning to retire, or a son or daughter is going away to college, or there is a new grandchild. All such events could be adding sufficient pressure to Mrs. Smith's daily responsibilities to make her feel overburdened or torn in many directions. Without such additional burdens she might have felt quite comfortable in helping her mother meet her needs.

Framing a hypothesis must include the perspective of Mrs. Smith's mother — the ostensible object of family concern. When seen in person, mother (let's call her Mrs. Jones) may be quite startlingly different from what the worker visualized when talking with the Smiths. We have no way of knowing, before meeting her, whether she feels neglected or smothered by attention, or whether she is so absorbed by her grief that she is hardly aware of her daughter's presence. Perhaps Mrs. Jones waited on her husband hand and foot and can hardly organize her life in his absence. Perhaps he took care of everything and she never had to make a decision. Perhaps failing memory and grief combine to make Mrs. Jones vague about whether she is talking to her daughter or to her own mother. Or perhaps none of the above hold. The point is that Mrs. Jones must be encountered in her own right and not remain a shadowy presence on the borders of someone else's life.

Encouraging and focusing communication. Having a genuinely interested listener is delightful for anybody and may be especially gratifying to those who, because of lack of mobility or the loss of former friends and kinfolk, have few social contacts. This is the situation of many older persons. On the other hand, some elders are wary of outsiders and fearful that sharing information about themselves will lead to loss of autonomy. They may be somewhat reassured if their fears are identified and acknowledged as legitimate. This can be done in a generalized and nonaccusing way by comments such as "I know it's not easy to talk to a stranger about your personal life. I'd like to understand your situation a little better and tell you about the kinds of things my agency does. Of course, it will be up to you to decide whether you want to try using any of them."

Reminding clients that the interview has a purpose and that decisions on how they want to conduct their lives will be left up to them may make the encounter less threatening.

The most important aspect of any interview is to hear what the client has to say and try to decipher its meaning to the client. The message should be "Go on; I'm with you; I want to understand" (Kadushin, 1983). If the client's story is extremely rambling and unfocused, the interviewer can provide some direction by a comment such as "I'm afraid I lost you there. I thought you were telling me about . . . ," or "I don't quite see the connection. Can you explain a little more?"

Active thinking. Active listening involves active thinking. Interviewers listen to what their interviewees are saying and respond to what is heard as well as to what is implied. They analyze the meaning and look for the common threads in the dialogue that constitute themes that the interviewee may not be conscious of conveying. Themes often emerge in initial interviews but are confirmed and expanded in subsequent ones.

In applying to a nursing service, the daughter of an eighty-six-year-old woman described her mother as bedridden for three years with a slowly progressive, debilitating muscular disease. Her physical condition, however, did not affect her mother's caring personality; she spent her days worrying and being concerned about others. She was preoccupied with the health of her children, demanded constant reports on their well-being, and admonished them to take care of themselves and each other. The daughter found that this underscored her anguish about her mother's condition and her love for this selfless woman who only cared about others despite her own tragic illness.

The interviewer asked if there was a reason for her mother's concern about the family's health, which the daughter denied. She responded that her mother had always cared too much and asked for accounts of every action and event, because otherwise she would worry. The interviewer commented that this must have felt somewhat confining. The daughter became pensive and then stated that she had never thought of it in that way but, yes, maybe it was so.

It would have been easy for the interviewer to accept the daughter's characterization of the mother at face value. Instead, she first ascertained whether the mother's concern about the health of her family was based in fact and began to identify a theme in her own mind. She speculated that the mother's need to be in control preceded her illness and that the daughter had never admitted to herself how resentful she was of this control or how trapped she felt by her inability to separate her mother's needs from her own. The revelation of the nature of the dynamics in this family would now also help the interviewer prepare the nurse who was being contracted to serve the mother to understand her patient better.

Themes are determined not only by listening but also by observation. Fidgeting, averting one's eyes, scowling, sitting on the edge of one's chair, smiling when it seems inappropriate to the subject at hand — in other words, body language — assist interviewers in ascertaining what their interviewees mean to convey, consciously or unconsciously.

Special Circumstances Affecting Interviews with the Elderly

Interviews with elderly persons may pose complications not usually found in work with younger people. These include the following problems:

- Failing health
- Sensory losses
- Cognitive impairment

Even when prospective clients have no seriously debilitating handicaps, their age-related changes may affect both the progress and the quality of the interview. Lowered energy may dictate shorter interviews; reduced vision may preclude evening office hours or limit the client's ability to deal with written material; lessened mobility may demand in-home rather than office interviews; and the social and emotional changes experienced in the process of aging may affect the attitude, behavior, and level of involvement and cooperation of the older interviewee.

FAILING HEALTH

One of the most prevalent reasons for seeking help for an older person is the result of failing health. When a sudden illness strikes an older person, family members and the aged themselves often fall prone to believing the still-prevalent societal stereotypes about aging and regard the illness as a portent of a downhill slide toward permanent ill health. Although it is true that some acute episodes, such as coronary or cardiovascular attacks, can leave the patient with chronic disability, it should be remembered that most acute illnesses strike older persons as suddenly as they do younger ones and are usually curable. In contrast, chronic illnesses, such as arthritis, parkisonism, and senile dementias, develop gradually and, although rarely life-threatening, are not curable and can perhaps only be dealt with by controlling symptoms. The promise of a lifetime of pain and inconvenience, the need to change one's life-style, the potential need to rely on others, and the frustration of not being completely in command of one's body all impact on the older person's self-image and attitude toward self and others. In the interview situation the messages about these reactions may be openly stated or patently clear, or they may be covert, unconsciously hostile, or of depressed affect.

EFFECT OF SENSORY LOSSES

The diminution of sensory acuity affects one's ability to participate in interpersonal communication, including professional interviews. The senses most likely to be affected in the elderly are vision and hearing. Smell and taste may also diminish, but touch is usually unaffected and may be used to compensate for some of the other losses.

Interviewing persons with vision loss. Developing gradually and presenting inconvenience, frustration, and, sometimes, jeopardy are some of the sensory losses experienced by many older persons. In interview situations loss of vision and hearing are particularly limiting. A client who is unable to see the interviewer's appearance and facial expressions approaches the interview with less certainty; the discomfort of the unfamiliar situation is heightened because it is shared with an unseen stranger. Even if the vision loss is not total, some changes of aging, such as the yellowing of the eye lens, demand some special consideration. For instance, in an office visit bright light is not only welcome but essential, especially if any paperwork is required. Forms should be printed legibly, with much white space and in larger-than-usual print. Colors that seem excessively bright to younger people are a pleasing change for older persons, to whom pastel colors often appear pale and drab.

If the interviewer is not seen clearly or if the surroundings seem colorless and uninviting, the interviewer may communicate warmth and attention by using the one sense that is least prone to deteriorating in old age—namely, the sense of touch. A handshake, a comforting hand on the elbow as the client is being escorted to a chair, or a touch on the interviewee's hand as a gesture of empathy may all do much to assure a reticent or insecure person. As always, however, the client must be allowed to give the first indication of willingness to be touched, usually by initiating the action himself or herself. There are those for whom touching or any other form of personalized attention is objectionable, embarrassing, or intrusive, and it must then be avoided at all cost. It is therefore best to begin by situating oneself within reach but not so close as to appear confining.

Interviewing the hearing-impaired. For many older persons hearing loss complicates functioning even more than visual impairment. People who suffer hearing loss consider its principal hardship to lie in the real or perceived isolation they experience. Human communication depends on the ability to hear, so participating in conversation, maintaining social contacts, and conducting business result in great strain, frustration, and frequent embarrassment. Ascertaining what the client wants or setting up an appointment by telephone is prone to misunderstanding and mistakes; in-person interviews may be equally unsatisfactory if there is a lot of extraneous noise or if there is the possibility of being overheard by others when voices are raised. Obviously, maintaining continuity in the conversation and protecting confidentiality become trying experiences for both the hearing-impaired person and the interviewer. Especially when hearing loss is relatively new, many older people do not realize immediately or admit they are having hearing difficulties. Denial in older persons is particularly prevalent because admission of deficits minimizes their self-esteem and makes them afraid they might be advised to give up independent living. Some cope with this fear by being unwilling to consider the use of a hearing aid; their inability to hear correctly may then make them appear to be slow, inattentive, or even psychotic.

Despite possible denial on the part of the interviewee, an astute interviewer will recognize a hearing deficit if the interviewee leans forward and appears to be straining, favoring one ear by turning the head, or focusing on the interviewer's mouth.

Even when there is acceptance of a hearing disability and the need to wear a hearing aid, the older person remains handicapped. No hearing aid completely restores hearing. It amplifies sound — all sound — so that background noise and speech sounds are increased. As a result, the hearing-impaired person must learn to filter out the noise, which sometimes is so disturbing that it seems easier to turn the hearing aid off. This can also become a defense for those who do not always want to pay attention and prefer to tune out what is going on, who don't wish to face whatever is painful, or who are withdrawn, apathetic, or depressed. The interviewer must ascertain what motivates the interviewee's behavior and determine whether it is a coping strategy or a pathological reaction.

Hearing-impaired persons rely on other senses to help them understand others. They depend on reading lips, which most of us can do to some extent even without formal training. What interferes with lipreading for most hard-of-hearing persons is intensified for the old, who need good sight and good light and unimpaired ability to comprehend to make lipreading possible.

TECHNIQUES OF INTERVIEWING THE HEARING-IMPAIRED. Interviewers sensitive to the potential barriers to communication experienced with hearing loss will conduct their interviews in bright light, speak slowly, rephrase questions not immediately understood by substituting other words, and leave their mouths unobstructed, if possible. They can achieve this by removing pipes or cigarettes from the mouth when speaking and avoiding chewing gum—which are practices to be avoided in all interview situations, no matter who the clients are, in order to show respect. For clients with hearing deficits, consideration is also shown by minimizing, whenever possible, such background noises as radio, television, or the sounds of office activity. In public settings or in facilities where there are other people within earshot, it is not only thoughtful but also essential to locate a private, secluded corner where the interview will not be overheard. This is not to suggest that speaking with the hearing-impaired requires shouting, a common mistake made by hearing people. Shouting does not clarify sounds; rather, it may be heard as a booming of unintelligible sounds. Neither is an unnatural slowing of one's speech helpful; mouthing words, exaggerating them, or pausing after each word are both unnatural and harder to understand. Instead, one's effort should be focused on speaking distinctly but naturally and making sure that the interviewee is included in the dialogue and involved.

With hearing-impaired persons it is best to have even initial interviews in person. These may prove to be only screening interviews that clarify that the person does not require what the interviewer's organization has to offer. Nevertheless, helping someone to sort out what is or is not needed is also a service, and for people with hearing losses to know that there are those who do listen and do communicate is both validating and reassuring.

As in all interviews of older persons, the interviewer should be alert to signs of fatigue in the interviewee. The strain of listening may exhaust persons with hearing loss, just as physically frail persons or those with speech impediments (caused by illness, dental problems, or different cultural origins) may be able to tolerate only shorter interviews. It may therefore be advisable to schedule interviews more frequently, to compensate for their shorter duration.

COGNITIVE IMPAIRMENT

Interviews with cognitively impaired persons, although they are extremely difficult to conduct and often not very effective, are needed and important for diagnostic purposes. The interviewer relies on observation, tests client comprehension, and prepares both client and concerned others for further exploration of responses and resources. Because it is often difficult for the cognitively impaired person to concentrate on and retain what is being said, the interviewer keeps the interview simple and direct. In addition to watching for signs of frustration or fatigue, the interviewer is careful to anticipate the limits of endurance and curtails the interview when the client manifests agitation, confusion, or irritation or becomes immobilized. To avoid overburdening or overstimulating the client, the interviewer must usually be more active, more directive, and freer with interpretation, in order to give the person an opportunity to agree or negate, which is less demanding and perhaps more feasible than expecting that the person can evaluate and plan options and solutions.

This chapter has addressed some of the fundamentals of interviewing older persons. There are many special conditions, circumstances, and personality characteristics that affect the nature and progress of both initial and ongoing contacts by human service workers with older people. These will be addressed later, with the clear understanding that the interview is the basic tool of any helping professional.

CHAPTER 3

Engaging Families and Groups

Viewing the family as a system is a natural outgrowth of perceiving the individual in dynamic interaction with the social and physical environment (see Chapter 1). Close relatives, or those who share a common household, are most people's immediate environment.

The Family as a Minisystem

Recognition that what happens in the social environment affects individual functioning led to the development of family therapy as a mode of psychosocial intervention and to the specialty of family practice in medicine. However, until recently, these developments had little influence on work with older people, who were usually perceived as separate or even alienated from family interaction. Those who worked with "families" thought in terms of parents and young children or teenagers living in the same household. Grandparents and other relatives were rarely included in the definition of family, perhaps because most older adults do not live with their children or grandchildren. Since they were not present, their influence could be easily overlooked.

A NEW VIEW OF THE AGED IN THE FAMILY

The traditional view has been modified by a dramatic change in the demographic profile of the American family in the second half of the twentieth century, combined with more sophisticated research into kinship networks and their impact on individual development. The increase in longevity means that more and more adults have living parents and grandparents. The over-eighty-five-age group is the population segment that is increasing most rapidly, and these people are at greatest risk of physical and mental impairments that may cause them to need assistance from others. Despite the persistent myth of family abandonment, more than eighty percent of the elders needing assistance get it from family members — spouses, children, siblings, and other kin. Many of those providing care are themselves over sixty-five. This fact has led to major public concern about the social and economic implications of family caregiving.

Another type of family profile that is becoming more frequently noted is that of the disabled or retarded adult who is dependent for care on aging parents. Other aspects of the changing definition of family are the high rates of divorce and remarriage and the large proportion of women in the work force. For instance, an older couple whose children are grown up may have a son or daughter return to the parental home with young children who need care and attention or economic support. On the other hand, divorce may deprive grandparents of their accustomed contact with grandchildren, and remarriage may introduce a new set. Employed women may find job responsibilities conflicting with the needs of an ailing spouse, parent, or child, and caregiving responsibility may be particularly difficult if the woman is divorced, widowed, or never married and has no source of income other than employment.

These demographic changes have forced public and professional attention on older persons as family members. Researchers such as Brody (1981, 1985), Shanas (1979), and Sussman and Burchinal (1962) have documented multigenerational family interaction as a usual rather than an uncommon occurrence. Experts in family dynamics, such as Boszormenyi-Nagy and Spark (1973), Bowen (1978), Carter and McGoldrick (1980), and Williamson (1981), have presented viewpoints and treatment recommendations on how relationships among adult family members affect the functioning and further development of each person. Some family therapists bring grandparents and other relatives into family sessions even if they do not live with the persons who originally requested help.

ENGAGING THE FAMILY IN BEHALF OF AN OLDER MEMBER

Bringing older members into family sessions was developed as a strategy for helping younger adults deal with unfinished business in their relationships with parents. For most professionals in gerontology this is not the usual point of entry. What is more common is that someone, perhaps a family member, contacts a helping organization in behalf of an older person who appears to be in crisis because of physical illness or change in functioning. The caller may not see any connection between the impairment of the older person and the functioning of the rest of the family. Indeed, the caller may wish to establish distance between the condition of the "patient" and that of the supposedly healthy members of the family. It is a common human reaction to turn away from illness or disaster in the hope of staying uncontaminated, regardless of the age of the person(s) affected. If the "victim" is elderly, however, such reactions may be reinforced by ageism. ("Old" — "sick" — "ugly" — "useless" . . . "no, no, not me!") Ageism may be further reinforced when there is physical impairment, particularly if the caller does not see the affected person's daily functioning and imagines the effects of the impairment to be exaggerated because of age.

Another reason a family may wish to avoid being included in discussions in behalf of an older person may be that the elder is estranged from other family members because of long-standing relationship problems stemming from alcoholism, desertion of spouse or children, outright abuse, or other aversive behaviors. Even if no one likes the old person very much, however, it may still be possible to engage family members for a specific purpose.

 Mrs. Wilkins was asked by a hospital social service department to help in planning for her eighty-nine-year-old father, Mr. Grimble, who had broken his hip and could no longer manage alone in his third-floor walk-up apartment. Mrs. Wilkins replied that she had never loved her father or been loved by him and didn't want to see him now. The social worker responded, "We aren't asking you to love him, only to help plan for

him." Mrs. Wilkins agreed to come in for that purpose and later expressed relief that her action had helped to ease a long-standing resentment and guilt. She visited her father in the nursing home where he was placed and found him more mellow and receptive than she had remembered him in the past.

On the next visit Mrs. Wilkins brought her ten-year-old son Bob, who became fascinated with Mr. Grimble's stories of his experiences as a soldier. Thus, Mr. Grimble regained a family connection, Mrs. Wilkins experienced a degree of reconciliation, and Bob found a grandfather.

Family members may be quite concerned over the plight of an elder in trouble but need help in seeing the value of their involvement. The human service professional who receives a request in behalf of an elderly person can often engage the participation of the family by identifying with their distress, suggesting that the problems encountered by the elderly person must be affecting the rest of the family as well and asking for their help and input.

Example:

CALLER: *Can you recommend a good nursing home? Mother is not taking care of herself the way she used to. I'm afraid she's getting senile.*

HUMAN SERVICE PROFESSIONAL: *You sound really worried. When did you start noticing changes?*

C.: *I guess it's been getting worse gradually. My brother, who lives out of town, was really upset when he visited last week and found her in a dirty dress, with crumbs all over the floor. She was always so immaculate!*

H.S.P.: *Does your brother visit often?*

C.: *He used to, but he lives too far away now. He's come in now for the holidays.*

H.S.P.: *Yes, sometimes a person who has been away will notice changes that more frequent visitors miss. Does she have many visitors?*

C.: *Well—I see her every week, or my husband does. Her sister calls every day, but she doesn't get out much in winter. They used to go out together a lot before.*

H.S.P.: *Yes, that must be a real loss. Sometimes, when people are lonely, they lose interest in their appearance. But you need a thorough evaluation in order to decide whether anything should be done.*

C.: *Can you visit her and see what you think?*

H.S.P.: *We can certainly have someone visit her. But I think before we send anyone out, it would be helpful if those who know your mother best could meet with us and share their observations. That way, we could get a more complete picture of what's been going on.*

C.: *Well—I hate to bother everybody during the holidays. It's not really their problem, you know.*

H.S.P: *.You just told me that your brother was really upset by the changes he saw. Wouldn't it be reassuring for him to check out his observations with the others and be able to make suggestions? It sounds like he's really concerned.*

C.: *Yes—they've always been close. Maybe you're right. I'll talk to him and to my husband.*

H.S.P.: *Can her sister come too? She seems to have a lot of contact, even though it's by telephone.*

C.: *We can bring her if she's willing to come.*

H.S.P.: *She probably would if you asked her. It helps to have as many viewpoints as possible.*

C.: *I'll talk to them and let you know.*

This exchange illustrates several features that are often typical of initial contacts with family members. Here is a list:

- The caller usually has a solution in mind and must be helped to see that further information is needed before a recommendation can be made.
- Inquiring about others who are or have been involved may introduce additional information that can be used in beginning an assessment of the older person in a family context.
- Reluctance to involve other family members may be overcome by assuring them that their input is needed by the professionals in order to obtain a complete picture. This also helps to demystify the assessment process.
- If participating on a planning session is seen as "doing something," it can help to alleviate the anxiety of family members.

- Participation can be encouraged by reinforcing and building on information already offered rather than by ignoring or challenging it. ("Yes, that must have been a real loss. . . .")

It must be remembered that examples are meant to illustrate principles rather than to provide a script. The most important principle is that of offering the family reasons for participation that make sense to them.

INVOLVING THE OLDER PERSON IN FAMILY INTERVIEWS

Another aspect of family engagement is involving the older person in the process. Often, families are reluctant to have the older member, about whom they are concerned, present during the discussion. They are afraid that their relative's feelings will be hurt or that they cannot speak freely. Sometimes, they feel that the older person is too frail or too confused to be able to participate. Yet the presence and input of the older person are essential not only for a meaningful assessment but also for a viable plan of action.

One solution to such an impasse is to conduct several interviews: one (or more) with the older person alone, one with other concerned family members, and one with all of them together. More than one interview with older persons may be needed in order to gain their confidence and comfort in speaking freely. Elders may be cautious about opening up to a stranger. They are usually at least as anxious not to offend their relatives as their relatives are fearful of offending them. Their primary concern may be to avoid jeopardizing an important relationship. They may agree to an interview at the request of family members but hesitate to say anything that, if reported to the family, could put them in a bad light. They may need several opportunities to experience the interviewer's interest in their viewpoints and willingness not to repeat what they have said without their permission.

CONFIDENTIALITY IN FAMILY INTERVIEWS

Family members, old or young, may wonder if they can talk "off the record," or they may ask to be informed of what others have said. The interviewer's and/or agency's attitude toward such disclosures should be stated in the beginning. The stance most productive for family work is one that protects confidentiality but encourages sharing among family members. For instance:

- "I won't repeat what you tell me without your permission, but if you want your son and daughter-in-law to respect your wishes, you'll have to tell them how you feel."
- "I can't speak for your father, but in our next family meeting perhaps he can tell you himself."

This has the double advantage of protecting confidentiality and keeping the worker out of the position of go-between. "I want you to tell my daughter . . ." can be countered with "I can't speak for you, but I can help you speak for yourself. If you're worried about her reaction, let's talk about how you can present your idea so that she will listen and try to understand."

The same principles apply when the first contact has been with the older person and it then appears desirable to involve other family members. Older people are often reluctant to permit such involvement because they fear loss of autonomy or becoming an unwelcome burden to their children. Shame and embarrassment may also be factors.

Mr. Asmura dropped in at the Senior Center and asked if they could help him find a cheap apartment. He had moved in with his son's family to save expenses but was very unhappy there. "My daughter-in-law is always on my back," he said. "She won't let me smoke, she complains I look 'messy,' she tells me what to eat and where to sit — I can't call my soul my own."

The community worker wanted to get in touch with the son's family to see whether the problem could be resolved without resorting to a move. At first Mr. Asmura refused. "I'd be ashamed . . . I don't want to embarrass my son . . . he tries to be good to me." However, when it became apparent that even the smallest apartment was beyond Mr. Asmura's means, he reluctantly agreed.

When the worker called the family, she reached Mr. Asmura's daughter-in-law, who was initially defensive. "I'm doing everything I can, and let me tell you, it's not easy." The worker assured her she had no intention of criticizing anybody but knew it was sometimes hard for family members to talk about problems when they were so close to them.

Sometimes, an uninvolved outsider could help them work out a better solution.

Mrs. Asmura was cautiously receptive. "Maybe you're right, but I want my husband to be here too. Can you come in the evening? He doesn't get home until six."

As this illustration suggests, arranging family interviews requires flexibility of time and setting.

COUNSELING OBJECTIVES WITH MULTIGENERATIONAL FAMILIES

Counseling objectives are often determined by who is identified as the client—the older person, the younger family members, or the total kinship group. The nature of the helping organization may determine client identification. For instance, family service agencies may regard the available kinship network or the household of the caller as the primary client. Agencies geared to serve the elderly population are more likely to see the elder as the primary client, with other family members as potential resources. Hospitals and home health agencies see the person receiving medical attention as the mandated focus of concern. Older family members may thus be seen as primary clients, as persons affecting the problems experienced by some other targeted client, or as part of the total family system that is seen as the client group. In the latter case older persons may be seen as essential or peripheral to family functioning.

 Mr. Nicosias, who lives with his daughter Helene and her family, would be considered the primary client by the senior center that he attends. If Helene broke her leg and required home health care after her return home, Mr. Nicosias would probably not be considered a client unless he took care of his daughter on a day-to-day basis. If Helene and her husband had marital problems and consulted a family therapist, Mr. Nicosias would be considered part of the family system and therefore part of the client group.

Counseling goals are also affected by other family members' perceptions of the roles of their elders. Older members may be seen as contributing to family welfare, as needing the care of other members, or as liabilities to family functioning who must be "fixed" or removed.

Elders also vary in perceptions of their roles in respect to the rest of the family. They may see themselves as isolated or abandoned and thus needing to make all decisions without reference to other kin. This perception may hold whether or not there are blood relatives or interested friends available. Never-married persons or those who have no children may assume that they are without family, even when they are in close contact with siblings, nephews and nieces, or longtime friends. Other elders see themselves as entitled to the care of family members, however distantly related they may be. Others see themselves as obligated to contribute to the welfare of the ongoing family, even at the expense of their own needs.

Because of the variety of goals that may be sought by families or by individuals within families, there is no one goal that is appropriate to all situations. How, then, can professional helpers determine what goals they can accept or encourage?

Although no one goal is appropriate in all circumstances, there are broad classifications that may be used as guidelines. Some professionals see the primary goal of treatment as restoring or mobilizing family functioning in behalf of the elderly member who is experiencing difficulty (Silverstone and Burack-Weiss, 1983; Greene, 1986). The rest of the family is seen as auxiliary to the functioning of the older person and as possibly needing respite, assistance, or education in order to accomplish this task effectively. Such family mobilization may appear to be the most obvious need when the elder has severe physical, cognitive, or emotional impairments. However, it overlooks the possibility that elders may be capable of improvement in some aspect of their own functioning and/or of enhancing the welfare of the total family unit. Cohen and Eisdorfer (1986), for instance, have documented the ability of Alzheimer's disease patients to understand their illness, to be concerned about family welfare, and to respond to some forms of talk therapy.

As we noted earlier, family therapists see enabling the total family to function better as the goal of treatment. This is consistent with the view of many other professionals that empowerment of the client or client system should be the goal of intervention (Bloom, 1979; Germain and Gittelman, 1980; Maluccio, 1981; Parsons, Hernandez, and Jorgenson, 1988).

Whether the professional helper selects an auxiliary model of mobilizing the rest of the family in behalf of an elderly member or an empowerment model of helping the total family, including all generations, improve its functioning is likely to be determined by the setting and by the particular family's request. Not all families are interested in reviewing their total functioning; many would be satisfied to achieve adequate care of an elderly member with a somewhat lowered stress level for all concerned. Since major changes are difficult to accomplish and require large investments of time and energy, it may be useful to determine with the family what is the least amount of change that would alleviate the problem to an acceptable degree. Establishing such parameters will help to identify outcome expectations; if they present conflict for the various family members, this approach could avoid confusion and working at cross-purposes.

Process in family intervention. The most significant feature of family intervention is that it involves interaction with several individuals who, although they belong to an identified family unit, have different viewpoints and needs and may be engaged in a wide variety of life tasks. Small children learning to play with others, teenagers involved in school and career planning, young adults starting their own families, middle-aged adults juggling work, family responsibilities, and retirement planning, and older adults struggling with issues of dependency and autonomy make up a more diverse group than any other in our society. The family is virtually the only group that is not segregated by age, sex, or occupation. Its formidable task is to integrate the needs, abilities, and desires of its members into a mutually supportive whole while fostering individual achievement. Some families do this more successfully than others, but all families experience some successes and some failures. Each family defines success and failure in its own way, which may be different both from the definitions of other families and from the definitions of professional observers. Since families, like individuals, are apt to be defensive about perceived failures, they may be helped to gain confidence in themselves and in the professional interviewer if they are encouraged to talk about their successes.

Establishing rapport in multiperson interviews. When conducting a family interview, the professional must maintain both neutrality and empathy, encouraging all present to express their views of the problem and their hopes for its resolution. It is also important for the professional to maintain control of the interview situation. This can be done by establishing procedures at the outset. For instance, the interviewer may ask all present to introduce themselves and may also indicate the title or form of address that he or she prefers, such as "I'm Dr. Jones"; "I'm Miss Evans, the social worker on our team"; "My name is Kathleen Ebert, and I'm a nurse practitioner." Some interviewers prefer to give their first and last names and allow the family to decide which to use. This is fine if the interviewer is equally comfortable with either choice; but if a particular form of address is really preferred, it is better not to offer a choice. This may seem a minor point, but establishing identity is one means of managing an interview. It gives interviewees some idea of what to expect.

The interviewer will note where people sit in relation to each other. For instance, does an adult son sit beside his wife or beside his mother or between them? Does a couple sit side by side, while the aged father is relegated to a corner? The interviewer should make sure that all present can see and hear each other easily. If the older person (or someone else) is hard of hearing, the interviewer should make sure the seating arrangement facilitates communication. This conveys the message that everyone's input is important.

The interviewer may begin by asking everyone in turn to say why they came and what they hope to accomplish. If someone, perhaps the older person, says, "They brought me" or "My son told me to come," the interviewer may offer recognition that not knowing the purpose of the trip could make one puzzled or uneasy and reassert that everyone will have a chance to talk. If several people start talking at once or if one person wants to do all the talking, the interviewer may ask that they speak one at a time so that everyone's view can be heard. If some family members say little or nothing, the interviewer can specifically solicit and encourage the expression of their views.

Sometimes, one of the persons present will start describing the behavior of another. The interviewer can then ask the person who is being talked about for feedback and try to get the parties to talk directly to each other rather than about each other. If, on the other hand, everyone seems to be "ganging up" on one person, the interviewer may have to intervene more vigorously. This may be done by formally stating that blame and accusations are unproductive activities and will not be tolerated in the interview situation.

Another possibility is for the interviewer to comment on the role of the identified scapegoat, noting that he or she seems to have the job of making everybody else look good and, although that is an important role, perhaps other contributions are also possible. Such comments have the purpose of helping the family begin to reframe the problem by viewing it in a slightly different way.

To illustrate some of these principles, let us examine an interview at a health center with a family group consisting of Mr. and Mrs. Wiley; their twenty-year-old son Charles; Mrs. Wiley's seventy-eight-year-old mother, Mrs. Cox; and Mrs. Cox's seventy-five-year-old sister, Ruth Grant. The reason for the interview is family concern over Mrs. Cox's loss of interest in food, personal grooming, and the maintenance of her apartment.

In the interviewing room Mrs. Cox, a short, slender, gray-haired woman who appears uneasy, sits at one end of a couch. Her grandson, Charles, sits protectively beside her. Mr. and Mrs. Wiley sit next to each other, not quite facing Mrs. Cox and Charles. Ruth Grant sits at the opposite end of the couch, maintaining distance between herself and all the others. The interviewer takes a seat directly opposite Mrs. Cox but where she can easily make eye contact with all the others. After introductions have been completed, the interviewer begins.

> INTERVIEWER: *I'm glad to see you were all able to get here. I know you all have concerns, and it's important to hear everyone's point of view. Perhaps we could start by having each of you share your point of view of what's going on, why you're here, what you hope to accomplish together.*
>
> MR. WILEY: *Well, we're really worried about my wife's mother. We want to do the best thing for her and as quickly as possible.*
>
> CHARLES (plunging in before anyone else can speak): *I was really shocked when I came home from college this time, but I don't want Grandma railroaded. There's not that much rush!*
>
> MRS. COX (moving closer to him): *I'm sorry you've all been worried. I didn't mean to upset anyone.*
>
> MRS. GRANT: *I really don't know what the fuss is about. What's so different?*
>
> MRS. WILEY: *Surely you see that she looks different from six months ago? I made her put on a clean dress today—you don't realize what she's been wearing—and the apartment! She never used to keep it like that.*

(Mrs. Cox burrows deeper into the couch, hugging herself. Charles puts his arm around her.)

INT.: *Mrs. Cox, you look unhappy. How does all this seem to you?*

MRS. C.: *I wish you'd all quit fussing. None of those things are important anymore. When Harold died—it just didn't seem to matter.*

MRS. W.: *But Dad died more than a year ago. You weren't like this then. What will people think if you just let yourself go downhill?*

MRS. C.: *I don't care what they think, now that Rosie's gone too. I just want to be let alone.*

INT.: *Who is Rosie?*

MRS. C.: *My neighbor. She used to come in every day. She was such a comfort after Harold died. But now she's gone too. There's no one to make coffee for.*

INT.: *It sounds like Mr. Cox's death was really a blow—maybe more than anyone realized. Perhaps Rosie's death brought it all to the surface again and made it even harder.*

MRS. W.: *Mother was so devoted—she did everything for him. He was sick for a long time. But no matter how much she had to do, she always looked nice, and the house was always clean.*

MRS. G.: *I don't think any of you have the least notion of what it means to take care of a sick husband. I remember what it was like when John had his stroke. My sister and I talked every day, and she came over whenever she could. I don't know what I'd have done without her. You young folks just don't know. She's exhausted, that's all.*

INT.: *That's a very good point. Taking care of an invalid can be exhausting. But I wonder—maybe Mrs. Cox didn't pay much attention to her own health while she was so busy caring for her husband.*

MRS. C.: *No—I never had time to see a doctor.*

INT.: *And now that you have the time, you haven't the energy? That's understandable. But there may be a medical cause for some of your fatigue. If so, a doctor might be able to help you feel better.*

MRS. C.: *They can't cure old age. Send me to a nursing home, that's all they'd do. I don't want that.*

MRS. W.: *Mother, we'd never . . .*

MR. W.: *The point is, what's best for her health?*

CHAS.: *No! The point is, what does* she *want? She's entitled to peace and comfort, not to be sent to the junkyard like an old car!*

INT.: *Let's not get into solutions until we understand more about the problem. We already know that Mrs. Cox has suffered an important loss and that she expended a lot of energy caring for her husband. Despite having a caring family, she also needed her friend. There may be additional causes for her fatigue and feelings of hopelessness. Finding out about them doesn't commit you to any course of action. When you know as much as we can help you find out, the decisions are still yours.*

MRS. C.: *Well, I suppose it can't hurt. But I won't go to a home. If you don't like the way I keep house, you don't have to come.*

INT.: *We are nowhere near ready to recommend anything about living arrangements. But you should be aware that there are ways of helping people take care of themselves and their homes without moving them to an institution.*

CHAS.: *I'm for checking out anything. But it has to be what Grandma wants.*

MR. W.: *Let's see what the doctor has to say. Can you make an appointment for my mother-in-law?*

INT.: *Yes, I can give you some times. After the doctor has seen Mrs. Cox, we'll meet again to discuss what the findings were. There may be some lab tests needed too. Does that sound okay to you, Mrs. Cox?*

MRS. C.: *I guess so. I never did want to worry anybody.*

INT.: *We'll talk about it some more after you see the doctor. Your health is worth taking time over.*

MRS. W.: *We only want what's best for you, Mother.*

CHAS.: *Okay, but no funny business after I go back to school, hear? If they hassle you, Grandma, you just give me a call.*

MRS. W.: *Now, Charles . . .*

MRS. C.: *He always was a feisty one. Like his Grandpa.*

MR. W.: *When's the appointment?*

INT.: *I'll call you this afternoon or tomorrow, as soon as I can let you know what's available.*

In this illustration we see the interaction of a variety of viewpoints. Mr. Wiley was pushing for a solution and was somewhat

impatient with the process. Mrs. Wiley, who had originally requested the interview, said relatively little. Charles, whose dismay at
the changes in his grandmother had focused family attention on her,
was now more concerned that action in her behalf might be contrary to her wishes. Mrs. Cox herself was initially wary but able to
express her views when encouraged to do so. Ruth Grant moved
from reluctant participation to a position of strong advocacy and
presented information of which others had seemed unaware.

The interviewer encouraged expression, discouraged inter-
ruption and premature decisions, called attention to new information, and suggested next steps. She did not, however, take a position
on the meaning of the information provided. Mrs. Cox's self-neglect
might be due to depression following bereavement, but it might also
be the result of other factors, such as an undiagnosed disease
process, malnutrition, or early dementia. The interviewer did not
discount or contradict any member's input. She gave indirect praise
to Mrs. Grant for speaking out and responded to Mr. Wiley's impatience by offering to set a specific appointment. Since Charles was
already taking a position of advocacy for Mrs. Cox, the interviewer
left that role to him, merely assuring Mrs. Cox that no decisions
would be made without her participation. In another interview she
might have to take a stronger advocacy role in the absence of a
natural family ally or if sudden deterioration or change in Mrs. Cox's
functioning precipitated panic.

Meeting with the family after the medical review would keep
them all up to date and also provide an educational feature. Both
families and elders frequently lack information on normal aging as
well as on the nature and anticipated course of any specific adjustment or disability.

The principles that human service professionals apply in all
family interviews can be summarized as follows:

- Maintain neutrality and empathy.
- Encourage the expression of all views.
- Anticipate that individual views will change, both within
  interviews and between interviews. Be alert to any inci-
  dents that may have precipitated such changes, including
  further family discussion of the material.
- Be aware of power and decision-making structures within
  each family. Who makes decisions about what, and who

has influence over whom? Respect these structures and make use of them.

- Be aware of alliances within the family and how these may shift. *Do not* enter into an alliance with any member against the others.
- Facilitate communication by setting ground rules about interruptions, the length of time each person can speak, and expressions of accusation and blame. Encourage family members to express views to each other rather than about each other. Solicit views of those who tend to be silent.
- Clarify the purpose of the interview at the beginning, and conclude by reviewing next steps that have been agreed upon.
- Include an educational component by offering or interpreting information about aging and/or specific disabilities as these issues arise. Acquaint the family with other opportunities for obtaining information from physicians and other experts, through study groups, or through reading and media presentations.

Sources of conflict in multigeneration families. As we noted earlier, diversity of personalities and life tasks sometimes creates conflicting goals and expectations. Changes in circumstance may force reexamination of these. If Grandma has a stroke, she is not able to baby-sit or cook a holiday dinner. If Mother takes a job in order to help pay for college tuition or contribute to the family budget, she is not at home to keep house, be a PTA room mother, or take care of Grandpa. Longevity and the entry of most women into the labor force have created an expectation gap for many families. There is no longer a match between the things that need to be done and the people available to do them. Tasks formerly assumed to be the sole responsibility of wives and daughters may have to be shared with husbands and sons, grandchildren, siblings, other relatives, and paid or volunteer outside help. For a family to shift its pattern of expectations for various members is not easy.

Besides an expectation gap, there may be a priority gap. Which task needs, deserves, or gets the largest amount of available time—shopping with a college-bound daughter, taking Grandpa to the dentist, or writing a budget presentation for the board of directors? Faced with such choices, women sacrifice job responsibilities more frequently than do men (Sommers and Shields, 1987) and, as a result, have lower incomes and skimpier pensions. Other priority decisions have to do with family-of-origin obligations versus family-of-procreation responsibilities. If a son spends three evenings a week with his mother, his wife will probably object; if he decreases the accustomed amount of time, his mother may feel neglected. In this situation there are three people whose wishes must be taken into account: the husband, the wife, and the husband's mother. Each of these is engaged in a dyadic relationship with each of the others; mother–son; wife–husband; mother-in-law–daughter-in-law. Whether these relationships are hostile, congenial, neutral, or mixed, each dyad impinges on each of the others. Every additional family member increases the number of dyads impinging on the others. Suppose, for instance, that the wife also has aged parents, or that young children or grandchildren require care and attention. As the life span gets longer, it is not unusual for adults to have both aged parents and young grandchildren. Divorce and other disruptions in the grandchildren's homes may pull the grandparents into a child care role. Another increasingly frequent responsibility is the care of an adult disabled child or sibling. With more and more calls on the time and energy of mid-life adults, it is obvious that not all of these responsibilities can be borne by one person — that is, it is obvious to an outside observer, but not necessarily to the family embroiled in such conflicting claims. It may become the task of the outside observer/professional helper to guide the family in sorting out what has to be done, who is available to do it, and how the family's efforts may be augmented by resources outside the family. In this process it is not so much finding the resources that is the chief problem but, rather, helping the family visualize getting things done in ways to which they have not been accustomed (Montgomery and Prothero, 1986).

Resolution of conflict through negotiation. The first step in negotiation of differences is to discover what they are. Often, people assume that others know what they want and are surprised and hurt when their wishes are not fulfilled. Behavior may be ascribed to malice or indifference when it is actually the result of ignorance or misinterpretation. Getting people to say what they need or would like may be a slow process because of feelings of embarrassment or fear of hurting each other.

Once the desires of all parties have been expressed, the next steps are identifying the hindrances and thinking of alternative ways of accomplishing what is desired. Alternative solutions may be difficult to envision because it is usually easier for people to say what they don't like or want. The irritation caused by a particular behavior may loom so large that nothing short of its total removal seems sufficient.

Mr. and Mrs. Vincenti complained bitterly about each other's lack of understanding and helpfulness. Mrs. Vincenti, age sixty-eight, had been diagnosed with breast cancer and had undergone a modified mastectomy followed by radiation. For several months thereafter she was weepy and tired. Mr. Vincenti became impatient with what he perceived as laziness and malingering. The more he scolded, the more she cried. He told their doctor that everything would be fine if Mrs. Vincenti would just stop crying and lying on the couch in the daytime. She retorted that it was his yelling that made her cry.

The doctor explained to both of them that fatigue and tearfulness were not unusual symptoms after prolonged radiation; and he assured them that Mrs. Vincenti's cancer appeared to have been totally eradicated but that it would take time for her to regain her previous level of energy. This was helpful to the Vincentis, who had both been secretly afraid that Mrs. Vincenti was not getting well.

Although Mr. Vincenti felt more confident of his wife's recovery, he was still upset by her tears. He recalled seeing his mother cry and feeling helpless about it, and he hated feeling helpless. Mrs. Vincenti decided she would try to do her crying in private if Mr. Vincenti would try to avoid yelling. She had childhood memories of voices raised in anger that were as painful to her as Mr. Vincenti's memories of tears were to him.

Awareness of each other's feelings helped Mr. and Mrs. Vincenti modify — not eliminate — the behaviors that were especially distressing to each. Reassurance that Mrs. Vincenti was really on the road to recovery also reduced the need for such behaviors.

Identifying and modifying distressing behaviors may be a time-consuming process, especially when several people are involved.

Mrs. Finkelstein complained to her visiting nurse that she felt unwelcome in her daughter's home, where she had moved when severe arthritis made it too difficult for her to manage alone. The nurse made a referral to a family service agency. Mrs. Finkelstein agreed to a joint interview with her daughter, Mrs. Cohen, and her family.

In this interview several areas of conflict were identified. Mrs. Cohen felt that there were "five people in the house but only one vote"—that of her mother. Mrs. Finkelstein, on the other hand, felt that she had no "turf" of her own and that all her efforts to contribute to family welfare were discounted. Mr. Cohen was disturbed by the conflict between the two women and felt that his wife was being "put upon." Dorothy, age thirteen, felt intruded upon by having to share a room with her grandmother so that she could help her to the bathroom at night. Jered, age eight, was relatively oblivious to the tensions among the female members of the household. He didn't like it when his grandmother scolded, but he did enjoy her stories and the after-school treats she prepared.

A series of interviews was held to help the family find a more acceptable solution for all of them. Some of the interviews were with Mrs. Finkelstein alone, others involved her daughter and granddaughter and, occasionally, her son-in-law and grandson. As a result, some changes in the organization of space was achieved. Dorothy decided that she would rather share a room with her little brother than with her grandmother. This was recognized as a temporary measure, but the use of screens helped assure each child of a measure of privacy. Mrs. Finkelstein thus had a room of her own to which she could retreat. A commode was installed so that Mrs. Finkelstein did not have to depend on Dorothy's help to get to the bathroom at night, thus removing a source of friction. When the family planned to take a vacation, Mrs. Finkelstein said she would stay at home, provided that she could select the companion hired to stay with her during their absence. She participated in the companion interviews and selected the one she preferred. Her choice might not have been that of Mr. or Mrs. Cohen, but the vacation plan worked out well and set a precedent for future negotiation.

Joint and separate interviews. In the case of Mrs. Finkelstein and the Cohens joint sessions were combined with individual interviews. Since Mrs. Finkelstein had initiated contact with the helping organization and was asking for help in planning her own future, many of the interviews had the purpose of enabling her to clarify her own feelings and wishes. She needed time to mourn the loss of her independence and to fully express her disappointment and distress. Joint interviews with Mrs. Finkelstein and Mrs. Cohen were held periodically to help them learn to talk to each other, because the relationship between these two members of the household was felt by them to be most problematic and tension-producing. Others participated when issues of particular concern to them were being discussed — as, for instance, the question of Dorothy's and Jered's room.

Utilization of joint and separate interviews may also be appropriate when the older member is suffering from a disabling or dementing illness — such as amytrophic lateral sclerosis (commonly known as Lou Gehrig's disease), Parkinson's disease, or Alzheimer's disease — and has limited capacity for group participation but needs the opportunity to express his or her own concerns. The disabled person's participation in family interviews should not be ruled out altogether, however. Cohen and Eisdorfer (1986) have documented the ability of patients in the early stages of Alzheimer's disease to engage in planning and responding to talk therapy, and the same may be expected of sufferers of any of the other conditions that result in progressive deterioration. In these cases the patient should be involved as much as possible, but other family members, especially those directly involved in caring for the patient, will probably need more frequent contacts to receive support and information. A self-help group may be useful for this purpose, but regular meetings with the primary physician and other professional helpers are invaluable (Sommers and Shields, 1987).

Some compromises are workable; others are unworkable. The solution arrived at by Mrs. Finkelstein and the Cohens might be totally unacceptable to another family. No one solution should be considered optimal. All depends on the needs and wishes of the people involved. Taking all viewpoints into account is more likely to result in a viable solution.

Using and expanding the family system. Frequently, there are more people involved in a family network than those who initially identify themselves. Siblings, cousins, friends, and neighbors may make themselves available if asked to do so. Family members may not think of including any but the most immediate of their relatives, unless they are asked to identify all who have consistent contact with the older person. For instance, siblings are often very important to each other in old age, since they share history and memories unknown to others (Gold, 1987). Grandchildren often have another kind of bond. They are likely to have experienced fun and good times with the grandparents and avoided the tensions of the parent-child relationship. Grandparents are not usually responsible for bringing up their children's children; they just enjoy them and then send them home when the visit is over. As one rebellious adolescent grandson put it, half in jest and half seriously, "The reason grandma and I get along so well is because we share a common enemy—my mother!" But it is precisely because of the special nature of these relationships that the observations of persons who do not bear the primary responsibility for the older person are so valuable in completing the picture of the presented problem.

It is important to draw on the silent members of the family system, especially if the problem being experienced is the care of an ailing older person. The chief responsibility may have fallen on one person—usually a spouse, daughter, or daughter-in-law. Others may not have offered to help because they were unaware of the need or did not want to be intrusive. The primary caregiver may need help in learning how to ask for help from other family members, neighbors, and friends and can rehearse such requests with the helping professional. The professional can then also suggest that if other persons can provide some free time to the caregiver by spending a few hours with the patient, help with transportation to medical or other appointments, run errands or prepare some meals, the support experienced by the caregiver is greatly in excess of the amount of time actually expended (Zarit, Reever, and Bach-Peterson, 1980). Often, the chief problem caregivers express is that of feeling totally alone with the responsibility (Sommers and Shields, 1987). Young parents have each other, their own parents, and a host of experts to guide them in their task of child care, but those engaged in caring for frail elders frequently have no one who comes forward to offer assistance or support.

Sometimes, the caregiver is reluctant to use the help of other relatives. This may be due to rivalry or fear of appearing inadequate to the task. Professional intervention can help to validate the need and may include advocating with the other relatives as well as teaching the caregiver how to make his or her needs known to others.

Another kind of network expansion may be gained through the use of services such as adult day care, visiting nurses, or housekeeping assistance, if they are available and if the caregiver and patient are willing to use them. If one or the other is unwilling, exploration of the reasons and encouragement to experiment with small amounts of the least intrusive service may be helpful. Expanding one's view of a problem and one's resources for dealing with it is not easy and requires time to integrate new ideas. Professional intervention is more likely to be successful when the family is seen several times, rather than when there is an attempt to cram everything into a one-shot planning session.

The professional's understanding of the family system grows with each successive contact. Dynamic assessment begins with the first contact and continues until intervention is completed.

Use of Group Process

Like the family, a small group consists of diverse individuals. Unlike a family, its members are not part of a biosocial entity but come together for a particular purpose, sometimes self-selected, other times imposed by external factors. Examples of voluntary associations are discussion or study groups, self-help or peer support groups, treatment groups focused on a particular problem such as bereavement or recovery from stroke, and action-oriented groups such as tenants' organizations. Examples of involuntary gatherings are meetings that all tenants of a building are required to attend, orientation groups for new nursing home residents, and treatment or discharge planning groups in psychiatric hospitals in which certain categories of patients may be expected to participate. This section will deal only with self-chosen groups. The rationale is that these are serving a purpose that the members consider valid and worth the trouble of attending. As in adult education, self-directed learners are likely to be more highly motivated than captive audiences.

AUSPICES OF GROUPS

Many helping organizations include group intervention among their services offered to the elderly and their families. Hospitals and social service agencies often have groups that offer education, emotional support, and/or psychosocial therapy aimed at developing insight and effecting behavioral change. Such groups are usually led or facilitated by professionally trained persons, such as nurses, social workers, psychologists, or educators, or they may be led by peer counselors who have been trained by professionals for the specific task of group leadership and who work under supervision. Other groups have come into existence on their own, generated by the felt needs of people in a particular situation. Examples of self-help groups are those for family caregivers of patients suffering from Alzheimer's disease, widow-to-widow counseling groups, and recovery groups such as Alcoholics Anonymous. Such groups may have rotating leadership, with each member taking the responsibility for a specified length of time. They do not use professionals as group leaders but may ask them to come in as resource people. The common rationale uniting professionally led groups and self-help groups is that people in similar situations can learn from and support each other. The experience or advice of a peer "in the same boat" often carries more credibility than the same information or suggestion offered by a professional. At the very least, group members come to realize that they are not alone with their problem or unique in their reactions to it. An advantage of peer-led groups is that the members are less likely to look to the leader as the expert with answers. In consequence, they may develop their own self-confidence more quickly. This does not always happen, however. Members may also reinforce each other's discouragement or resort to mutual criticism or scapegoating. They also lack any knowledge base beyond their own; with new information or a broader viewpoint supplied by a professional leader, they are more likely to gain a different perspective on their situation. The most effective self-help groups are those in which the indigenous leaders have some knowledge of group dynamics and access to outside resources. A caregivers' group, for instance, might ask a physician to provide current information on diseases of aging, a nurse to teach bathing and transfer techniques, or a lawyer to advise on methods of estate planning. This could also be done if the group leader is a professional. Indeed, it might be easier for a professional to locate knowledgeable colleagues than for a group of laypersons to do so.

RECRUITMENT AND SELECTION OF GROUP MEMBERS

Recruitment of members for a group is usually the most time-consuming task of group leadership. It is advisable to locate at least twice as many potential members as are needed for a viable group, since there is bound to be attrition and some fluctuation in attendance. Therefore, if the desired size is eight to ten people, at least twenty should be recruited. If, in fact, more people appear than can be accommodated, it would be better to split them into two groups rather than to deal with one that is too large. The experience of most group leaders indicates that group attendance, especially in the formative stages, is erratic, that usually fewer people attend than have promised to come, and that group sizes tend to dwindle in time.

One means of recruitment is to place newspaper notices and distribute flyers inviting all interested persons to a first meeting of the proposed group. However, this has several disadvantages. The group may turn out to be far larger or far smaller than anticipated. One or two people may monopolize the discussion, provoking dissatisfaction and dropouts among the others. It is preferable to have interested persons call the group leader for further information. This allows for at least a telephone screening and gives a more accurate estimate of the number of people who will actually show up. Some group leaders insist on an in-person interview with each applicant. This provides a more dynamic assessment of the needs and characteristics of the potential members.

Selection criteria. In general, group membership is appropriate for those who share a common concern, are capable of interaction with others, and are willing to make a commitment to group attendance. Diversity of experience contributes to group potential; but if people perceive themselves or are perceived as totally different from the rest of the group, they may not be very comfortable or may not feel that the group offers anything to them. For instance, one widower in a group of eight widows might feel out of place; the presence of even one other man could help each to validate the other's experience, as well as adding a new dimension to the group. In caregiver groups it may be difficult to combine spouses and adult children because of differences in role perception.

Unsuitable group candidates include those with paranoid preoccupations or pet projects unlikely to be shared by the group. Those who are too cognitively impaired to participate in a conversation and those with severe hearing loss or speech impediments would have difficulty in groups where the rest of the members did not have such deficits. However, groups organized for persons sharing a particular problem, such as hearing loss, have been very successful.

SETTING GOALS WITH GROUPS

In groups formed under organizational auspices there are usually at least three sets of goals operating: the organization's goals, the leader's goals, and the various goals of the individual members. These must be reconciled if the group is to function. For instance, the organization may plan for a support group in order to satisfy the mandate of a funding source. The group leader may see the group as an opportunity to share feelings and learn about the experiences of others. The majority of group members may prefer an educational format because they think it would best help them achieve mastery of the tasks they face. These goals, while different, are compatible. Sharing individual experiences and reactions can take place in the context of getting new information about the problems being faced, and new learning may stimulate discussion of individual situations, thus facilitating integration of the material. However, if the organization sees group work as primarily a cost containment or public relations strategy, or if the group leader is trying to fulfill an educational requirement by fostering a particular kind of group, the needs of the group members may be overlooked or misunderstood. The goals of organization, leader, and group can be different, but they must not be in conflict. If they are, the group will not function very long or very effectively.

In helping the group to sort out its own goals, the leader must be sensitive to the fact that different people want different things. These may include new learning, mastery of a task, interaction of knowledge, emotional support, change in attitude or behavior, and change in environmental circumstance. If there are several major issues that group members want to address, it may be possible to gain agreement on assigning a portion of time to each. For instance, a group might decide to devote half an hour per session to talking about current experiences of members, one hour to structured learning, and half an hour to resource sharing. Or the members might agree to devote different amounts of time in different sessions to specific issues.

GROUP PROCESS AS THE INSTRUMENT OF CHANGE

In the early stages of group development, members usually relate primarily to the leader rather than to each other. As they become more comfortable in the group setting, they feel freer to communicate directly with each other, supporting, challenging, or expanding on the viewpoints of other members. The group leader facilitates this by encouraging each member to speak out and by soliciting the reactions of other members to what is said, rather than by responding directly to each speaker. What group members eventually gain from the experience is an understanding that there are many ways of looking at any situation, that people solve their problems in different ways, and that they may be contributing to their own difficulties in ways they do not realize.

Martha Relling stated that her children never help her yet made it clear, both from her story and in her interaction in the group, that she never lets them know she needs any help. When she explained that this was so as not to "burden" her children and friends, the group responded that she was standoffish and foolish not to be open with her children. The very fact that group members perceived her behavior in another way than what seemed obvious to her was quite a revelation to Mrs. Relling.

Duration of groups. Groups may meet for a set period of time or may be open-ended, lasting as long as the members are interested in meeting. Short-term groups typically meet once a week for six to eight sessions. Open-ended groups are more likely to meet once or twice a month. For most people an ongoing time commitment on a more frequent basis is difficult to maintain. Ongoing groups that meet once a week may have different people in attendance at each session. This may not be problematic if there is a core group of regular attenders, but a cohesive group will not develop unless most of the same people attend each session. Regular, frequent attendance may be easier to facilitate if the members are drawn from a senior center, clinic, church, or some other setting that they have shared reasons for visiting. In the absence of such a setting it may be feasible to have less frequent meetings in order to increase the likelihood of a more stable attendance pattern.

Termination in group intervention. In short-term groups termination and separation are major issues. After establishing an atmosphere of trust and sharing, members are confronted with the prospect of losing what they have built up together. This may be particularly difficult for older people, who are frequently dealing with many other losses. It is therefore important for the leader to address the issue of termination and its meanings to the group members before the final session. Some leaders talk about the endpoint of the group in the very first session and continue to refer to it at each succeeding session: "This is our first meeting. We will have seven more. The last session will be on October 15th." And "This is our fifth meeting. We have three sessions left." Such comments can be used to help group members think about what they have accomplished, what they still want to accomplish, what they will do when the group ends, and how the gains they have made will carry over into the next phase of their lives. Sometimes, group members keep in touch with each other after the group ends and thus augment each other's social and support networks. Not everyone wishes to do this, however, and it should not be urged on the group as a solution.

Termination issues are less clear-cut in ongoing groups. Members continue attending as long as they wish to do so or drop out and return periodically. The departure of a longtime member may be felt as a loss by the rest of the group, however.

At the Greenwood Senior Center ten to fifteen members had met regularly for three years. They had begun as a current-events discussion group but evolved into a forum for sharing the events in their own lives rather than those reported in the news media. When Grace Livingston broke her hip and had to go to a nursing home, the rest of the members were very gloomy for several weeks. It was not only that they missed Grace but that her accident reminded them of their own frailty. What had happened to Grace could happen to any of them. One man stayed away from the group for three weeks because the reminder was too painful for him. Others brought cookies "to cheer us up" or called to check on each other more frequently.

Staying away and drawing closer are both means of dealing with separation and feelings of loss. The group leader, if there is one, can help the members identify their feelings of loss, connect them to their various behaviors (for example, staying away or baking cookies), and thus make the mourning experience explicit instead of implicit.

Groups and families are both social networks for individuals. Both have points of entry and exit, stages of development, accomplishments and failures, gains and losses. In both networks, what can be explicitly shared is more fully enjoyed and more easily endured.

CHAPTER 4

Assessment: Assembling the Building Blocks

Assessment is a technique and series of procedures that precede the delivery of services or treatment and serve to determine the appropriate amount and level of care or assistance. The purpose of conducting an assessment is to arrive at a body of information about the old person and his or her situation that will be used by the client and the helping organization in response to needs, whether these have surfaced during a particular crisis or have existed as long-standing problems. There is an expectation that an assessment of an older person results in recommendations intended to either ameliorate or alleviate problems or simply to ensure the maintenance of current functioning.

Multiple Purposes of Assessment

In addition to determining the immediate need for service, assessment may serve several other purposes, such as preventive consultation to help client and/or family avoid precipitous and ill-considered action, or in-depth evaluation for long-range planning. In most organizational settings that rely on assessments, this method of examining the issues has both clinical and administrative management functions.

MINIMAL AND SELECTIVE INTERVENTION: A KEY CONCEPT

Whether the goal is to effect change or prevent deterioration, the guiding principle in conducting an assessment of an older person should be to arrive at a treatment or service plan based on minimal and selective intervention — that is, offering only as much or as little service as is needed to continue or stimulate the client's optimal functioning and decision making. Implicit in such an approach is the conviction that the more autonomy an individual retains in conducting the affairs of daily existence, the more he or she will strive to continue to do so. If, often with the best intentions, help is offered prematurely or to excess, it may have an eroding effect on the person's self-esteem and sense of independence (McKnight, 1977).

ASSESSMENT AS A CLINICAL FUNCTION

The clinical intent of assessment is to provide a means of looking at the client in a comprehensive fashion and to arrive at information that will be used in the planning process by the client and the agency. The assessing professional uses a physio-psycho-social approach, which includes environmental understanding, interpretation of observations and findings, and setting of goals that ensure appropriate use of resources and services.

For the client the assessment process offers relief and support at a time of difficulty; ascertains potential for help, both in terms of availability of services and the client's willingness and ability to use them; and clarifies the situation and problem areas, offering the client an opportunity for self-evaluation. Both the client and the helping professional are concerned with the examination and diagnosis of problems, determination of service needs, exploration of options and resources, costs, and the development of appropriate and available service plans.

ASSESSMENT AS A MANAGEMENT TOOL

Simultaneously with the clinical process, the assessment fulfills managerial requirements. Effective administration and management require systematized data collection, efficiency, and standardization. To this end, an agency or service organization has the responsibility to develop a methodology that will make explicit its position and policies and allow for means of accountability and codification of data. An effective assessment integrates both the clinical and the managerial functions, resulting in a plan that is both helpful to the client and consistent with organizational policy.

Initial Phase of Assessment

It is essential to involve the old person in the assessment process as early as possible. This is a step often overlooked by anxious families and even by referring agencies. The assumption may be that the old person is too disabled or the situation too critical to allow for the "luxury" of consulting the person who will become the actual client. However, such a shortcut usually wastes time in the long run. Old persons are likely to refuse or sabotage the plans proposed for their supposed benefit, unless they have been involved in developing them. For adults to have control over their lives snatched away arbitrarily is both threatening and demeaning. Nor do they lose the ability to make decisions because they have passed a certain birthday, become ill, or encounter a crisis. Even those with severe cognitive or sensory impairments can usually be engaged in at least some discussion of their needs and preferred ways of meeting them. At the very least they should be entitled to veto power. Therefore, professional helpers must always attempt to involve potential clients in discussing changes and services being suggested in their behalf.

UNDERSTANDING THE INITIAL REQUEST

Assessment is the gateway to service. It enables the practitioner to help the client and, whenever possible, the family to gain a clearer understanding of the problem and the range of options that may help resolve it. However, assessment is rarely requested as such. Most people call a helping organization with a specific service in mind, which they believe will alleviate a problem for themselves and their spouses, friends, or relatives. If the person who receives the call responds only with the criteria of eligibility for that service, the underlying purpose of the call may be totally missed. Active listening must begin with the first request for help, whether the person who responds is a telephone operator for a service provider or a trained intake worker in a social service agency.

 Mr. Frankel called an agency to request Meals on Wheels. The intake worker, mindful of the fact that the availability of such meals was limited, told Mr. Frankel that, since he was not housebound nor recently discharged from the hospital, he was not eligible. Mr. Frankel subsequently called someone else in the agency and complained bitterly about the "unfeeling" treatment he had received. What emerged was that Mr. Frankel, although in fairly good health himself, had a wife who, because of Alzheimer's disease, had lost her ability to cook or keep house. Mr. Frankel had taken over the other household tasks, but he had never learned how to cook, and the total care of his wife left him little energy or inclination to learn. He had not mentioned his wife's condition to the intake worker BECAUSE SHE HAD NOT ASKED.

DISCOVERING THE PRECIPITANT

When a request for information or service is made, the alert human service worker will always ask: "Why now?" What has happened in the old person's or family's life to create a need for service today rather than last week or last month? If there is no obvious change in circumstances, such as recent illness or bereavement, for example, the precipitant for this request may be an anniversary of an illness or death, or it may lie in the old person's support system — the people who make up the social environment. Perhaps a relative, friend, or neighbor who provided help with shopping or household tasks is planning a vacation or is in the throes of some personal crisis that makes him or her less available to the old person. Such a loss may be social as well as purely practical; the shopping chores may be necessary, but the visits and human contact are essential antidotes for loneliness and isolation.

DISCOVERING THE MEANING OF THE PRECIPITANT

Not only the trigger event itself but also the meaning of the event to the caller, the old person, and/or others in the family are essential to a complete assessment. The assessment worker must not assume that the precipitant means the same to the caller as it does to the worker, or that it means the same to the caller as to the potential client, if they are not one and the same.

A niece called to inquire about services for her aunt, Mrs. Rodriguez, who had Parkinson's disease. The condition had been diagnosed some time earlier, but the niece had become concerned when, at a family gathering, Mrs. Rodriguez had not been able to hold a teacup without spilling.

When the assessment worker called Mrs. Rodriguez to set an appointment, the woman was quite resistant. She finally agreed to a visit when the worker assured her that she was under no obligation to accept any service—she only wanted to let her know what was available. It would be up to Mrs. Rodriguez to decide whether she wanted to use anything. During the visit Mrs. Rodriguez appeared quite anxious. Encouraged to talk about her situation, she finally revealed that she was very fearful that her family wanted to put her in a nursing home. That was her interpretation of their concern over the teacup incident. Once she was reassured that less radical measures were available, she calmed down and expressed interest in hearing about them.

DISCOVERING THE MEANING OF THE SOLUTION

The first question in assessment, "Why now?", is therefore followed by "What does this mean to you/your family/your aged relative?" These questions are important because the reasons people request service are not always those the agency has in mind. A family may request evaluation of their elder's needs because they hope to facilitate entry into a nursing home that has a long waiting list, because their doctor told them to, or because they hope to reduce the older person's complaints and criticisms by providing additional services or counseling. Or they may be going on vacation and want to know what resources would be available to their older relative during their absence. An old person may inquire about service in order to get what her next-door neighbor gets, to pacify an anxious son or daughter who wants her to "do something," or perhaps to have an excuse to talk to someone. Knowing what the caller hopes to achieve helps the assessment worker focus further discussion so as to develop a helpful and realistic plan of intervention. The role of the worker is to gather data, not for its own sake but in order to develop a sound basis for further action.

Here are some principles to keep in mind during initial contacts.

- Distress is often expressed as a request for a tangible service or information.
- Knowing the precipitant helps clarify the nature of the distress. It is also essential to understand the meaning of the precipitant and the proposed solution to both the caller and the older person, if they are not the same.
- If the caller is not the old person, he or she may be helped to see the need to involve that person, if it can be shown that this will alleviate the distress of the caller.

Middle Phase of Assessment

The understanding that emerges from the initial contacts—sometimes referred to as "information and referral" or "screening"—constitutes the beginning of the comprehensive assessment, once client, family, and agency have agreed that this is the appropriate next step. The process usually consists of in-person contacts with the old person, the family (if available and interested), and any others directly involved in the situation that presents the problem. Since the purpose is to obtain information for and about the client, there is an advantage to conducting the assessment in the client's own surroundings. Not only is being at home more comfortable and, in the case of frail older persons, more practical, but a home visit also enhances the assessor's understanding of the client's environment, circumstances, condition, and functioning. Regardless of the location of the interviews, however, the professional's task is to help the old person and the family explore options, analyze alternatives, and emerge with a sound plan and, if indicated, a coordinated service package.

There are several principles that should guide the assessing worker in helping the clients take stock and evaluate the need for next steps.

- *Minimal intervention* is the philosophical position that old persons are helped most effectively if given only as much help and service as is absolutely necessary. This means taking a chance on less rather than more in order to test and strengthen the older person's capacity for self-help.
- *Self-determination* acknowledges the right of each individual to determine his or her own destiny, even if this defies the standards or values of those who are advising or helping.
- *Respecting autonomy* means allowing adults to act in their own behalf and exercise their own choices. If a person appears at risk because of confusion, abuse, or neglect, the danger must be very carefully weighed before intrusive measures are resorted to.

Assessment is most comprehensive when it is conducted in multidisciplinary fashion, utilizing the contributions of several professional specialties. Although the basic team most commonly consists of social worker, nurse, and perhaps an internist or general practitioner, thorough diagnostic procedures to deepen understanding may include such specialists as psychiatrists, neurologists, cardiovascular diagnosticians, dentists, audiologists, ophthalmologists, architects, occupational therapists, and physiotherapists. Use of projective tests administered by a psychologist may be a helpful nonverbal approach in understanding the needs of inarticulate or confused persons. These specialized procedures should not be resorted to automatically or routinely but coordinated and interpreted in a planned fashion if the client's functioning presents unanswered questions. Such a team approach can be most helpful in achieving a comprehensive, or holistic, understanding of the old person, but specialists are not always available. Whether or not they are, however, it is always most important to pay attention to the old person's account of his or her concerns as well as to consider the information that can be added by family, friends, and other associates.

Whether the assessment is conducted by a team or by one practitioner, the process should cover medical data; nutritional and other health issues; psychiatric and emotional considerations; the social milieu and its utilization; economic facts and problems; and the attitudinal, relationship, coping, and behavioral patterns that constitute the individual's uniqueness. Collecting these can be expedited by data-gathering instruments, but the involvement of the practitioner is essential for their interpretation. As current facts and previous history are discussed with clients, family, and professional sources and the interactions among them are observed, a more vivid and accurate picture of the client's functioning emerges.

Because the information to be evaluated is so complex, it is helpful to have an outline that can serve as an organizing instrument. The checklist below may prove useful for this purpose.

CHECKLIST FOR ASSESSMENT DATA:
A HOLISTIC VIEW

   I. Social Functioning
      A. Current coping methods
      B. Previous coping methods
      C. Social history
         1. Major life events
         2. Family structure and patterns of interaction
  II. Physical functioning
      A. Current medical problems
      B. Observed functional capacity to deal with activities of daily living
      C. Medical history
 III. Psychological functioning
      A. Affect (level of emotional expression)
      B. Cognitive abilities
      C. Mental state
      D. Nature of relationship formations
         1. With assessing worker
         2. With others (observed and reported)
      E. Psychiatric history, if any
  IV. Environmental functioning
      A. Living conditions
      B. Financial/economic circumstances
      C. Changes from former life-style

    V. Exploration of external resources
- A. Informal support network (family, friends, neighbors, and so on)
- B. Community services
- C. Financial assistance programs
- D. Subsidies

There are a number of models in existence that are designed to help assessing interviewers organize their data. Some—such as those of Pfeifer (1977), Kane and Kane (1981), and Brink (1986)—describe various measurement and rating methods in considerable detail. These are particularly useful if the information being gathered will also be used for research purposes. Others—such as those of Silverstone and Burack-Weiss (1983) and Greene (1986)—present models that link family assessment to the functional needs of elders. All of them provide ways of obtaining useful information; however, the sheer volume of methods can be overwhelming and intimidating when one is considering how best to gain information about a particular client. The following checklist, using material from a number of sources and building in greater detail on the checklist above, can assist the practitioner in both interviewing and documentation.

    I. Social functioning
- A. Current coping methods
  1. Who made the first contact to present the problem?
  2. What is the relationship of the caller to the old person whose problem is being reported?
  3. What is the nature of the request?
  4. Why now?
  5. Apparent precipitant or trigger event
  6. Worker's view of meaning of precipitant to prospective client/family
- B. Previous coping methods
  1. Has there been a similar crisis in the past?
  2. How did the client/family deal with it?
  3. What is the client's/family's preferred solution?
  4. What do the client/family hope to achieve through the preferred solution?
  5. What were the previous attempts to solve this current problem?

    D. Social history
       1. Major life events
          a. Early personal history
          b. Marriage, birth of children, deaths
          c. Has there been a recent bereavement (loss of spouse, relative, friend, pet, role, or self-image)?
       2. Family structure and patterns of interaction
          a. Who is currently involved with the client?
          b. What is the level of involvement?
          c. How do involved persons feel about the situation?
          d. What is the family/network structure?
          e. How have relationships changed over time?
          f. Is there disagreement between family members as to desirable solution to current problem?
          g. Is there evidence of conflict in life tasks/stages among family members, including the old person (second marriage, retirement, new baby)?
          h. Is the client at risk of abuse, neglect (including self-neglect), or exploitation? How serious and/or immediate is the danger?
       3. Social network
          a. Does the client have significant relationships outside the family?
          b. Observed interactions with others
          c. Reported interactions (give source)
          d. Socialization, activity interests of client
          e. Work history (including current work, if any)
       4. Interaction with professional helpers
          a. How does the client relate to the worker?
          b. What are the worker's reactions to the client? (Indicate any strong positive or negative feelings evoked by the client or the situation.)
          c. How does the client relate to other professional helpers (doctors, home help, service personnel)?
II. Physical functioning
    A. Current medical problems
       1. Client view of current medical status
       2. Medical conditions that cause limitations
    B. Observed functional capacity to deal with activities of daily living
       1. Observed client functioning—indicate whether client is

unable to do or performs with difficulty any of the
following tasks:

    a. walking (indoors, outdoors)
    b. dressing
    c. administering self-medication
    d. climbing stairs
    e. bathing/grooming
    f. eating
    g. preparing meals
    h. housekeeping
    i. doing laundry
    j. transferring from bed to chair
    k. toileting (note if incontinent)
    l. shopping
    m. engaging in sexual activity
    n. using telephone
    o. managing finances
    p. reading/writing
    q. using public or private transportation

  2. Observed client appearance
    a. Dress
    b. Personal hygiene/grooming
    c. Gait
    d. Evidence of energy level/mobility

  3. Observed client responses to interview
    a. Eye contact
    b. Affect/manner
    c. Evidence of visual/hearing problems
    d. Speech patterns (slow response, words jumbled, talks nonstop, jumps from topic to topic, limited or no fluency in English, gives only yes or no answers, and so on)

C. Medical history
  1. Obtain source of medical information
  2. Review currency of contact with health professionals
  3. Note any specific medical condition that causes limitations

III. Psychological functioning
  A. Affect (level of emotional expression)
    1. How does the client react to the problem, limitations, or health deficits?

      2. What is the client's observed attitude/stance toward the worker?

  B. Cognitive abilities

      1. Orientation to reality

      2. Long-term and short-term memory

      3. Judgment

      4. Evidence of client wandering or getting lost

  C. Mental state

      1. Client self-concept (Is it similar to or different from perceptions reported by others?)

      2. Vegetative signs of depression (disturbed eating and/or sleeping patterns, diminished sexual drive, and so on)

      3. Other signs of depression: apparent sadness (distinguish from normal grieving); self-blame; flat affect; slow response; inability to experience pleasure; agitation or confusion

      4. Verbal and behavioral clues (If the client is described by others as depressed, withdrawn, or manipulative, how did the behavior manifest itself?)

      5. Evidence of hallucinations, delusions, phobias, obsessions

  D. Nature of relationship formations

      1. With assessing worker

      2. With others (observed and reported)

      3. Observed/reported coping strategies (denial, avoidance, reliance on others, overcompensation)

      4. Effectiveness of coping strategies (for whom?)

      5. Dependency patterns (on whom and for what?)

  E. Psychiatric history, if any

      1. Suicidal ideation, or previous suicide attempts (reported by client or others)

      2. Previous psychiatric history or psychiatric hospitalization

IV. Environmental functioning

  A. Living conditions

      1. Neighborhood

         a. What type of neighborhood is it (urban, rural, family, commercial)?

         b. Is transportation available/accessible?

         c. Is shopping accessible?

      2. Building

         a. Appearance

         b. Upkeep

      c. Safety features

      d. Barriers to mobility (stairs, disrepair, and so on)

   3. Interior of dwelling

      a. Hygiene (clean/dirty; evidence of odors or spoiled food; adequacy of bathroom equipment; evidence of roaches, mice, or other vermin?)

      b. Safety and well-being (living space neat/cluttered; adequacy of food supply; adequacy of cooking/storage facilities; evidence of fire or other hazards — note burned pots or cigarette burns; indoor temperature; clocks and calendar set correctly; scatter rugs; access to telephone?)

      c. Other observations: (family pictures; decorations; boxes not unpacked; condition of furniture; pets; behavior or maintenance of pets; evidence of interests and hobbies?)

  B. Financial/economic circumstances

  C. Changes from former life-style

 V. Exploration of external resources

  A. Informal support network (family, friends, neighbors, and so on)

  B. Community services

  C. Financial assistance programs

  D. Subsidies

This detailed outline can guide human service workers regardless of their professional disciplines. However, in certain settings where assessments are conducted by teams of workers with different specializations, their individual evaluations must be added to the overall assessment. These should include a reflection of the degree of crisis, factors pertaining to the life stage of the assessed client(s), and salient need. If there are differences of opinion among team members, these should also be clarified and recorded.

The concluding item of any assessment is the recommended plan of action. The plan includes the following:

1. Worker/team/agency recommendations for services or other actions, including referrals to other appropriate sources of help. Indicate how these relate to client/family goals.

2. Client/family acceptance and rejection of recommendations. Indicate which portion of the plan has been mutually agreed upon and accepted.
3. Next actions to be taken by agency, worker, client, and family. Indicate the time frame for these.
4. Short-term and long-range plans. Identify and distinguish between them.
5. Time frame for evaluating whether goals have been achieved.

USE AND MISUSE OF INSTRUMENTS

Regardless of the model or combination of models selected, it should be emphasized that although such instruments are valuable for the organization and presentation of data, their use is an adjunct to, not a substitute for, professional judgment. It must also be emphasized that most instruments address the need for all the information one eventually needs to amass for long-term treatment or intervention. However, most older persons cannot sustain, in one sitting, the energy needed to deal with such a comprehensive, lengthy, and focused approach. The assessing worker must be sensitive to allowing the client to make tangential comments, which are often more revealing than the facts, and to allow for rest stops. It is better to divide the assessment process into several interviews than to exhaust the client in one long session.

Another hazard in the assessment process is that many special-purpose instruments may be used in the evaluation of one client's needs. For instance, there may be one questionnaire for housing, another for financial eligibility, and still another for in-home services. Much of the same material may be covered in each, and the repetition can be exhausting and confusing to the client and can result in duplication of effort for the busy interviewer.

Because of the tendency to see the instrument as a "test" to be passed or failed, there is also the likelihood that the client will experience anxiety, which may affect the overall score or outcome. Sensitivity to the client's reactions is therefore paramount at all times.

 Mr. and Mrs. Marcus, a couple in their eighties, had applied for day care for the husband. The assessing nurse, in the course of her evaluation, asked questions to test his recent and remote memory and orientation to

time, place, and person. Mr. Marcus became so fearful of giving the
wrong answer that he panicked and was unable to give any answers at
all. His wife, in turn, became extremely upset at this "evidence" that her
husband's condition was much worse than she had supposed. Convinced
that "his mind was gone," she began to think in terms of institutional
care. This was unfortunate, because although Mr. Marcus was exper-
iencing some memory deficits, they did not interfere seriously with
his day-to-day functioning.

The reaction of Mr. and Mrs. Marcus also reflects a cultural
bias that invests test scores with greater credibility than may be
warranted. The same thing often happens with the interpretation of
test scores for children. However, the elderly are particularly vulnerable to such misinterpretations, both their own and those of the
person conducting the assessment. They are likely to have less
energy and fewer advocates to help them contest a mistaken assessment, as well as being handicapped by the societal expectation of
negative findings about old people. It is therefore incumbent upon
the assessing workers to be extremely sensitive to the effect of the
assessment process itself on the person being assessed.

It is important to remember that the measurement of phenomena affects the phenomena measured (Mahoney and Arnhoff,
1978). As we stated earlier, there is always the expectation that the
old person initiates, or at least participates in making, the request for
help. The objective of the assessment is therefore not only to understand the old person but also to involve him or her and offer
choices in the decision-making process.

HOW MUCH ASSESSMENT IS NECESSARY?

Not all assessments require an equally extensive outlay of
time. A request for help with household chores, for instance, may
not take as much time or take as many factors into account as would
a need for a total change in life-style. Nevertheless, even in an
apparently simple request the underlying issues may be very complex indeed. The nature of the request does not necessarily indicate
how much assessment will be needed.

 Mrs. Callahan called a service-providing agency to request housekeeping
help. During the first home visit the assessing worker discovered that
Mrs. Callahan had recently returned from a rehabilitation center, where

she had been sent after her right leg had been amputated owing to uncontrollable circulatory problems. Her left leg was now swollen and discolored, and she was fearful of the possibility of a second amputation. She was living alone in a second-floor walk-up apartment that not only precluded access to the world outside her door but also made her extremely vulnerable in case of fire or other emergency. Although she had two stepsons who were concerned about her, both were living in distant cities. Her local support system consisted of a cousin who was elderly and in poor health, a few friends, and nurses in the rehabilitation facility who had taken an interest in her. It was obvious that Mrs. Callahan needed a great deal more than help with household chores. Her chief need, in fact, was for someone with whom she could discuss her situation in order to arrive at decisions that would be both realistic and personally acceptable.

Sometimes, in situations such as Mrs. Callahan's, the need is obvious to everyone except the client. However, Mrs. Callahan was eager to find someone in whom she could confide safely, who could help her to facilitate decisions when she was ready to make them, and who could help her confront reality (in this case the potential loss of her remaining leg) without condemning her fears and vacillations. In other words, she wanted a counselor.

In this instance the request and proposed solution offered by the elderly client was appropriate but insufficient. Providing housekeeping service alone, even though it was clearly needed, would have been an inadequate response to the client's total situation. Minimal intervention does not mean doing the least possible but, rather, providing just the amount of service that meets the client's immediate needs, without undercutting his or her coping capacities to plan and contemplate next steps. Introducing a counselor into Mrs. Callahan's situation also lays the foundation for future discussion of potential change of apartments, introduction of assistive devices to assure greater safety and mobility, and the client's wresting with the grief and fear that resulted from the amputation and her deteriorating health, as well as her consequent isolation.

The intent of assessment is not solely to lead the client to a concrete solution or to counseling. The assessing agency may not be able to provide either. Rather, the intent is to help the client grasp the implications of the current situation so as to be more knowledgeable in the search for appropriate resources. A parallel approach is that of the Mayo Clinic in Rochester, Minnesota, which offers a comprehensive medical diagnostic service but then usually refers patients to physicians in their own community. In contrast to this diagnostic facility's methods, however, the assessment process is the same whether or not the assessing agency is also capable of supplying services, because the assessment findings can, and should be, communicated to the client and family and to referral sources, should they turn out to be required. It must be noted that the assessment serves the functions of not only identifying service or other needs but also clarifying that no help is needed and reaffirming for the client and family that the situation at present is under adequate control. Thus, the assessment process also serves to validate the client's resourcefulness, coping ability, and functional sufficiency.

Final Phase of Assessment

Although assessment is often invaluable in helping elderly people and their families sort out issues and arrive at decisions, it is not an end in itself. Its object is to guide the client and family to develop a plan that will meet the identified needs, using resources that are *available, acceptable* to the clients, and *affordable* through their own means or through community or government subsidies for which they are eligible.

Often, more than one solution is available. In that case client and family preference, far more than professional recommendation, will, and should, govern the outcome. To paraphrase an old proverb, the professional proposes, but the client disposes. A successful assessment is not necessarily one that results in the client's acceptance of the solution the assessing worker considers most desirable but one that adds to the data base on which the client and family can make a decision. The most valuable outcome of assessment may be the client's and the family's discovery that they have a choice and are not locked into a situation over which they have no control.

SETTING REASONABLE AND REACHABLE GOALS

The goals that emerge from assessment may include maintenance of the status quo, services to prevent or delay further deterioration, or support in the face of inevitable decline. Often, the need presented by the client, and more particularly by the family, is for clarification of the changes—cognitive, physiological, or behavioral—to ascertain if now is the time for making alternative living plans. They may be greatly reassured to learn that professional judgment validates their own sense of what is happening, that they are handling it well, and that no change is needed; or alternatively, if the situation has become intolerable for them, that they are justified in seeking relief.

The professional who has invested a great deal of time in assessment may feel frustrated if the outcome is merely justification of the status quo—namely, that all should remain as it is. Yet the relief to the client and family may be immense; and if the old person is spared the trauma of a change in his or her life or an unnecessary move, this may do more than any amount of service to prolong life and enhance its quality. Often, the best prescription is to be brave and do nothing.

However, the goal emerging from assessment may be one of helping the old person to improve functioning and/or life-style significantly. The means to achieve such a goal may range from securing a more benign environment to helping the client improve interpersonal relationships and enhance self-esteem. Of course, it is always more gratifying to the professional to be a facilitator of change; and where change is necessary or desirable to the client, such gratification is valid. However, it is essential to make sure that the client does see the need and potential benefit of any change. In other words, the goals of professional and client must be congruent. An agreed-upon goal is the essence of therapeutic alliance; without it the professional and the client will be working at cross-purposes, with disappointment as the inevitable result for both.

THE QUESTION OF TREATABILITY

The foregoing discussion of the need for congruent goals raises the often vexing question of treatability. Can old people really change and grow? Basing their findings on research, experience, and observation, gerontological practitioners are convinced that old persons can and do adapt to changing circumstances and find the process enriching, whether it is accomplished with or without therapeutic assistance. In assessing the potential for treatability, the clinician must avoid two hazards: the temptation to impose his or her own goals on the client and the tendency to underestimate the client's capacity for growth. The old person's eagerness to change something in his or her life pattern — far more than age, symptoms, or previous history — determines the possibility of achieving the change. Closely linked to this is the level of hope in the professional. If the practitioner believes that change is possible, the existence of that belief constitutes a powerful reinforcement to the motivation of the client, who might otherwise succumb to the social stereotype that "at your age, what difference does it make?"

When one is assessing the motivation for change, it is important to distinguish between words and actions. Many people, especially if they have had extensive experience with helping organizations, can "talk a good fight" and sound as if they are interested in effecting change when, in fact, they are not. Others, who may not be particularly articulate or familiar with the jargon of intervention, show their determination to change their lives for the better by their actions — by actually getting down to work and doing something. This difference is illustrated by several clients who used the services of the same agency over a period of several years.

Mrs. Angelini, a dramatic and engaging woman in her seventies, talked at great length about her relationships with others and her estimate of herself but, in fact, made no changes in these. She also made it clear that she did not wish to do so.

Another client, Mrs. Benson, a ninety-year-old with severe hearing loss and no family, seized every opportunity to improve her life-style. This ranged from getting a better hearing aid to applying for and obtaining a housing subsidy so that she could have a richer social life in an apartment building of senior citizens.

A third client, Mr. Cardman, lost his wife when he was in his eighties. At first he used the agency and his assigned counselor as a sounding board to help him deal with his grief. Then he moved on to reflect on his life and arrive at some decisions and ways to implement them.

Both Mrs. Angelini and Mr. Cardman were articulate and introspective, but Mr. Cardman used these characteristics to achieve change, while Mrs. Angelini used them, very skillfully, to avoid change. Mrs. Benson, who was neither articulate nor introspective, nevertheless used the agency to help herself improve the quality of her life.

In the assessment of the potential for and actuality of change, client behavior is a more accurate indicator than words. Improvement does not depend on gaining insight and still less on talking as if one has "seen the light" but, rather, on demonstrating by action the motivation to make things better for oneself.

ASSESSMENT AS A LINK TO SERVICE PROVISION

When the assessing organization also provides services, whether these consist solely of assistance with daily needs or include counseling and planning, the assessment process paves the way for the client's utilization of these services. If the client has difficulty in navigating the often complex service arrangements, or if dealing with several service providers becomes confusing, a worker who facilitates these linkages for the client, often called the case manager, is very helpful. The assessing worker may or may not serve as a case manager, but the experience of discussing and evaluating one's needs with a professional makes forming a relationship with a case manager and service personnel a natural next step — that is, if the assessment process has been perceived as helpful and productive.

Need for Reassessment

If assessment has resulted in practical services, ongoing case management, or counseling, a procedure for periodic reassessments should be built into the plan. This serves to update earlier conclusions, considers the effects of services provided, and allows for indicated adjustments.

As important as it is to establish goals, it is also essential to determine whether the agreed-upon plan is meeting these goals, when they have been met, and when they are no longer appropriate. This can best be done within a time frame set during the initial assessment. Concrete, specific goals are easier to reassess than more global ones, such as "providing emotional support" or "maintaining independence." If the intent is to provide assistance during recuperation from illness or injury, to mobilize or reconstitute a support network, or to facilitate the process of grief, it is possible to measure the extent to which these aims have been reached. The question raised in the assessment then becomes: Can the helping agency's presence be withdrawn? Is the client ready to take on a new task, with or without help? Or is the support system so minimal, and the physical or emotional disability of the client so extensive, that a helping presence will probably be required on a permanent basis? Even when the latter appears to be true, the support system, the level of disability, and the coping capacity of the client need to be reexamined periodically. There is always the possibility of unanticipated change.

Once a service is in place, time pressures can make it easy to allow subsequent contacts with the client to become superficial. For instance, Gubrium (1975) describes five-to-fifteen-minute interviews held in preparation for staff meetings about residents in a nursing home, which consisted mainly of social chitchat. Unless the resident happened to be upset or complained about something, the social facade was accepted without question as evidence of good adjustment. On the other hand, even a minor complaint was seen as evidence of a potentially major personality problem. Reassessments, although not necessarily as lengthy as initial assessments, must examine enough dimensions of the client's situation to elicit real information. Some of this may be obtained from others in addition to the client: family members, service providers, volunteer visitors, and the like. The questions "What is different now?" and "What has happened since the last contact?" always need to be addressed.

Dilemma of Economics and Professional Practice

Professional judgment, although essential to the provision of individualized service, is not always easily quantified. Even those who subscribe to similar goals and standards of intervention do not always agree on what should be done, how much, or for how long. Individual interpretation of standards is fundamental to independent professional practice in all disciplines. On the other hand, providers of human services have become increasingly dependent on funding sources, both governmental and private, which stress accountability and uniformity of service delivery.

Put another way, in the clinical sense assessment is a therapeutic tool and thus a service in itself; however, values and standards of practice performance are often in conflict with the results expected for documentation and accountability. For instance, if a scoring instrument is intended to measure the need for concrete services that are made possible by a funding grant, the efforts of the assessing worker to renew the client's confidence in his or her own coping capacities that result in no service will receive no acknowledgment by the funding source, since no service units will have been generated. The dilemma lies in the fact that demands for clinical expertise may not fit the world in which cost-effectiveness and unit counts often take precedence over practice considerations.

Administrative concerns with the methodology of assessment address such questions as what services to provide, whom to serve, how to organize to make assessments and services accessible, how to define geographic boundaries and ascertain economic and demographic characteristics of the population served, and how to determine staffing needs. The instruments used for this purpose are factual, based on universal criteria. Such standardization is essential: It guarantees consistency and efficiency, allows for means of accountability and codification, helps uncover service gaps and define service needs and direction, and contributes to the building of a general body of knowledge. Viewed in this way, quantifying instruments can be effective, provided that their purpose is clear and coordinated with organizational policies and that staff who apply the instruments are professionally oriented and stringently trained.

The dilemma in the productive execution of assessments — whose purpose is to respond to client needs in an informed, supportive, and well-planed way — lies in the potential conflicts between clinical management and administrative management. Although there is an acknowledged need for standardization and a systematic approach to information gathering, instruments used to measure and codify must also incorporate a measure of professional quality based on clinical judgment, which is often not easily quantifiable.

Furthermore, to truly reflect the intended goal of the assessment process, any instrument used must include clear statements of position and agency policy. Somewhere between the extremes of "I have a good heart and want to help old people" and the near-punitive method of scoring the deficits of aging—which forces clients to view sickness as a benefit that leads to service (that is, the sicker the client, the greater the eligibility for service and the higher the reimbursement to the service provider)—lies the concept of minimal intervention. As we mentioned above, this consists of fostering continued independence, encouraging alternative coping patterns, and protecting the person's decision-making capacity by giving only the amount of service that is essential to the client's continued autonomy. Minimal intervention as a desired goal is frequently reflected in the assessment tools already in existence; what is not nearly as well addressed is that offering less service is not always cost-effective in dollars and cents, since it may require extensive clinical intervention and encouragement. Funding sources are geared to pay for specifically stated activities, whereas selective nonactivity based on clinical judgment and assessment may in fact be as costly or even more so, both in terms of nonreimbursable time and potential loss of service provision income. Nonetheless, although this cannot be measured in hard currency, the effort spent in minimizing service utilization by strengthening self-sufficiency may yield rich personal dividends to the clients.

This dilemma makes it imperative for service-providing organizations to develop clear definitions of their assessment strategies and the means of documenting the effects of these in maintaining client independence and optimal functioning. Such documentation can provide leverage with funding sources and help counteract the tendency to measure programs solely in terms of units of concrete service rather than in terms of the effects of service (or nonservice) on the functioning and well-being of elderly clients. This indicates that professional workers have a responsibility to consider the administrative implications of their interventions, even if they are not administrators, managers, or legislators. Those who would maintain standards of clinical excellence cannot afford to ignore economic reality.

CHAPTER 5

Counseling: Basic Philosophy and Generic Techniques

Once a dynamic assessment has determined what plan of action is most appropriate, how shall the plan be implemented?

Old age is a time of rapid change—and often of change perceived as loss, such as retirement, widowhood, physical or mental deterioration, and shrinkage of one's social network and economic resources. As the population in this vulnerable age group increases, a variety of remedies, services, and responses have come into being, many of which did not exist even a few years ago. These are of two major kinds: bringing auxiliary services into the older person's environment and changing or restructuring that environment. Responses of the first kind include special transportation, meals on wheels, and in-home services ranging from simple companionship, through chore/housekeeping and home repair services, to skilled nursing care in the home. Responses of the second kind, namely, those that offer a change of environment, include specialized recreation or community centers, adult day-care facilities, housing designed for the aged, retirement communities, and nursing homes.

Hospitals, clinics, social service agencies, and private practitioners have begun to specialize in the treatment of problems of the elderly on numerous levels, choosing from and combining the range of services and responses mentioned above. At the same time, there has been increasing recognition that older people are entitled to and capable of using counseling or therapeutic treatment to sort out their problems.

The variety of problem-solving choices can thus be rather overwhelming. As we saw in Chapter 4, a systematic assessment of an individual's needs and preferences can help to narrow down a problem, but a plan recommended is not the same as a plan implemented.

One common element among the responses just noted is that they all have to be talked about in order to help the client arrive at and carry through a plan of action. The technique required in each exploration of options is discussion — to determine availability, compare advantages and disadvantages, and, above all, establish their meaning to the client.

In-depth extended discussion may indeed be the principal instrument used to help clients effect change. It is used to identify and refocus the stated problem or situation, mobilize client and family strengths, clarify resistance to change, resolve or modify conflicts, and, overall, help each client achieve a better fit between what is available and what is acceptable. A series of such discussions — usually called counseling, psychotherapy, or clinical intervention — may be used with individuals, couples, families, or small groups.

In addition to considering client feelings and perceptions, the discussion may focus on specific services that may alleviate the problem. If one or more of these services is agreed to, the professional may also be responsible for locating and monitoring the service(s), interpreting the service(s) to the client, and perhaps acting as the client's advocate with service providers if difficulties occur or persist. If these functions are added to the original discussion mode, the process is usually called case management or care management. The same label may be used if the service involves negotiating a change in environment, but the process is likely to take longer, involve more people, and stir up even more intense feelings.

It is sometimes supposed that counseling requires special skills but that case management is simple and routine because the services being managed are concrete and specific. Nothing could be further from the truth. The services involved usually mean a change in self-image and life-style for the person receiving them, and this fact has profound emotional repercussions. Services that affect one's daily routine, especially those involving food and shelter, often stir up an immense amount of primitive feeling and seemingly irrational behavior. The case manager is constantly challenged to understand the meaning of the behavior and to be a representative of external reality while acknowledging the power and validity of the feelings involved — one's own, the client's, and the service provider's. Anyone who supposes that counselors or therapists deal with the intricacies of emotion but that case managers deal only with concrete services has never encountered the reality of an old person in confrontation with a service system. The apparently simple theory of matching services to deficits is not so simple in practice (Burack-Weiss, 1988).

Basic Definitions for Counseling and Case Management

A characteristic feature of work with the elderly is that provision of assistive services may often be intertwined with planning and interpersonal or psychological treatment. These two aspects are often provided by different people, although they may be combined. Following are some basic definitions of the interpersonal and service components and their interrelationship.

INTERPERSONAL TREATMENT OR COUNSELING

The primary socialization of every human being takes place in an interpersonal context. The ability to relate to others — initially developed in the family — is a skill used throughout life in all kinds of social situations. The hostess who keeps a dinner party going smoothly, the teacher who controls a classroom successfully, the employer who defuses an office quarrel, or the director of a senior citizen center who controls the behavior of disruptive members are all utilizing this basic skill. As society has moved from a focus on materials to a focus on service, more and more attention has been devoted to the study and development of interpersonal skills. Some professions, such as psychiatry, clinical psychology, clinical social work, and family therapy, deal primarily with the study of the interpersonal context — what makes it work and how to correct it when it has gone wrong. Practitioners in these disciplines may subscribe to one or more of a variety of theoretical models — psychodynamic, behaviorist, cognitive-emotional, or family systems, to name some of the major ones — and utilize a wide range of techniques and strategies. A common element in these diverse approaches (with the possible exception of classic behaviorism) is that they seek to understand the meaning system of the client and use the treatment relationship as the primary instrument of change.

CASE MANAGEMENT

Intervention with the elderly often includes locating a variety of services. Because of the complexity of the number of agencies that provide services (or in certain geographic areas, the scarcity of such agencies), extensive knowledge of resources (and their availability) is required. This means knowing about the eligibility requirements of public agencies and their funding capacities, which are apt to change frequently, and the variety of other services available through the private sector. Case management may be performed in a variety of settings by practitioners representing a wide range of backgrounds, such as nursing, social work, public service employment, recreation work, and rehabilitation, to name a few. Professionals whose primary service is the treatment of interpersonal relationships sometimes also provide case management. As we noted above, case managers need to be aware of the emotional impact of the services they deal in and, if their clients also have interpersonal therapists, to collaborate with those persons.

Such collaboration will be facilitated if case managers as well as counselors understand the nature of the counseling process. Like any other process, it has beginning, middle, and end stages, with specific tasks appropriate to each. The remainder of this chapter describes the beginning, middle, and concluding phases of individual counseling. Many of the problems that arise in the counseling process also occur in the course of case management, and illustrations are drawn from both. It must be noted that professional counseling should not be undertaken by those who are not trained or licensed to practice it.

Beginning Phase of Counseling

The first steps in developing a treatment relationship are as follows:

- Listening actively
- Setting congruent goals
- Establishing an initial contract

Active listening was discussed in Chapter 2 in terms of its role in initial contacts with clients or family members. In the early phase of counseling the purpose of active listening is to identify themes important to the client, especially those that may be different from the problem originally presented.

 While living alone in her apartment after her husband's death, Mrs. Dover had suffered several falls resulting in fractures. Her daughters urged her to move to a long-term-care facility, and she finally agreed to apply. In the application interview, however, she spoke several times about the loss of another daughter, who had died at the age of five.

Mrs. Dover's preoccupation with this event might have been seen as a digression, an attempt to avoid talking about a move, or as evidence of reduced ability to concentrate or of limited attention span. The fact that she kept returning to the same theme with considerable intensity of feeling, however, might suggest that the loss of her daughter and the impending loss of her home were connected in some way.

 When the counselor asked Mrs. Dover if the thought of giving up her apartment reminded her of the loss of her daughter, she immediately began to speak of her apartment, how much she had enjoyed decorating and maintaining it, the independence it represented, and how sad she felt about giving it up.

Mrs. Dover had to mourn the loss of her current life-style before she could address planning another. She gave the interviewer clues to this need by her repeated references to an earlier loss.

Listening for underlying or divergent themes enables the counselor to help the client identify the most salient need or the problem of greatest concern and is a necessary prelude to setting the goals to be worked on in the counseling process.

SETTING CONGRUENT GOALS

The first phase in the process of intervention is clarifying the situation as it appears to the people involved in it. The next step is determining how the agency or the professional they have approached can help with the presented problem and with setting goals that are acceptable to all—including those of the helper or helping organization. This may require refocusing or reframing the nature of the problem as viewed by one or more of the potential clients. In Chapter 2, we saw how the practitioner helped the daughter, Mrs. Smith, move from a simple request for meals to consideration of a planning session involving her husband and her mother. It was possible, indeed likely, that each of these three involved persons had different hopes or fears of what might be accomplished. The goal of giving Mrs. Smith some relief from her caregiving tasks by supplying her mother with other forms of assistance would have worked only if everyone really wanted that to happen. The mother, Mrs. Jones, might have been fearful of losing contact with her daughter; Mrs. Smith might have anticipated feeling guilty if she were to spend less time with her mother; and Mr. Smith might really have preferred to see his mother-in-law move to a retirement home so that he and his wife could travel. With so many conflicting agendas the plan for substitute care would probably not have worked. If, however, the underlying fears and preferences were brought into the open, a compromise solution was more likely to be achieved.

Establishing congruent goals usually involves both a long-range vision and a series of small incremental steps. Suppose, for instance, that Mrs. Jones really needed help with heavy housecleaning chores but was uneasy about having a stranger in her house. The first step might have been to help her make a list of tasks that needed doing. How long would each take? Would the helper be needed for a whole day or only a few hours? The next step would have been to assemble a list of possible providers. Mrs. Jones could then be encouraged to make calls inquiring about availability and cost. It would have been better for her to do this, if at all possible, because the more control she would feel, the less fearful she was likely to be. If she was hesitant about trying, the presence of a familiar person, such as her daughter or the professional, might have made the unfamiliar task less formidable. A long-range goal could thus be broken down into a series of smaller ones, and establishing the goal would have merged naturally into developing the plan for its implementation.

ESTABLISHING AN INITIAL CONTRACT

The plan for implementation is sometimes called a contract. The contract may be a formal written document, signed by all the parties thereto, or it may be a simple verbal agreement. The essential components are an understanding of what goal is to be accomplished, the activities to be undertaken in order to achieve it, who is responsible for each of the activities, a time frame for evaluating progress, and, if applicable, a fee for the service and who is to pay it.

In the Smith-Jones example, the contract might be something like this:

- *Goals:* To help Mrs. Jones gain more control over her life and to help Mrs. Smith conserve time and energy for herself.
- *Means:* Obtain regular housekeeping help for Mrs. Jones.
- *Activities:* Make a list of tasks to be performed by the housekeeper, obtain names of providers, call to inquire about services, interview applicants, schedule housekeeping visits, and review the effectiveness of the service and Mrs. Jones' satisfaction with it.
- *Time frame:* One month.
- *Assigned responsibilities:* The professional worker will meet with Mrs. Jones and Mrs. Smith to help them draw up a list of tasks, will give them a list of providers of housekeeping services, will meet with them again to review the service, and will be available for additional meetings or calls, if necessary. Mrs. Jones will specify tasks and call the providers. She and Mrs. Smith will interview applicants together. Mrs. Jones will select the one she prefers.

Mrs. Jones and/or the Smiths will arrange payment for the housekeeper and also pay for the professional time of the practitioner, if applicable.

It may appear that this is an elaborate set of activities to accomplish a simple housecleaning visit. However, the absence of such an agreement is likely to result in frustration and confusion. Suppose the worker agrees to find a housekeeper and send her to Mrs. Jones, without involving Mrs. Jones in the process. If Mrs. Jones is ambivalent about making a change and feels no ownership in the plan for getting her a housekeeper, she is likely to find something wrong with each candidate. One is available too late in the day, another too early, another is careless about scrubbing corners, a fourth is too slow, and a fifth arrives and is dismissed because Mrs. Jones's granddaughter is coming to visit. By this time the professional has made a dozen calls, has accomplished nothing, and probably feels like wringing not only her own hands but also the client's neck.

Mrs. Smith is also feeling disappointed and angry. Rather than confronting her mother, she is likely to vent her anger on the professional, who has failed to deliver the expected magic.

A contract gives all the people involved a measure of ownership in the plan and responsibility for its success. This applies equally to the service provision, case management, or counseling. Even if no other services are involved, a contract for counseling, like the contract for using concrete services, should specify the problem to be worked on, the goals of treatment, and the activities expected of both counselor and client(s).

A couple are experiencing marital conflict since the husband's retirement. The two have come to a family therapist stating different goals. The wife wants her husband to stop telling her how to organize her kitchen, and the husband wants his wife to stop nagging him about getting more exercise.

The first step in counseling may be to help the couple identify a goal that they both want to achieve—possibly to have fewer quarrels. They may then agree to spend several sessions talking with the therapist about how this might be accomplished and what seems to be blocking it. The treatment focus is on convincing both clients that they have a shared responsibility in the resolution of their conflict.

Some therapists give "homework assignments." They may ask clients to keep records of certain behaviors or feelings or to plan and carry out some activity and report on it in the next session. The specific assignment is not as important as making the point that the clients must feel that they own the problem and are working at resolving it, not waiting passively for the mystique of therapy to take it away.

Besides the principle of shared responsibility, another important element of a contract is time. How much time is to be devoted to this particular problem, what will it cost, and how will the clients and the therapist know whether the work is successful? Reviewing the original goal periodically can help determine to what extent it is being met and whether it still needs to be worked on. The couple who wants to have fewer quarrels may discover that when they don't quarrel, they don't talk at all. They may switch from the goal of fewer quarrels to finding a more satisfactory way to communicate.

There is nothing sacred about the initial goal; it can and should be modified whenever appropriate in the continuing process of dynamic assessment. Reviewing whether the initial goal has been met helps determine if it is still the goal of choice and may indicate when one has moved into the next phase.

Middle Phase of Counseling

The tasks of the beginning phase of counseling, as we have seen, are engaging the client(s) in identifying salient needs, setting congruent goals, and establishing an initial contract. The counselor has been able to help the clients overcome their reluctance to ask for help and mobilize their hopefulness.

RESISTANCE, REFRAMING, AND PARTIAL RESOLUTION

Counselor and client(s) start to work together. Then the phenomenon of resistance begins to emerge. Clients may complain that the plan of action isn't working or isn't really necessary. They may forget or cancel appointments. If services in addition to counseling are involved, there may be cancellations, complaints, and frequent requests for changes of schedule. Why does this happen?

The basic reason for resistance is that change is difficult and often scary. It may be easier to continue as before, because the unsatisfactory situation is at least familiar.

Anderson and Stewart (1983) point out that people usually seek help not because they want change but because they have been unsuccessful in accommodating to change. Retirement, widowhood, departure or return of children, and the onset of illness are common occurrences in old age. These events and many others produce changes with which it is often difficult to deal. The unspoken hope of the client may be that the counselor will be able to make things revert to the way they were before or to stop a family member from reacting to change in a particular way.

Another aspect of resistance is disappointment that the hoped-for change requires a lot of effort and time. Initial optimism may then give way to discouragement or, at the very least, result in ambivalent reactions.

Ambivalence is the ability to feel several different and often contradictory ways at the same time. Reluctance to cope with change on the one hand is countered by hope for some more satisfactory resolution on the other, and the person vacillates between these two extremes. The counselor must be aware of both poles of the ambivalence so as not to be overwhelmed by one or the other.

Reluctance and hope may be brought into closer alignment through reframing—expanding the focus of the problem to allow for solutions that might otherwise appear mutually exclusive. For example, the couple mentioned earlier started out by saying, "I want my husband to stop criticizing my housekeeping" and "I want my wife to stop nagging me about exercise." Pointing out that their roles had changed since the husband's retirement helped them recognize that the issue was broader than the behaviors of which each complained.

Resistance is often related to fear of offending or hurting someone important to the client. The older person who is struggling to manage three flights of stairs may be resistant to the suggestion that family members might help locate something more suitable and might respond: "Don't bother my son" or "My daughter has her own problems." The suggestion that they might be hurt by not being told of mother's difficulties may introduce a new idea.

Resistance based on fear of being "a burden" may also be related to the fear of losing autonomy if family members, particularly adult children, are asked for help. The fear is that they may take over, with their own solutions, and leave the older person with no share in decision making.

The fear of, or demand for, an all-or-nothing solution fuels a great deal of the resistance of older people and also family members. All-or-nothing solutions may be suggested by statements like the following:

- "If I tell the children I don't feel so good, they'll want to put me in a nursing home."
- "If I ask Mother what she really wants, she'll insist on moving in with me. I couldn't stand that."
- "If my son knew I had a housekeeper, he'd never bother to visit."

Such expectations are not necessarily realistic appraisals of the family members' actual feelings. But even if they do reflect reality, clients who have painted themselves into this kind of corner may be helped to partialize the problem and to define what kind of response, or what range of responses, would be acceptable. Thus, they could offer a counterproposal and arrive at a partial solution at least. It may be suggested that perhaps the children would not seize on an institutional solution if they knew what other options were available. If the daughter can define the limits of her involvement, she and her mother may be able to work out an alternative living arrangement acceptable to both. If the son can become aware of his parent's need for social contact (more than the practical housekeeping help only), not only would he not stop visiting but he would perhaps also attribute greater significance to his visits.

The essence of partial resolution is compromise and flexibility. The person who dreads an all-or-nothing solution may need help in spelling out what is negotiable and what is not.

Frustration with client resistance. Helping the client spell out what is negotiable is not always as easy as it sounds. Human beings are not purely rational creatures. Often, they appear to be bundles of conflicting emotions, demanding a solution in one breath and refusing all available options in the next. Every suggestion may be met with "Yes, but . . ." This is very frustrating for professionals who feel that, as agents of change, they ought to be making something happen. They may be deflected from the task of helping clients arrive at a truly autonomous decision and feel that their job is to convince the client of the rightness of a particular course of action. In this they may be supported by pressure from family members, referring agencies, and the clients themselves, who beg, "Tell me what to do!" while refusing to do anything.

Forcing a course of action on an unwilling client is not only unprofessional but also practically impossible. People have infinitely many creative ways of avoiding unwanted actions. One of the most common is to agree to a proposal but make no effort to follow through, despite promises to do so. Phone numbers are lost or forgotten, appointments are not kept or canceled, bills go unpaid, and the whole machinery of implementation grinds to a halt.

Human service workers with the elderly sometimes ascribe such behavior to memory loss, an excuse that is rarely invoked with resistant younger people. Memory loss may, of course, be a factor, and identifying such a deficit should be part of the assessment process. But even when some memory deficits exist, the effect of ambivalence cannot be overlooked; indeed, it may be intensified.

TECHNIQUES FOR GETTING UNSTUCK

What techniques can a human service worker use to keep the helping process moving or get out of the bog of inaction? The following discussion describes several methods:

- Feedback and clarification
- Reflection and hypothesis
- Exploration
- Offering alternatives
- Confrontation

Feedback and clarification. The worker may restate the client's words and ask if they were heard correctly, as in the following example.

CLIENT: *That boy is so unreliable! He said he'd come and take me shopping, but he hasn't.*

WORKER: *Your son didn't come last week?*

CLIENT: *Oh, he came last week. I mean, he didn't come this week.*

The worker might then ask for further clarification, such as how these arrangements are usually made, or what the client does about shopping needs between visits. The answer might suggest that supplies are not really the issue. For instance, she may have had the groceries delivered or gone with a neighbor. The real issue then becomes clear, and she can be helped to acknowledge it: She misses her son and wishes to see him more often.

Reflection and hypothesis. The worker may restate the client's dissatisfaction, suggesting a reason for it.

WORKER: *It sounds like you're disappointed that he doesn't visit more often.*

Such a suggestion may bring out a variety of responses, such as:

CLIENT: *I worry when he doesn't call.*

Or

I don't care if he doesn't want to come. It's that wife of his who won't let him.

Or

I just wish he'd keep his promises. Just like his father . . . promise anything, but when it's time to do it, where is he?

Exploration. The worker may test the hypothesis by further exploring the issues suggested by the response. In the example given, one might inquire about the relationship that appears problematic and whether the client would be interested in opening the lines of communication. This may indicate whether the client is distressed enough about the situation to attempt some change or whether complaining is a sufficient outlet. Not all complaints require action. However, if the client appears interested in some kind of change, the worker could begin to explore how that might happen. In this instance the worker might ask the client if she had ever talked to her son about her wishes. Such a question may also elicit a variety of responses:

> CLIENT: *Oh, yes, but he never listens.*
>
> Or
>
> *He just gets angry if I ask him to do more.*
>
> Or
>
> *I told you, his wife is the problem. It's no use talking to* HER.

The worker might then ask the client for more details of how she talks to her son.

> WORKER: *What do you say when you call him?*
>
> Or
>
> *What would you like to tell him?*

Responses to this are often quite vague and global:

> CLIENT: *I just tell him he should be more responsible.*
>
> Or
>
> *If he's a good son, he'd know what I need.*
>
> Or
>
> *I tell him I don't feel so good. He should know what that means. If he doesn't, what can I do?*

Offering alternatives. If a client's efforts have not been successful, they may be open to other approaches. In the current example the worker might suggest using "I" messages instead of "You" messages. For instance, the client might try saying "I need help shopping this week because . . ." instead of "You are irresponsible." Some professionals use role playing or tape-record parts of the interviews, playing them back in order to help clients identify their own behaviors and how others react to them. If the worker is considerably younger than the client, however, this teaching-relearning approach may not work very effectively, because it may be threatening to both of them. This is a better method to use in a group setting, such as a community center. As a group or class, the participants can share experiences and try behaviors on each other, with the worker acting as facilitator or resource person. The reactions of peers in such situations are both more convincing and less threatening that those of a younger professional person acting as coach.

The client who does not have access to a group can, however, be helped to specify what he or she would like to say to a child or "significant other"—friend, sibling, landlord, doctor—as preparation for a discussion of needs or feelings. If such a discussion is to take place during an interview with the old person and those with whom the person has had communication difficulties, the worker may pave the way, if the person agrees, or review the results after the meeting has taken place. Such an approach can help the client be more specific, less accusing or less anxious, and the worker avoids the pitfalls of acting as an uninvited teacher.

Confrontation. Confrontation as a technique is both essential and risky. It involves pointing out discrepancies or inconsistencies in client behavior but without being critical or punitive. This can be very tricky if the worker is frustrated by inaction and the client is defensive. The professional worker must keep in mind that the object of confrontation is not to win an argument but to share an observation with the client that will be helpful and not hurtful. It is to bring the client useful "news about the self," as psychologist David Gutmann defines counseling.

Confrontation may begin, very gently, with the acknowledgment of ambivalence. For instance:

- "You'd like your daughter to help more, but you hate to ask her."
- "You could really use some help in the house, but you know it won't be done the way you used to do it."
- "When you feel lonely, it may be hard to think about making new friends. Kind of like the first day of school, or starting a new job."

The point is to acknowledge ambivalence, without criticizing it, by emphasizing the normality of feeling several ways at the same time.

The next step in confrontation is sharing an observation of how the client's behavior interferes with the client's own goals. Again, it is important not to condemn the feelings that lead to such behavior.

For example, an elderly man may be caring for a wife who is suffering from a dementing illness such as Alzheimer's disease. He knows, at least intellectually, that there are many things she can't remember; but when he gets frustrated by her slowness, he yells at her. This makes her more agitated, which makes him try even harder to control her behavior by scolding. At the same time, he feels very guilty about abusing the sick woman. The worker might try to help him relate these conflicted feelings to his behavior.

> WORKER: *Mr. Grey, I know you feel terrible about your wife's condition. It's painful to see her like that—so different from what she used to be. And you're trying so hard to take care of her. It's understandable that sometimes you get so frustrated that you yell at her. But you see what happens—she just gets worse.*
>
> MR. GREY: *Well, but what can I do? Sometimes, it just gets to me. There must be some way to make her behave.*
>
> WORKER: *There are some ways to make it easier for both of you. Let's go over some of them.*

This kind of introduction may make Mr. Grey more receptive to learning techniques for dealing with demented or memory-impaired people; scolding him for insensitivity would only harden his defensive stance.

Confrontation of client behavior combined with acceptance of feelings may be called "carefrontation" (Siegel, 1986). It challenges clients to examine their own contribution to the problem while supporting them as persons. "Support" is sometimes taken to mean agreement with everything the client says or does, but this is a misconception. Encouraging the client in futile or destructive behavior is not supportive. It does not promote true self-determination, because it deprives the client of a portion of the data needed for informed decision making, namely, an awareness of his or her own part in the situation.

Self-awareness includes awareness of contradictory feelings and wishes. Sometimes, carefrontation can help both worker and client identify which pole of the ambivalence is stronger. The following example illustrates this.

Both Mr. and Mrs. Davis, a couple in their seventies, had various chronic physical problems, for which they received regular medical care. Mrs. Davis also had cataracts for which surgery was planned but had been postponed owing to a long and debilitating bout of pneumonia. She had nearly recovered from this when Mr. Davis also contracted pneumonia. His doctor kept him under close observation but did not think his condition warranted hospitalization. Mrs. Davis, however, was frantic. She saw nothing in their future but further deterioration and isolation.

She begged their son to move them to the city where he lived, but he refused, ostensibly because of his wife's opposition. He did agree to help them move to a more protected setting, if necessary, after Mrs. Davis's eye surgery. He consulted with the couple's doctor, who felt there was no immediate crisis. Mrs. Davis interpreted this as abandonment. She cried constantly and also complained about the part-time help she had with the heavier household tasks, feeling it was inadequate and unsatisfactory.

The worker, who had been meeting regularly with the couple during this series of events, was unsure of how to understand Mrs. Davis's distress. On the one hand, both she and her husband were making slow by steady recoveries; on the other hand, Mrs. Davis's discouragement seemed to be increasing daily. Was she asking for permission to give up?

Finally, the worker told Mrs. Davis that if she really felt she could not cope any longer, she could ask their doctor to arrange for immediate placement in a nursing home, at least until they regained more strength. The worker stated that she had observed that Mrs. Davis was doing all that had to be done for her own and her husband's care, and she believed that Mrs. Davis was doing better than she herself realized. However, if she preferred an institutional alternative, it was available.

Mrs. Davis was shocked. "How could you advise me to go to a nursing home?" she demanded. "I thought you'd try to talk me out of it!"

The worker assured Mrs. Davis that she was not advising placement but thought Mrs. Davis was flirting with the idea as an escape.

Although dissatisfied with her situation and disappointed in her son, Mrs. Davis decided she did not want placement.

This intervention clarified that Mrs. Davis was not asking permission to give up. It also brought to Mrs. Davis's attention that she appeared to be asking to be relieved of responsibility and that others might take her at her word if she persisted. Her reaction to the suggestion of placement was, in effect, "Never mind what I say; pay attention to what I mean." Confrontation helped the client become aware of what she really did mean.

Another confrontation took place around the issue of Mrs. Davis's dissatisfaction with her household help. She had had several helpers but never kept one for very long. When the worker commented on this, Mrs. Davis was again surprised.

> WORKER: *Let's see, you've had six housekeepers this year and haven't liked any of them. I wonder why that is.*
>
> MRS. DAVIS: *My goodness, you make me sound so crabby and critical. I'm really very easy to get along with. I never make demands. Take the one I've got now. She doesn't do what I want, but I never say anything.*
>
> WORKER: *If you don't tell her what you want, how is she to know?*
>
> MRS. DAVIS: *But I don't want to make her angry. You know how touchy they are.*

The worker might have interpreted the last comment as a racial or class-related slur. Instead, she continued to focus on the issue of clear instructions. In this way Mrs. Davis began to see how she could take action to get some of her needs met, instead of passively waiting for someone else to figure out what she wanted and then weeping and feeling helpless if she did not get it.

Confrontation is not a global, once-and-for-all intervention. It is done in small steps. It helps the clients see themselves in segments so that they can integrate any new information about themselves. For instance, Mrs. Davis may well be a clinging, passive person whose dependency and unrealistic expectations create difficulties for her in other relationships besides the one with her housekeeper. To try to tell her that in one interview would be overwhelming. The most probable result would be an increase in her feelings of hopelessness, rage, disappointment with the worker, and precipitous withdrawal from seeking further professional help. If, however, she can learn a more effective method of dealing with her housekeeper, she may eventually, and with continued assistance from the practitioner, be able to transfer that learning to other relationships.

Here, again, we see that counseling and case management, both of which may be provided by human service workers, are related interventions. Clients' styles of relating to service providers and to family members form one pattern, which is determined by the clients' perception of self and others. This is true even when a client's style of relating to family, professionals, and service providers seems very different. For instance, a client may be meek and compliant with his doctor ("Yes, doctor"), and helpless and clinging with his daughter ("What shall I do? I can't do that!"), and demeaning and critical of his housekeeper ("You never do anything right"), thus presenting no apparent consistency. Such a combination of behaviors would suggest that he can only be assertive with those he perceives as inferior and/or expendable. Still, these apparent inconsistencies are characteristic of his pattern of interaction with people and thus consistent with his style.

ACTION AS FACILITATOR OF TREATMENT

Not all therapeutic interventions are verbal. Treatment can be facilitated not only by speech but also by action. This includes actions of the professional worker and actions of the client that are suggested, encouraged, or acknowledged by the professional.

In an interview between a young social worker and an elderly client, Mrs. Haines, who had recently undergone the amputation of one leg, the client expressed a concern about her ability to continue caring for herself. The social worker listened and assured Mrs. Haines that help was available if needed. Then she asked for a glass of water. Mrs. Haines wheeled herself into the kitchen, poured a glass of water, and brought it back to the worker, who thanked her and commented on her efficiency.

The request, and the client's success in fulfilling it, emphasized the client's competence and the worker's recognition of it. The spoken words then drew the client's attention to what she had just done. Referring to a fact in the here-and-now was more effective than relying on a report from the past or a speculation about the future. Of course, it wouldn't have worked if the client had not actually been capable of fulfilling the request. Asking for the impossible only sets the client up for failure.

Sometimes, a professional may deliberately step out of the role of expert and ask the client to become a teacher. This is particularly valuable when working with the elderly, who are thereby enabled to draw on the experiences of a lifetime and to feel validated when they can share the knowledge and wisdom thus accumulated. Although placing clients in a teaching role is a counseling technique, it can also be used by a variety of professionals, as illustrated by the following two examples.

Mr. Makovsky, who was depressed by the loss of mobility after a stroke, regained some of his self-esteem when his home health aide asked for chess lessons. They played for a few minutes each day after Mr. Makovsky's bath, and the aide was greatly encouraged by his pupil's progress. It gave him a sense that he was still contributing to the life around him and was not totally defined by his near-useless body.

Again, asking the client to become a teacher emphasizes capability rather than deficit. An occupational therapist experienced a similar success when she asked her client, Mrs. Ogilvie, to teach her how to make pastry.

Mrs. Ogilvie, who suffered from Parkinson's disease, had severe tremors in her hands. She could no longer roll out the pastry herself, but she could supervise the process, with a sharp eye for mistakes. After the first lesson she tasted the results. "Hmm," she commented, "not too bad. Not as good as mine, of course, but you'll learn."

From the experience of teaching the occupational therapist, Mrs. Ogilvie gained enough confidence to teach her daily companion to prepare the kind of meals she liked; and thus she regained a measure of control over her life, which she had feared had been lost forever.

Placing clients in a teaching role allows them to act on their competencies rather than merely describing them. It also allows the professional to become a model for the role of learner. Persons experiencing disabilities or role changes often have to learn new skills or new ways of using old skills. The professional in the role of learner demonstrates that learning can be expansive, gratifying, and dignified rather than demeaning.

Whether verbal or action-focused, a treatment relationship involves (at least) two people: the professional counselor and the client(s). Each of them brings to the relationship not only the conscious and rational aspects of their work together but also hopes, fears, fantasies, and reactions to the personality of the other. Of these, they are often totally or partially unaware.

IMPORTANCE OF EVOKED FEELINGS IN TREATMENT

Transference and countertransference are terms often used in the professional literature to refer to feelings evoked in the treatment relationship. These terms originated in psychoanalysis, where they initially signified only the unconscious feelings evoked in the client by the therapist (transference) or in the therapist by the client (countertransference). They are now often used to include reactions of which either or both parties may be conscious, even if the reasons underlying the reactions are not fully understood. Therefore, the term *evoked feeling* seems more accurate and comprehensive. The value of the original terms lies in the fact that they indicate the direction of the feeling — that is, from client to therapist (transference) or from therapist to client (countertransference).

Many of the feelings evoked in therapist and/or client are carryovers from past encounters or situations that each has experienced. This is, of course, not limited to therapeutic or other professional relationships. We all interpret present happenings in the light of previous experience; that is the function of memory. What goes on all the time, in all relationships, is singled out for study in the therapeutic relationship because of its impact on the progress of treatment. Understanding evoked feelings can clarify assessment and advance the treatment process. Ignored or misunderstood, such feelings can impede or undermine the process.

Old clients and young counselors. The raw material of the evoked feeling (or transference/countertransference) situation is inherent in the helping process itself. The client comes with hopes for amelioration and fears of criticism or rejection. The content of both is formed by images of the past, of other helpers or authority figures, such as parents, teachers, doctors, or welfare workers. For an older person, who may be seeking professional help for the first time, the situation may be rendered more unfamiliar by the fact that the would-be helper is likely to be younger than the client and may be of different ethnic or social background. This may also be a hurdle for the counselor or other human service worker. He or she hopes to provide effective help and has undergone some kind of professional preparation for that purpose. This education is now to be put to the test by application to persons who may be old enough to be one's parents or grandparents. Furthermore, these young people cannot augment their training by drawing on their own experience of old age, because they haven't had it yet. They may feel like airplane pilots, flying blind and totally dependent on instruments for their flight plan.

As they gain familiarity with their own feelings and those of their clients, however, they discover that they can indeed be helpful, not as authority figures but as confidants, mirrors, advocates, and facilitators. The clients, too, discover that chronological age does not confer or withhold the ability to be truly helpful.

Fitting current reality into life experience. Given all of the above, it is not surprising that the older person may see the human service worker in the role of child or grandchild and anticipate affectionate service and companionship or, conversely, be put off by the perception of inexperience. The child/grandchild role may also be comfortable or uncomfortable for the worker. It is easy to get drawn into the familial expectation and find oneself running errands or making social visits without quite realizing what is going on. This is particularly seductive if the old person is, or seems to be, bereft of close family ties, or if the worker accepts the old person's distrust of the worker's professional capabilities because of youth and inexperience. (Age is relative: To an eighty-year-old, a fifty-year-old is still young enough to be a son, perhaps still regarded as a child.) However, accepting the child/grandchild role unwittingly is counterproductive. It eats up the worker's time without expanding the client's social resources and sets the client up for another loss when the case is closed or the worker moves on to another agency or position. It also limits the worker's ability to serve more than a very few clients.

There are ways, however, of making conscious use of the youthful role. One of them was described in an example in the previous section, in which the worker deliberately stepped out of the expert role and invited the client to become the teacher. Another method is to encourage reminiscence or life review (Butler, 1963). The client may be encouraged to review his or her life story, perhaps with the aid of a tape recorder, as a legacy to oncoming generations. The life review thus serves as an enhancer of self-esteem, and as such, it may effect some beneficial changes in the current mode of living. The worker may facilitate this process through active interest, comments, and questions about the changes that the elder has observed.

In general, if the role of a counselor promotes client capability and extends areas of client control, the relationship is being put to productive use. If it promotes passivity and *exclusive* dependency on the counselor, it is counterproductive. "Exclusive" is the critical distinction. A treatment relationship that promotes trust and confidence will, of course, involve some dependency. But the intent should be to make the dependency transitional—a means to something more permanent and valuable—not an end in itself. In other words, by developing confidence in and dependency on the counselor, the client learns to trust those feelings and to carry them over to other, consistently available social relationships.

Idealization and disappointment. As treatment progresses, the client may develop very positive feelings about the counselor. These may be expressed in such terms as "I've never been able to talk this way to anyone else," or "Nobody has ever helped me like you have." Inevitably, this idealization will prove faulty, and the client will be disappointed. Such disappointment may come about as the result of the counselor's failure to understand something the client says, inability to provide a service the client wants, or unavailability owing to vacation, illness, or other responsibilities. Then, the client may protest, "How could you say such a thing?"; or "You could do it if you really wanted to"; or "Why are you people always at meetings?" If the counselor has been seduced into taking the initial idealization at face value, this may result in later feelings of professional inadequacy and guilt, or anger and resentment, or both. The counselor may suppose that feelings of disappointment in the client indicate therapeutic failure. The underlying assumption may be as follows:

- "All feelings are legitimate; therefore all desires are fulfillable. If I can't fulfill them, I must be a failure as a counselor."

or

- "I should be able to fulfill all legitimate desires. If I can't, the client's wishes are illegitimate and unjustifiable." (One way in which this reaction is frequently expressed is "the client is manipulative.")

Both these reactions stem from a rescue fantasy — that is, a conviction that any human condition can be remedied, if one works hard enough at it. This fantasy is an occupational hazard to which all helping professionals are apt to be vulnerable. The underlying assumption overlooks the fact that idealization and disappointment are components of all human relationships and an inescapable and inherent element of the human condition.

Remnants of infant longing for the total love and attention of the mother or mother substitute linger in even the best-adjusted adults and are reactivated and intensified in times of stress. Such longing cannot be fulfilled in actuality, but it can be acknowledged and its normality recognized. Doing so will help prevent discouragement in professionals and disappointment, shame, and rage in clients.

The counselor can deal with the dilemma posed by idealization and human fallibility by acknowledging feelings while admitting inability to meet all needs. Then, the client's experience of disappointment may be used as a springboard for exploring other relationships in which the client was disappointed and what happened as a result. Did the client withdraw from the disappointing relationship? Continue in it while feeling resentful or hopeless? Develop expectations of being failed or let down in other relationships? If the counselor demonstrates willingness to continue working with the client, accepting the feelings of disappointment without feeling guilty about them, the client may be enabled to accept the real but limited benefits of a "good enough" relationship instead of hopelessly yearning for a perfect one (Winnicott, 1965). Such a learning experience may then carry over into other relationships.

Dealing with negative feelings. Instead of dealing with idealization, the counselor may have to deal with frequent expressions of hostility and denigration, such as "Nobody can help me"; "If you knew what you were doing, I'd have gotten that service long ago"; "All professionals are frauds"; and the like. Some criticisms, of course, may be justified. Any allegation of misunderstanding or mishandling should be acknowledged, explored, and, if possible, corrected. However, if the criticism is constant, regardless of circumstance, it is likely to be an expression of client personality rather than a realistic appraisal of the situation.

Anger is a natural reaction to unjustified criticism. How can professionals deal with global expressions of hostility, sarcasm, or deprecation and with their own resentment thereof?

Scolding and arguing are usually not effective; they merely pull the professional into the client's pattern of blame and recrimination. Acknowledgment of feelings without acceptance of blame may help defuse a barrage of accusation. It is paradoxical that people who seem most abrasive and attacking may feel that they actually have very little impact on their environment. They step up the volume of complaints out of a sense that no one hears them. Acknowledgment of their distress sometimes results in a startling change of attitude. This is more likely to be true if the outburst is reactive to a particular situation rather than characteristic of client reaction to any situation.

For the chronically hostile person the most effective response may be clearly indicating the limits of one's tolerance of the behavior, without being drawn into an argument about it. "I can't hear you when you're shouting"; "I can't send you a housekeeper if you call her a dirty so-and-so"; or "You can't come back to the Center if you hit people" are examples of such limit setting. In a treatment relationship it may be helpful for the counselor to acknowledge the impact of the depreciation. The following example illustrates how this may be done.

Miss Cotter had been having a series of unproductive interviews with Mr. Ratner, a seventy-five-year-old man who talked at great length about the inadequacy of Miss Cotter compared with all the other professionals he had known, particularly her immediate predecessor. Miss Cotter had attempted to acknowledge his disappointment at losing his previous worker, but the barrage continued. Finally, she said, "I know you were very disappointed when Mrs. Brown left, but I'm getting awfully tired of hearing about it. I feel very frustrated, and that makes it hard for me to listen to you." Mr. Ratner looked surprised, commented, "I guess I do run on," and allowed Miss Cotter to shift the interview to another topic. In subsequent interviews, although his typical sarcasm was still in evidence, he showed that he could control its expression and address issues of concern to him without constantly attacking his helper.

Miss Cotter's confrontation took the form of an "I" message ("I feel frustrated") rather than a "You" message ("You are attacking me"). Mr. Ratner's response indicated his ability to control his behavior and reflected the value the relationship had for him, despite his verbal deprecation.

It is important to remember that in an ongoing relationship positive or idealized feelings about one's helping professional carry the potential for disappointment, and expressions of negative feeling also have a positive underside. The professional must try to avoid being seduced by positive, or unduly dismayed by negative, components of feelings. This is another element in the process of dynamic assessment.

Concluding Phase of Counseling

The hopes and disappointments inherent in the counseling relationship also impact on plans for its conclusion. This is true of all treatment relationships; however, termination with elderly clients may have special difficulties for both client and professional helper. Older people may be in chronically unstable situations because of physical frailty and unpredictable deterioration. They may have an extremely limited network of social supports, owing to the death or mobility of friends and family members. Some are isolated because of poor social skills or abrasive personalities. Such factors may incline the client to cling to the human service worker and may induce the worker to prolong the relationship even when the original goals of treatment have been met.

Sometimes, the professional helpers may be tempted to maintain a relationship just because it is gratifying. The client is so enjoyable and has made so much progress that one is reluctant to close the case.

Mrs. Jordan was a delight to everyone who worked with her — social workers, nurses, shopping assistants, housekeepers, even bus drivers were charmed by her graciousness, unfailing courtesy, and resourcefulness. She had suffered a stroke that had left her partially paralyzed, but after a long rehabilitation process she had learned to manage in her own apartment with a wheelchair and minimal services. Her physical and occupational therapists adored her, were extremely proud of her success, and dreaded the day when Medicare would no longer pay for treatment because she had reached maximum recovery. The case manager in charge of her household help found excuses to visit nearly every month. Mrs. Jordan always had some issue she wanted to talk about. To be sure, she had much the same kind of conversation with her many friends. But her gratitude and charm were such a pleasant change from complaints and criticisms doled out by her other clients that the case manager did not want to end this relationship.

In contrast, a relationship may also be maintained even when little has been accomplished and the client seems unmotivated. In such a case, the worker hopes that trying harder and longer will result in some kind of breakthrough. Such efforts are usually doomed to futility and should not be continued unless the client is clearly at risk.

Sometimes, indeed, a professional connection with an older person must be maintained for a very long period, perhaps for the duration of the client's life. Some people not only have lost their natural networks but also lack the physical, cognitive, or emotional resources to develop new ones. In such cases a connection to the helping organization rather than to the individual worker is what should be fostered. It is the nature of the professional scene that workers move from job to job and that earning a reputation for one's accomplishments usually results in relinquishing current tasks in order to take on more challenging assignments. Therefore, it is important not to allow a client to believe that any professional relationship will last forever.

Engaging in a professional helping relationship involves a paradox. In order to be helpful, the worker must gain entry into the client's life and mesh with the client's system; but it is equally important to be able to extricate oneself without injury to the client. For this reason the essentially time-limited nature of the relationship should be built into the client's expectations from the beginning and reinforced as treatment progresses. This can be done initially by building a time frame into the contract. The frame may be modified or extended, if appropriate, but always with the understanding that there will be an endpoint.

During the middle phase of counseling, if this is provided under the auspices of an organization, the client can be reminded that the present worker will not always be available but that others will provide backup and can be called upon in case of need. Specific plans can be made for the client to contact the worker's supervisor, other designated persons in the helping organization, and/or individuals in the client's natural network. Practitioners in private practice are also well advised to assure that they can provide coverage in their absence and have resources that guarantee continuity, should it become necessary. Scheduled vacations are good opportunities to rehearse for eventual termination. When the worker returns, the client's functioning during the period of absence can be reviewed, including the reliance on and use of other resources.

Helping clients learn how to expand their social networks is often an appropriate counseling issue. This may include tasks as diverse as meeting new friends, communicating more effectively with adult children, supervising household helpers, or advocating for oneself in the public service system. In such situations the worker should function as a bridge or transitional object, not as a permanent substitute. Allowing oneself to become the client's total support system leads to burnout for the worker and disappointment for the client. It reinforces the fear that no one is reliable or can really help and decreases, rather than increases, the client's ability to trust others and use what is available.

Periodic reviews of what has been accomplished and what remains to be done are part of the ongoing assessment that underlies the helping process. Such assessment helps sustain realistic hope and prepare for eventual termination, which is the end phase of dynamic assessment. The basic principle to bear in mind is that termination is not an issue to be addressed solely in the concluding phase of counseling. It is a reality that should be acknowledged from the very beginning and built into the helping process at every step of the client/worker interaction.

PART TWO

Ongoing Work: Understanding Problems of Aging

CHAPTER 6

Physical Decline

Health problems are among the most frequent reasons for professional interventions with the elderly. These problems range from severely disabling illnesses to chronic conditions whose principal effect is inconvenience. The seriousness of the diagnosis does not necessarily define the degree of disability. Rather, it is the attitude of the patient toward the condition, its meaning, and its possible treatment that is critical in the management of the illness and the patient's ability to cope with whatever disabling symptoms accompany the diagnosis.

A professional objective in intervention is to help clients sustain or regain the greatest possible measure of autonomy and control of their lives. Enabling them to obtain needed services may be a part of this process, and these services are considered a form of treatment, as are recommendations to obtain medical attention. For example, in addition to obtaining medical evaluation and treatment, an arthritic client may benefit from an elevator building, a housekeeper, and/or an exercise class. However, none of these will work without the client's consent and cooperation. These depend, in great part, on the meaning to the client of both the condition and the suggested treatment. Therefore, of paramount importance in offering professional help is the psychological support given to the patient's concept of illness.

 Mrs. Carlson, who suffers from arthritic knees, lives in a third-floor walk-up apartment. Despite the inconvenience, she is very much attached to her familiar neighborhood. She also regards household help as intrusive and demeaning and considers exercise unladylike. Therefore, she prefers to put up with her aches and pains and do nothing. In her case shame at being disabled and fear of further deterioration, which she prefers to deny, also contribute to her reluctance to seek relief. For her, professional intervention may consist most constructively of allowing her to continue as she chooses until such time as she is able to acknowledge that she must make some change in her life-style.

In contrast to Mrs. Carlson, elders who do not see arthritis as a threat to identity or self-worth are more likely to accept their limitations with good humor and work around them with ingenuity. They may be quite creative in compensating for their symptoms, like Mrs. Carter, who, when her hands became too stiff to wring out a sweater, rolled it in a large bath towel and sat on it. She even joked about her use of "sitting power" as an alternative form of energy.

Age-Related Changes

It is not uncommon for elders, their families, and even professional helpers to attribute all difficulties, discomforts, and deficits to "the aging process" (Butler, 1975; Leventhal and Prohaska, 1986). It is very important to distinguish normal aging from disease, which is abnormal at any age. Some changes most likely to be noticed in the aging body after age seventy-five are decrease in sensory acuity, slowing of motor activity and reflexes, decrease in reserves of energy, and decrease in the body's ability to maintain temperature control. The rate of decrease in relation to age is different for every person. Thus, one cannot assume the development of age-related decline without appropriate medical testing.

CHANGES IN VISION

The aging eye becomes more farsighted, so reading fine print and other close work become more difficult, but, again, at different rates for different persons. The typical, half-jesting explanation is that "my arms aren't long enough to hold the newspaper." Even those who have never worn glasses are likely to need them for reading by the time they are in their forties. Those who have been nearsighted, on the other hand, may find that their vision actually improves. As the lens of the eye yellows and thickens with age, color discrimination also decreases, so it is more difficult to perceive subtle differences in shade and tone. It is easy to trip over a step in poor light because it fades into its background. Bright, strong colors not only are more appealing but also make it easier to orient oneself to one's environment. A strip of bright yellow tape on each tread of a stairway guides the eye and helps prevent falls. Good light, properly shaded to avoid glare, prevents eye strain and makes reading easier and walking safer.

Cataracts and glaucoma, while by no means inevitable, are common eye diseases in old age. Cataracts can generally be corrected by surgery. Glaucoma, an insidious process that damages the retina, may show no symptoms until the damage is far advanced but can be detected by a very simple test. Yearly tests for glaucoma are recommended for all persons over forty.

CHANGES IN HEARING

The aging ear also tends to lose acuity, especially the ability to disentangle several competing sounds. The loss may be noticeable only at certain pitches (high or low) or in certain settings. Some people can hear better on the telephone; others can communicate only if they can see the persons to whom they are talking. Sometimes, telephone amplifiers help. Hearings aids may help a great deal if they are properly fitted. However, even the best are limited in their effectiveness because they magnify all sound equally; background noise is not filtered out. Therefore, often the hearing-impaired person's greatest difficulty is distinguishing conversations from competing noises.

It is tentatively estimated that 30 percent of persons over sixty-five suffer from significant hearing loss and that two-thirds of the population is affected to some extent by age eighty (Rupp, 1970; Darbyshire, 1984). One of the chief consequences of hearing impairment is social isolation. People drop out of social activities because it is so hard to follow a conversation. Their withdrawal and lack of responsiveness may lead others to believe that they are unfriendly, stupid, or "senile." They may also resist using hearing aids, both because of their limitations and because there is more social stigma attached to wearing a hearing aid than to glasses or contact lenses. People of all ages wear glasses, sometimes for purely decorative purposes, but only the impaired and the elderly wear hearing aids. If a hearing device could be designed to look like the earphones worn by youthful joggers, the stigma might be decreased.

Hearing-impaired people may have an easier time communicating one-on-one and in good light, where they can clearly see the faces of their conversational partners. Other tips for talking with the hearing-impaired were described in Chapter 2.

In groups a meeting may be more successful if the acoustics can be adjusted to the hearing abilities of the members (Plomp and Duquesnoy, 1980). For instance, in a church group, many of whose members were over sixty-five, there were frequent complaints that even with a microphone the speaker could not be heard. Sound was distorted by an echo effect. When a carpet was installed, the difference was amazing. Not only was the room warmer and more attractive, but the disturbing echoes were also muffled.

CHANGES IN SMELL, TASTE, AND TOUCH

Smell and taste become less acute with age. Food may not taste as good as it used to, but the dulling of these senses is not likely to create risk or even serious inconvenience. However, it must be considered that lessened enjoyment of food may affect a person's nutritional levels adversely, and this bears watching.

Fingertip sensitivity also decreases with age, and it may be more difficult to manage small buttons or tiny hearing-aid batteries. However, the pleasure of touching does not decrease. Hugging, holding hands, kissing a lover, or fondling a grandchild are as warmly delightful as ever, when they are available. Unfortunately, although the sense of touch does not diminish, opportunities for touching often do. Widowhood, the absence of friends or relatives, the social stereotype that makes aged people unattractive and therefore untouchable — all these may add up to a sensory deficit that is both painful and unnecessary.

MYTHS AND REALITIES OF SEXUAL CHANGE

It is commonly believed that older persons lose interest in and capability for sexual activity. Indeed, evidence of such interest and activity often stirs anxiety in younger persons. However, research and practice indicate that active sexuality does continue in the later years, with some changes in pace but no loss of interest (Starr and Weiner, 1981). Loss of sexual function may be related to disease but more often than not can be resumed after recovery. However, older people may be too embarrassed to consult their doctors about the possibility. The doctor may not bring it up either, assuming that no question means no problem or, perhaps, that the whole idea is inappropriate anyhow (Butler and Lewis, 1976). Other inhibitors of sexuality include loss of a spouse, the difficulty of remarriage for older women (because, among other reasons, they far outnumber men), and the frequent objections of family members, particularly adult children, to remarriage even when a match is contemplated (Schaie and Willis, 1986).

Professionals need to be sensitive to the continuing sexual needs of their elderly clients and to offer opportunities for discussion of these in both initial assessment and ongoing work. Conflict between elderly spouses, for instance, is as likely to have a sexual component as is conflict in any other age group. It is unfortunate that assessment instruments for the elderly do not routinely include sexual function among the other functions being examined; the result is that the whole issue is apt to be overlooked.

THE INTERNAL THERMOSTAT

The aging body has less ability to control its internal temperature, making elderly people more vulnerable to both heat and cold (Hayter, 1980; Kurtz, 1982). For this reason, older people often prefer a higher room temperature and warmer clothing than their younger relatives find necessary. They are also more likely to succumb to heat exhaustion in summer and hypothermia in winter, if not protected from extremes of temperature. In cold weather layers of warm clothing; mittens and boots to protect fingers and toes from frostbite; and caps, scarfs, or face masks to protect ears, noses, and lungs from extremely cold air are essential protective devices. During periods of intense heat, use of air conditioners or fans, plenty of liquids, and restriction from unnecessary activity may be lifesaving.

SLOWING DOWN

As the body ages, everything slows down. It takes longer to do familiar tasks. The trip to the supermarket that was once completed in an hour may now take two or three because the body requires a more deliberate pace. Going up and down stairs or climbing onto a bus, which were once done without conscious effort, may become tasks requiring concentration and care. Decreased flexibility in joints and muscles makes balance harder to maintain. Elders affected by such difficulties wisely maintain a deliberate speed for fear that haste might result in falls and fractures.

On the other hand, those who make a practice of regular and vigorous exercise may have faster reaction times than much younger adults who do not exercise (Botwinick, 1978; Spirduso and Clifford, 1978). Exercise can also help maintain flexibility and range of motion. Those who suffer from arthritis may find aquatic exercise less tiring because the water supports much of the body's weight. Warm water is also refreshing for tired muscles.

CHANGES IN ENERGY LEVEL

As people get older, they tire more quickly. Youngsters at a "slumber party" can giggle and chatter into the morning hours, while their weary sponsors doze. A twenty-year-old college student can sit up all night finishing a term paper and go to classes the next day with no ill effects. Her forty-five-year-old father, however, no longer has such reserves of energy. Nevertheless, even seventy-year-olds sometimes exhibit great stamina. "When my mother and I spend the day shopping, I come home exhausted, but she is ready to go out again," says a puzzled forty-year-old. Neugarten (1968) suggests that many women report increased vigor after menopause. However, in the later years, although motivation and activity levels may remain high, the reserves of energy needed to sustain them are not as great as they once were. Fatigue sets in sooner, which is one of the exasperations of old age.

 A seventy-eight-year-old woman, involved in many projects, complained to her doctor that she "ran out of steam" by three o'clock every afternoon and that sometimes her feet swelled. He advised her to get more rest and elevate her feet frequently during the day. "How can I keep my feet up when I have to get the newsletter out this week?" she objected.

Energy reserves, though decreasing, can be improved by sufficient rest, moderate exercise, and good nutrition. Many old people have inadequate diets because of eating alone or lack of interest in cooking, neglected teeth or poorly fitting dentures, or the difficulty of getting out to shop. Poverty may also be a factor, but many people with adequate incomes do not get the nutrients they need. It is easier to subsist on tea and crackers or to open a can of soup than to brave the elements in search of better food. With lessened food intake appetite decreases and fatigue increases. The vicious circle thus begun may end in hospitalization for malnutrition.

Such inroads on energy are not inevitable. Proper dental care (sometimes neglected because it is not covered by Medicare) can take the discomfort out of eating. Nutrition sites for the elderly offer low-cost meals in conjunction with companionship and interesting activities. For the homebound, Meals on Wheels, also known as Home Delivered Meals, may be an option. Sometimes, neighbors arrange to prepare meals together or take turns, thus sharing the cooking tasks and avoiding solitude. It behooves human service workers, once they become involved with persons at risk of malnutrition, to explore what the clients have available to them and to recommend the most appropriate and accessible service. However, workers must first ascertain what expectations there might be for the clients' low energy levels, making certain that these are not physical symptoms of illness. If it is determined that the reasons for improper nourishment lie in remediable circumstances such as dental care or need for assistance through services, workers must engage the clients in a discussion of help and ease their acceptance thereof before a crisis occurs. Of course, many older people do not come to the attention of professional helpers. Nonetheless, they have many opportunities to learn about improving their nutrition. Human service workers may conduct health education programs at senior centers and clinics and can speak to church groups and other gatherings to disseminate information and increase awareness. Aside from education, their task is to encourage the elderly to take responsibility for their own health and fitness and, above all, to encourage them, when necessary, to substitute wisdom for energy.

Acute and Chronic Illness

One of the hazards of advancing years is the increased risk of illness and disability. Although most people over sixty-five are healthy, the statistical likelihood of illness increases year by year and is highest in the upper age brackets. The greatest incidence of hospital admissions, prescription and nonprescription drug use, home health visits, and nursing home residency occurs in the years after eighty. Acute and chronic illnesses not only are more likely to occur in the later years but also are more debilitating in their effects. A healthy younger person can usually recover from a bout of flu or even pneumonia quite rapidly; for an older person it will take much longer. If the old person is already suffering from one of several chronic conditions, such as diabetes or high blood pressure (86 percent of all older people have at least one chronic illness), the impact is likely to be increased and the recovery period further prolonged. A common situation among the very old is having to cope with a number of chronic illnesses that are occasionally exacerbated by acute episodes (Nahemow and Ponsada, 1983).

MANAGEMENT OF CHRONIC ILLNESS

Controlling a chronic condition—such as diabetes, parkinsonism, or colitis—may involve both medication and strict attention to diet and other routines. Even with the most careful monitoring, the disease may flare up or worsen progressively. It is not surprising that patients sometimes feel that the benefits are not worth the restrictions posed by the treatment. If one restricts the pleasures of life but gets worse anyhow, what is the point? Consequently, some cheat occasionally, others binge, and some ignore instructions altogether. This can be very frustrating for professionals who are trying to help the patient keep the disease under control. The temptation may be to berate and scold the person into compliance. This will usually not work; indeed, it is likely to have the opposite effect and may even drive the person away from treatment. A more effective strategy is to acknowledge the patient's frustration and discouragement sympathetically, agree that the disease may flare up despite compliance, and then point out that, in the long run, compliance will result in more good days and fewer bad ones.

Some conditions are difficult to manage because several diseases are present at the same time, and the treatment that benefits one aggravates another. For instance, arthritis is so common in older years that few escape it altogether. For most it is a nuisance rather than a disability. Its more severe manifestations can be treated by exercise, medication, and sometimes surgery to replace severely damaged joints. However, an arthritic who has heart disease may need exercise for arthritis and rest for the heart. Or a heart patient who takes anticoagulants to prevent blood clots may reactivate a bleeding ulcer. Patients may become confused by these contradictions and conclude that the doctor is incompetent. They often need lessons in how to talk with doctors. Rather than discontinue treatment, they can be helped to frame questions, describe symptoms, and participate in an ongoing consultation on their own health care. The elderly as a group may have had little practice in doing so. They grew up in an era when it was not considered appropriate to question a doctor about diagnosis or treatment. It may require a lot of discussion, reassurance, and, perhaps, role playing to convince an old person that understanding one's own health is an entitlement, not a favor.

The goals of treatment, even for a single illness, may not be totally compatible. In severe arthritis, for instance, the goals may be freedom from pain and increase of mobility. If exercise is painful, patients may find it difficult to tolerate unless they are highly motivated to regain mobility.

Writer Dorothy Canfield Fisher (1956) describes one such determined old lady, her own great-grandmother. Nearly immobilized by "rheumatics," she insisted that two of her sons come every day and walk her up and down until her joints unlocked. She screamed with pain, but woe to the sons if they tried to stop. She insisted on continuing, "hollering" with every step, until she was "limbered up" enough to get through the rest of the day.

Professional helpers often find themselves in the same position as this woman's sons, tempted to save older persons from pain and agony. But the decision of whether or not to carry on is not theirs to make. It is governed by the will and self-determination of the person who is trading temporary discomfort for longer-range benefits. Only when clients or patients put themselves in jeopardy of serious harm should helping persons suggest more realistic coping methods and stand by in support of the emotionally painful loss that accompanies the acknowledgment of one's limitations.

HAZARDS OF MEDICATION

Older people use more drugs, both prescription and nonprescription, than other segments of the population. They are often subject to several simultaneous illnesses and therefore take a greater variety of medications than younger people (Warheit, Arey, and Swanson, 1976). They are also likely to be consulting a number of different specialists and may not inform each about the medications prescribed by others (Ascione et al., 1980). Indeed, they tend not to question their doctors about their medications but accept whatever information is given to them (AARP, 1984).

Prescribed medications may interact adversely with each other or with nonprescription medicines, especially if the patients rely on the latter without informing their physicians. Standard dosages, as they are used with younger persons, may be excessive for older people, who are more sensitive due to metabolic changes and slower absorption and elimination rates. In addition, many older people tend to self-medicate inappropriately: When pain and discomfort are particularly severe, they may decide to take more pills than were prescribed; on a good day they may decide to omit or lessen the dosage. They may also have difficulty swallowing pills and not be aware that this can be overcome by the use of gelatin capsules, crushing and mixing with food, and other practical solutions. Or they may simply be denying the existence of a problem and therefore reject the need for treatment. Such inconsistencies and behavioral messages not only make it difficult to monitor the progress of the disease and rate of recovery or maintenance but also can create havoc in the body. This is still further complicated by the fact that because medications are expensive, many older people will try to stretch or save their medications so as to minimize their expense. For all these reasons old people may be at risk of adverse drug reactions.

Managing a complex array of medications is a challenge. It may involve remembering to take a pill in the morning, another with meals, and still another every other day, plus eye drops three times a day. Many people have to take six or eight medications or even more. It is easy to get mixed up. For a person with some degree of memory loss this is almost inevitable, unless there is a structured system for knowing what to take when. Another problem is that labels may be difficult to read without a magnifying glass, or instructions may be ambiguous. Adverse drug reactions can result in hospitalization; or hospitalization for other reasons may reveal drug toxicity as part of the problem or even as the underlying problem.

COPING WITH MULTIPLE MEDICATIONS

To provide structure for a bewildering array of pills, family members or a visiting nurse may set up medications to be taken over the course of several days or a week, using egg carton compartments or similar containers labeled with the day or time to be taken. Frequent monitoring of such a system may be necessary to determine whether it is working effectively. Such monitoring is essential not only to ensure that the patient is following instructions but also to determine the level of patient tolerance to the current prescriptions.

Medication counseling and education are intended to help older people reduce misinformation and misunderstanding in order to manage their medications more effectively and to be alert to reactions that may require adjustments in dosage. Such instruction is most likely to be given by pharmacists or nurses to augment the instructions given by physicians. The framework described by Lesage and Zwygart-Stauffacher (1988) provides guidelines for determining how much people already know and what they need to learn. It includes four areas of exploration:

1. The medications (prescription and nonprescription) actually being used

2. The sources of information underlying the elder's (or caregiver's) knowledge of medications
3. The specific goals of drug therapy and whether they have been achieved
4. The presence of signs or symptoms that may be associated with adverse drug reactions.

The third item is especially significant because the goals of the prescriber and the goals of the patient may be different. For instance, the patient's goal may be to feel better or to function better; the prescriber may be using criteria such as reducing weight or blood pressure. Discovering that there is a discrepancy can enable the educator to facilitate communication between the prescriber and the patient. The educator or other professional rightly tries to determine whether there is compliance with the prescriber's instructions; however, it is not enough to try to prevent noncompliance. The old person's (or caregiver's) understanding of medications, their purpose, and their effects is a better protection against drug misuse (Weintraub, 1984).

Group education, feedback, and follow-up are also important strategies for enabling older people to become partners in their own care (Hammerlund, Ostrom, and Kethley, 1985). Oral instruction may be reinforced by written handouts, which can be kept and referred to by the older persons. Group instruction via lectures, health fairs, and other consciousness-raising events provides another form of reinforcement. Follow-up contacts help determine how well the original instructions were understood. The availability of a health professional, such as a nurse or pharmacist, at senior housing, senior centers, or other neighborhood gathering places adds another source of information and opportunity to get answers to questions.

ALCOHOL USE AND ABUSE

Alcohol use creates two different complications in health management. The first is that alcohol interacts with other drugs and may limit or intensify their effects. It must therefore be taken into account as a possible factor in the effectiveness of medication. Even if the alcohol and the other drug are consumed many hours apart, there may be an interaction.

The second complication is that old people, like younger ones, may become dependent on alcohol; that is, they may become alcoholics. The majority of aged alcoholics have been addicted for many years, but a significant number become alcoholics only in old age. Their dependence may have developed insidiously as a reaction to loss, isolation, or physical pain, and they may have turned to alcohol as an antidepressant or tranquilizer.

Treatment of alchoholism in the elderly. Late-onset alcoholics can often be treated very successfully if they are identified. Group treatment is beneficial for elderly alcoholics, as it is for younger chemically dependent persons, but it is usually more effective if the members of the group are age peers (Schiff, 1988). However, elderly alcoholics may remain unidentified and untreated. There is often a reluctance to believe that the elderly can be substance abusers, and the possibility is not checked out routinely. Elderly alcoholics may also escape notice because they are frequently retired, living alone, and no longer driving. Therefore, they are not confronted with their addiction because of problems in the workplace, family conflict, or driving while intoxicated. Family members, indeed, may be reluctant to encourage treatment even if they are aware of the problem because they do not wish to deprive the old person of an alleged "pleasure" when so few are available. Addiction is not a pleasure, however; it is a compulsion accompanied by shame, self-isolation, and increasing despair. Professional helpers must be sensitive to these feelings and be particularly aware that alcoholism is not only a chemical dependency but also the result of inner emptiness. Addressing the externally imposed losses experienced by many older persons is important but is very often only part of the broader picture.

Enabling an addicted person to enter a treatment situation may require extensive outreach, perhaps even beginning with offers of concrete assistance unrelated to the drinking problem. Peers who have successfully undergone treatment can often act as effective outreach agents, for they can both empathize with and confront the shame and denial (Rathbone-McCuan, 1988).

SUDDEN OR CATASTROPHIC ILLNESS

Sometimes, a person who has enjoyed robust health for seventy years or more is suddenly laid low by a stroke, a heart attack, a hip fracture, or a devastating diagnosis such as cancer. Then, it is not only the illness itself that must be dealt with but also the terrifyingly sudden change from health to illness. The victim may react with rage and denial or with numbness and apparent resignation to the worst. Persons faced with such a situation are better prepared to deal with it if they have had some previous success in overcoming a serious problem, whether or not it was health-related. However, it may be difficult to translate the former achievement into a new idiom if one has never felt physically vulnerable. Men who have had an athletic or macho self-image may have a harder time than women, who are less likely to have that particular self-expectation.

 Mr. MacDuffy was sixty-four when he suffered a heart attack. He had been a cross-country skier and Little League coach and was indignant at the idea that his heart had let him down. In fact, he didn't believe it and constantly pushed himself beyond the limits of activity advised by his doctor. To no one's surprise except his own, he suffered a relapse. He recovered, but he became severely depressed.

Mr. MacDuffy found the change from invincible skier to invalid too great a shock. It gave him the psychological equivalent of diver's bends, a condition wherein the muscles tighten and become rigid from the impact of a dive. Time and support may enable him to gain a more realistic outlook. Paradoxically, he might have been fortunate to have had an earlier brush with illness — like Mr. Richards.

 Mr. Richards had suffered from rheumatic heart disease as a child but made a good recovery. In his forties he had an ulcer attack, underwent surgery, and was restricted to a very bland diet. He was good-natured about it and made a point of enjoying to the fullest whatever foods and beverages he was permitted. In his sixties he was diagnosed as having cancer. He underwent surgery and recovered. Then, the cancer recurred in

another site. In a period of eighteen years he had five recurrences. Each time, he cooperated cheerfully with all his specialists and continued to enjoy life—whatever he could enjoy at any given moment. He finally succumbed to the disease at eighty-three, having far outlived his initial prognosis. In his last months he was very frail but still enjoyed walks in good weather, occasional lunches with friends, lively conversations with his wife, and reading his beloved books.

Potential for Rehabilitation

Damaged hearts heal; stroke victims regain mobility; fractured hip joints can be pinned or even replaced and bear weight again—not always, but frequently enough to make the effort worthwhile. Whether or not rehabilitation succeeds depends on many variables: the body's general health, the level of support by attending physicians and other therapists, state-of-the-art technology and its availability, and the motivation of the patient. The last element is the most important of all. Nothing can compensate for the lack of hope and determination of the patient to get better, though the encouragement of family, friends, and professionals can shore that up.

Popular literature is full of stories of those who have overcome immense physical odds, such as severe burns, prolonged exposure, wartime injuries, neurological disorders, and cancer. The ages of the protagonists in such stories range from childhood to middle age, but rarely are the heroes old people. Here is an exception.

Charlamae Jackson, a seventy-two-year-old black woman, suffered a stroke in her home. She was hospitalized; and when her condition stabilized, she was moved to a rehabilitation unit for physical therapy. But the doctors did not think she was a very good candidate. When she tried to stand, her balance was poor. She did not seem to understand instructions for transferring from bed to chair or toilet. Even if she eventually learned these techniques, there was no one at home to take care of her. They thought she would be better off in a nursing home.

When Mrs. Jackson heard these recommendations, she was furious. "How do you know I can't learn?" she stormed. "You haven't even let me try!" Cautioned about the dangers of falling, she retorted, "I don't see why you're so worried. If anyone falls it will be me, not you." She was so adamant that she won a six-week extension of her originally scheduled one-week stay. She worked daily at the parallel bars, did all the exercises, and struggled to learn the transfer techniques. At the end of six weeks she could walk with a walker, maneuver a wheelchair, and apply the transfer techniques. She was ready to go home, but she still had no one to help her with the many tasks she could not perform unaided, such as bathing, shopping, housekeeping, and transportation.

Mrs. Jackson had a plan, however. Although her physical abilities were somewhat depleted, her organizational skills were as good as ever. She mobilized her family and friends. The grandchildren could take turns checking on her and running errands for her after school. Her daughter, who worked, would shop on weekends and prepare some meals for later reheating. A neighbor who was a retired nurse agreed to come in twice a week to give her a bath. Through the Ladies' Aid Society she located several women who would take turns cleaning, doing laundry, and preparing some simple meals. (They didn't dare say "no" to a past president!) And a cousin was willing to drive and escort Mrs. Jackson in her folding wheelchair to medical appointments.

So Mrs. Jackson went home, having thumbed her nose at fate and confounded the experts. But no one wrote up her achievement for the newspapers or the Reader's Digest.

Mrs. Jackson organized her discharge plan by means of single-minded determination, networking, and a touch of intimidation. Being the sort of person to whom people are afraid to say "no" can be a real advantage in the struggle against physical disability. Mrs. Jackson also had the advantage of knowing exactly what she wanted and having a wide variety of family members and acquaintances who could help her achieve it.

Even those who do not have as many resources available to them as Mrs. Jackson can preserve their independence and maintain control despite physical disability. The rapid growth in home health care and the availability of human service workers as case managers has made it possible to provide very complex care in the home. In the case of a stroke victim about to be discharged from the hospital, for example, a professional would begin by ascertaining the patient's desires, the availability of family or other supportive care, and the complexity of the patient's needs, both physical and psychological. If the patient is to return home, some environmental adaptations may be needed. Grab bars in the bathroom; rental or purchase of a wheelchair, walker, or hospital bed; additional lighting; elimination of scatter rugs or carpeting for ease of wheelchair maneuverability; storage space for medical supplies; and designation of a refrigerator shelf for medications are all easily arranged. Occupational therapists specialize in home visits that determine required changes and help implement them.

For other tasks that include hands-on care, such as bathing, range of motion, change of dressings, injections, and the like, nursing care can be obtained from many reputable home health agencies. Those who qualify under Medicare are eligible for these services, as well as for nonmedical services such as social services, occupational therapy, speech therapy, and home care. Under Medicare, 25 percent of approved time can also be spent on other than hands-on care, such as cooking and laundry. Non-Medicare patients can obtain all these services on a fee-for-service basis and, in some instances, may be eligible for subsidized home care. The availability of services is growing, partially because hospital stays are shorter and partly because home care is driven by consumer demands.

Coping Strategies

The ability to utilize available services and the interest in doing so varies significantly and is seldom determined by the degree of disability or nature of the older person's physical problem. It is almost always dependent on the personality and coping capacity of the individual and the patient's concept of his or her illness. Personalities run the gamut from active to passive, from accepting to abrasive, and from making the most of reality to rejecting it out of hand, substituting a personal view. The old may be frail in body, but they are strong in spirit, whether or not this spirit serves them well and whether or not it meets the expectations and standards of others. As Ronald Blythe (1979) put it, "The old do not want outreach, they want association."

DISCOUNTING THE ODDS

When faced with catastrophe, the old, as well as others, have two choices: give in to the seemingly inevitable or buck the odds, even if the chance of success seems remote. Mrs. Jackson's doctors, for instance, thought her chances of recovery were poor, given her age and diagnosis. Statistically, they were probably correct.

Mrs. Jackson, however, refused to be intimidated by statistics. She insisted on being allowed to try and argued with the doctors until she won her point. In this she showed the characteristics of what Siegel (1986) calls "exceptional patients"—those who are so invested in their own health that they are unwilling to leave it in the hands of experts.

AGGRESSIVENESS VERSUS PASSIVITY

Passivity during a crisis is counterproductive at any age and particularly so for the old. Younger persons may be encouraged to fight their own battles for health and other needs, but societal expectations that the elderly will be—should be—frail, confused, and incompetent may deprive them of external supports. Sheldon Tobin (1987) describes how his mother-in-law, when hospitalized, attempted to be a compliant "good patient" but soon withdrew into apathy and apparent confusion. When encouraged to speak up for herself, however, she began objecting to nursing routines and questioning the doctor about her diagnosis and treatment. She also started getting out of bed and regained her orientation to place and time. Despite these evidences of improvement her family was deeply embarrassed by her behavior. She had ceased to be a "good patient" and become "ornery." One is reminded of parents' fury when their three-year-old has a tantrum in the grocery store, or when they are summoned to the principal's office to discuss their teenager's truancy. It is not the actual destructiveness of the child's behavior that is infuriating but the parents' feelings that they have been made to look ridiculous or inadequate in the eyes of their neighbors or persons of authority.

BLAMING THE ENVIRONMENT

It is not unusual for those who suffer from physical and other deficits to blame and criticize others. An old person's reaction to hearing loss may be to accuse others of lying or spreading malicious rumors. Failing vision or memory loss, with consequent difficulty in finding things, may precipitate accusations of stealing. Such ascriptions of blame are very distressing to family, friends, and employees, but it is less devastating to the individual to place the responsibility for the trouble outside oneself. Otherwise, perception of inadequacy may lead to preoccupation with deficits, panic, or withdrawal into depression. Survival prospects are much better for people who are sharp-tongued, feisty, and even downright nasty (Wacker, 1985). Practice wisdom among those who have had long experience with the elderly holds that the "squeaking wheel gets the oil" and "a little paranoia is a good preservative" in old age.

DENIAL AND TRANSCENDENCE

Rather than complain, the old may ignore or deny deficits.

Ninety-year-old Mrs. Greenstein insists on walking everywhere in her neighborhood, despite a severely arthritic hip. The walks are tiring and painful, but she insists on getting, under her own steam, to the bank, the grocery store, the dentist, and the beauty parlor. She can easily afford to take a taxi but won't bother to call one. Despite the resulting fatigue the exercise probably helps her maintain the usability of her hip, and purposeful activity certainly helps her avoid boredom and depression. Nevertheless, if a friend offers her a ride, she accepts. Going with a friend is a social outing, whereas calling a cab would be acknowledging disability.

Mrs. Greenstein's walks do not put her at risk of anything worse than fatigue, unless she insists on going out in slippery weather. Even more dramatic examples of transcending their disabilities are Miss Pinkham, who at eighty still insists on cleaning out her own roof gutters, and ninety-year-old Mr. Ross, whose daughter-in-law found him perched precariously on a ladder washing his outside windows. "What will the neighbors think!" she protested, imagining charges of exploitation and neglect. "Humph!" replied the old man. "They aren't going to wash my windows, are they?"

Others with more serious ailments, such as damaged hearts or high blood pressure, may risk collapse by toiling up and down stairs with bags of groceries, shoveling snow, managing a booth at the church rummage sale, or getting to the weekly bridge or bingo game. Maintaining identity and purpose in life may be more important to them than physical safety. Given the choice of "dropping in harness" or rusting in a rocking chair, they vastly prefer the former, despite the protestations of family, friends, and physicians that they are courting an early death. In any case those who have survived into their eighties and beyond do not fear death as much as disability and inactivity. One such woman, trying to reassure her anxious son that she was not overextending herself, said: "Don't worry, dear. In any case, I won't die young!"

Robert Peck (1968) described such behavior as "body transcendence" and regarded its accomplishment as one of the normal tasks of old age. Failure to master this task, in his view, resulted in "body preoccupation."

SOMATIZATION AND HYPOCHONDRIA

Some people (old and young) take the opposite tack and become extremely concerned about every physical symptom. Pains in the chest, stomach, or elsewhere; breathlessness; feelings of weakness; rapid heartbeat; and many other discomforts may be sources of complaint. Doctors may be unable to find any organic basis for the symptoms. Being assured that "everything is fine" only convinces the patient that the doctor is incompetent or uninterested. Dismissing the doctor, the patient searches for another who will find the cause of the mysterious malady and do something about it. Some physicians subject patients to a battery of tests, not because they expect to find anything but because they hope to convince the patient that everything possible has been done. They may even do exploratory surgery. This confirms for the patient that there indeed is an organic problem. Then, if nothing shows up, the patient is again disappointed and has spent a lot of money needlessly. The doctor is also frustrated by the endless calls and complaints that seem purely fanciful. The physician may suggest a psychiatric or psychological evaluation when no organic basis for the problem is found. This recommendation is rarely accepted. Such is the vicious cycle of hypochondria.

What becomes clear to professionals working with persons suffering from hypochondriasis is that the most obvious responses that suggest themselves, such as the ones described above, are ineffective because the underlying causes are emotional and usually of a neurotic nature. A response offered to explain away the symptoms of which the person complains does not achieve the desired result because the person needs the reported disease as a defense. It serves to shift anxiety about oneself and others and feelings of deprivation to the less threatening and more socially acceptable concern with one's health. Generally, assuming the sick role buys patients a certain amount of social sanction: it is acceptable to be dependent when ill and thus exempt from social responsibility. In addition, preoccupation with one's body offers a substitute activity when other meaningful activities are no longer readily available.

If an emotional explanation for the symptoms is rejected, and tests and surgery only reinforce the patient's conviction that the problem is indeed organic, what can be done? First and foremost, professionals must accept and make the point that the hypochondriac is indeed suffering from an illness—being aware, but not necessarily stating their suspicions, that the complaints stem from psychological need. Butler and Lewis (1982) suggest that if the doctor makes appointments and telephone reassurance available when requested and assures the patient of interest and willingness to help as much as possible, the symptoms and associated anxiety are more likely to subside. A placebo prescription may also be effective, although some doctors consider the use of placebos dishonest. However, Siegel (1986) believes that the effectiveness of placebos, even in studies of organic illnesses, indicates a degree of power in the mind to cure the body that is largely untapped and unacknowledged.

In hypochondria pain and distress are experienced as real, although no organic basis can be found. In somatization, on the other hand, organic illness seems to occur in response to stress. Like the anxious student who gets a sore throat or breaks out in a rash when exams are due, the anxious older person may come down with the flu or be hospitalized for chest pains when the family is due to go on vacation. Both the student and the old person are likely to be accused of malingering; however, the symptoms are not faked. What happens is that an organ of the body becomes the vehicle for expression of anxiety or stress, and a physical reaction occurs regardless of whether or not the person expresses the distress verbally as well.

FEAR AND DEPENDENCY

Somewhat different from hypochondria (the experience of emotional pain as physical) and somatization (the development of illness in reaction to stress) is an excessively fearful reaction to an organic illness.

Mrs. Peterson had been quite healthy until she suffered a heart attack at the age of eighty-two. She made a good recovery but became extremely fearful about staying alone in her apartment. She frequently called an emergency hospital service complaining of chest pain or rapid heartbeat. She would be taken to the emergency room and examined, then sent home again. She also called her son frequently, often in the middle of the night, complaining of pain or inability to manage. A live-in companion was installed but did not relieve Mrs. Peterson's anxiety or limit her frantic calls to family and paramedics. After a few months she had to give up her apartment and move to a nursing home, not because of her weakened heart but because of her intractable panic. In the nursing home she did well, partly because there were people and activities to distract her from her preoccupation with illness, but also because there was always a charge nurse on her floor and a doctor on call. The availability of medical personnel made Mrs. Peterson feel safe for the first time since leaving the hospital.

Hypochondria, somatization, and panic reactions resulting in extreme dependency are all distressing to the patient and difficult for family, associates, and professionals. How can they be considered to be coping strategies? Are they not, rather, evidence of noncoping? To answer these questions, we must consider the social effects of illness, or the "sick role."

Illness, however caused or experienced, provides a legitimate escape from a stressful situation. Fear and feelings of inadequacy or helplessness do not dispense one from responsibility for managing one's life, but physical illness does. It is usually perceived as something outside the individual's control and therefore something for which he or she cannot be blamed. Emotions, on the other hand, are more likely to be perceived as within the individual's control. This probably accounts for much of the resistance to psychiatric diagnoses and recommendations.

Another advantage of illness is that it entitles one to the assistance and attention of others. It is a socially acceptable means of admitting dependency and asking for help. However, if the illness is perceived as imaginary—that is, within the control of the patient—help and sympathy are likely to be withdrawn or given grudgingly. This is an additional reason for resistance to psychological explanations of illness: they not only delegitimize the person's distress but also result in loss of support. This perception is not limited to the old; most people find it easier to announce they need an operation than to admit they need to see a psychiatrist.

LEARNED HELPLESSNESS

The concept of "learned helplessness" (Seligman, 1975) is that people become passive when they feel they have no control over events or over the management of their lives. Some people have had a lifelong experience of lack of control; for others it occurs in old age. They view a sudden bout with illness or even minor surgery as assaults on their bodies and portents of future problems. They begin to think of their lives as finite and experience a (sometimes temporary and sometimes permanent) loss of equilibrium and confidence. Mrs. Peterson had always felt that she was in charge of her life until she had the heart attack. Then, she discovered that she could not fend off the mysterious malady that had struck her down and that might strike again at any moment.

Differences in Perception

The same set of external circumstances that stimulated Mrs. Jackson to fight back, to refuse to accept what happened to her as destiny, turned Mrs. Peterson into a quivering bundle of terror. Why did they react so differently? Why did one consider her life half-full, but the other only saw hers as half-empty? Perhaps, in absolute terms, both were unrealistic. The statistical odds against Mrs. Jackson's ability to continue in independent living were greater than she would admit, and the statistical risks for Mrs. Peterson's having another heart attack were less than she feared. Nevertheless, each did the best she could with the situation as she perceived it.

As a wise physician once observed, there is no such thing as a 25 percent chance of something happening, as far as one individual is concerned. For each person it either happens or it doesn't. So the chances are either 100 percent or zero. One person goes after the one-in-a-hundred chance of success, but another will not risk a one-in-a-hundred chance of failure. In most cases the bases of decision are neither rational nor conscious but seem obvious to the person concerned. Sometimes, such perceptions can be altered by experience or by psychotherapeutic interaction and support.

Anticipation of Death

Old people think about death more often than younger people but are less anxious about it (Kalish, 1976). Planning for one's estate, making and updating a will, and even arranging for one's funeral are part of the daily business of managing one's affairs. Planning the details of a memorial service, perhaps writing a statement of one's most cherished beliefs or a "moral legacy" for one's children or grandchildren, may be part of maintaining both one's sense of self and one's links to the community.

Although the old may fear death less than the young, they dread prolonged invalidism and "being a burden" to themselves and others. For this reason the technology available for prolonging life, even when the patient is in a vegetative state, is less promise than nightmare. To be unable to die—to continue for weeks, months, or even years in pain or insensibility, becoming an inescapable emotional and financial burden to one's family—is, in the eyes of many, a fate literally worse than death.

MAINTAINING CONTROL AT THE END OF LIFE

Much has been written about the legal and ethical aspects of withdrawing treatment or life supports. In some cases this may be done even without prior instructions from the patient; in other cases it may be refused despite repeated requests. These ambiguities have led many people to try to make their wishes known in advance through the instrument of a Living Will. This is a document that states the circumstances under which an individual does not wish to have "heroic measures" used to prolong life. In general, this applies only to terminal illness, not to conditions that, although unresponsive to treatment, are not likely to result in death in the near future. Living Wills are not legally binding in most states but do furnish evidence of the person's wishes. It is best to advise a person considering such a document to discuss the Living Will with his or her physician and to file copies with the doctor as well as with close relatives, who might find themselves in a decision-making position in behalf of the patient at some future time.

Because of the limitations of a Living Will, many people choose to use a Durable Power of Attorney for Health Care. This document names a person—usually a spouse, child, or trusted friend—who will act as the individual's agent in decisions regarding health care if he or she becomes unable to make such decisions. Because anyone can be named as agent, the Durable Power of Attorney is more flexible than the Living Will, which makes it useful for those who have no close relatives. However, it should also be discussed with physicians and family members, because not only the person designated as agent but also others likely to be concerned. For instance, if one child is appointed the agent, other children should also be made aware of the appointment. However, if the designee becomes unavailable, perhaps by moving away or becoming disabled, a new document must be prepared to name a replacement.

INTERVENTION WITH THE DYING

Those diagnosed as terminally ill are often avoided by both family members and professionals. Yet those so designated need human contact as much as they ever did, perhaps more. They need, above all, to be treated as continuing members of the human family, not as if they were already dead. They need friends and relatives who will allow them to talk about death if they want to or about other things if they prefer. If these are not available, for whatever reasons, professional helpers can play a significant role: they must explain the nature of treatment and prepare the patients for whatever discomforts result therefrom; they answer the dying persons' questions honestly and help them live with the answers; they provide emotional support and assure patients of their continuing presence and interest, regardless of the outcome of their diseases. One patient, dying of terminal cancer (Graham, 1982), called these actions by professionals an assurance of "safe conduct" to the end of one's life.

THE HOSPICE CONCEPT

Hospitals are designed for acute care, with every procedure selected to promote cure. Even before the era of Diagnostic Related Groups (DRGs), a method of predetermining payment to hospitals, hospitals had little to offer a sick person who had no prospect of recovery. The hospice concept, as an alternative, offers comfort, pain relief, and emotional support, whether in special in-patient units or in the patients' homes. The hospice movement began in England, under the direction of Dr. Cicely Saunders. In the United States it has spread rapidly during the 1980s and is now widely available. Reimbursable through Medicare, hospice care has enabled many patients to receive humane and dignified treatment and to die at home or in a homelike atmosphere in the company of their loved ones.

Unfortunately, hospice care is only available to those who have been diagnosed as having a life expectancy of three to six months or less. This leaves out thousands who are not technically terminally ill but who wrestle with the discomforts of prolonged chronic disability. They too need compassion, dignity, and the continuing experience of being part of the human condition. Human service professionals can offer them such recognition and thus support the ability of the aged to adapt to, cope with, and accept treatment in the face of their physical decline.

CHAPTER 7

Socially Distressing Symptoms and Behaviors

If a person's behavior is sufficiently distressing or disruptive to the social milieu, the social milieu will eject the offender. In Alaska, we are told, the Eskimos abandon their unproductive elders on ice floes. Here, depending on the nature of the offense and the age of the offender, prisons, psychiatric hospitals, or nursing homes may be regarded as acting in the same way.

This is not to say that psychiatric hospitalization or nursing home placement is punitive in its intent or effect, or inappropriate for older persons or those in need of constant care, treatment, and supervision. The point being made is that when placement is sought, the reasons may sometimes have more to do with hiding socially unacceptable symptoms or easing family anxiety than with responding to the actual needs of the afflicted older person. On the other hand, psychiatric or nursing home care may, in fact, be the best choices in some circumstances. Families who try to avoid such resources at all cost may be doing their disabled relatives (and often themselves) a serious disservice.

It is important for professionals to understand some of the behaviors that families and society often find particularly difficult to tolerate. The behaviors we describe here are not intended to represent a complete inventory of socially unacceptable symptoms, nor are they to be viewed as diagnostic entities. Rather, they are examined in terms of their impact on those involved with the afflicted persons and their effect on the availability of support and care. Our discussion includes suggestions for management that may make the behaviors easier to deal with and will consider how the needs of the impaired elderly can be met without overwhelming their concerned relatives.

The behaviors that are most frequently brought to the attention of practitioners are those that distress families or society at large, and these may emanate from physical, environmental, cognitive, or psychological causes. Although the list presented here is not exhaustive, it should help professionals and those interested in older persons to separate the observation of symptoms and their implications from the anxiety reactions they evoke, and serve to establish principles of intervention.

Socially Distressing Physical Symptoms

Physical symptoms may create distress because they evoke helplessness, revulsion, or fear in the observer as well as the sufferer.

PAIN

One of the most difficult symptoms to deal with, for both the sufferer and the observers, is severe pain. The person experiencing the pain can think of nothing else; the observers are helpless to alleviate it. Because the helplessness is so difficult to endure, the sufferer may be bundled off to a hospital or nursing home, where relatives will not have to watch the agony. Despite the recognition that the motivation for this action is to obtain treatment and relief for the person experiencing the pain, removal from familiar surroundings adds a sense of isolation to the physical suffering.

Extreme pain is associated with some forms of cancer and is one of the chief reasons that the disease is so dreaded. The hospice movement, which has gained momentum in recent years, has grown largely in response to cancer and other painful terminal illnesses. Its intent is to offer support, care, and pain control at home or in a homelike environment as an alternative to the cure-focused acute care usually found in hospitals. The principal goals of the hospice method are the alleviation of pain without impairment of consciousness, and the maintenance of the patient's significant social relationships (Stoddard, 1978). As the number of hospices increases throughout the country, so do the options for the terminally ill and their families.

Not all intense pain, however, is caused by fatal illness. For instance, arthritis, especially rheumatoid arthritis, can keep victims in daily misery. No one dies of it, although some wish they could. No "miracle drug" has thus far proven both safe and effective. Pain, coupled with hopelessness, has driven some sufferers to attempt suicide. Constant complaints may drive their relatives to consider institutional care.

When pain is chronic, the most crucial elements in its control are the mental attitude of the patient, the strength of the family unit, and support from the doctor. An encouraging and imaginative physician can do a great deal to maintain an attitude of hopefulness in patient and family. Old-fashioned remedies such as heat and aspirin, coupled with moderate exercise, can do much to reduce discomfort and maintain a range of motion. A hot bath, especially with a whirlpool attachment, may work a temporary miracle. Imagination comes into play in considering what kinds of assistance, equipment, or activity could serve to reduce discomfort. Consulting a physical or occupational therapist may also be helpful.

When a doctor says that nothing can be done, it usually means no cure is possible at present. It almost never means that no alleviation is possible, given the combined efforts of physician, patient, and family to make use of whatever is available. The physician's investment in alleviating the patient's discomfort can go far beyond the prescription of pain-controlling medications. By recommending a range of remedies or activities, the doctor can reassure the patient, who feels comforted by "doing something." The doctor's level of hope, as well as the patient's, may also be reinforced when calling on other members of the professional team. Reflecting on the various potential interventions and pooling their expertise to make the patient's condition more manageable is encouraging to all concerned.

True hopelessness resides only in the unwillingness of the patient or the relatives to make use of help. Sometimes, this arises from dissatisfaction with partial success. If total cure is not possible, some people refuse to make any effort on their own behalf, preferring to rail against fate. Sooner or later, their hopelessness is likely to infect their support system, and those who have tried to help will withdraw. Intervention by a professional may inject some hope and consequent motivation into such patients. The discipline to which the professional belongs, whether it be medicine, nursing, physical therapy, occupational therapy, or social work, is less important than the hope the individual can inspire.

INCONTINENCE

Another physical symptom distressing to both patient and family is incontinence of urine or, worse yet, of feces. Loss of control of the processes of elimination often creates embarrassment to the patient and revulsion in the observers. It also makes an immense amount of work for those caring for the patient.

If the primary caregiver is an aged spouse, the constant necessity for linen changes, laundry, and cleaning up accidents may be beyond available strength or tolerance. Aside from the physical effort involved, the symptom itself is likely to produce intense rage in both the sufferer and the caregivers. The regression to a babyhood level of functioning may precipitate changes in role and self-image not only in the patient but also in the caregiver. It is not unusual to see caregiver and patient locked in a bitter battle reminiscent of an exasperated mother trying to toilet train a recalcitrant two-year-old. The caregiver rails and scolds; the patient sometimes seems to gain a perverse satisfaction from causing trouble, as if the symptom provides a means of getting even with the caregiver, the situation, and the sense of helplessness. The weapon that enabled the child to retaliate against all-powerful grown-ups may thus be resorted to once more in old age, and noncooperation may be a cover for the humiliation of being unable to control one's own body. And for the caregiver frustration and helplessness may engender guilt and a deep sense of personal failure. After all, did not the spouses promise to take each other "for better or for worse"?

A childless husband and wife lived in independent accommodations despite considerable physical frailty. Mr. Shiver, at age ninety, was

diabetic, irritable, doubly incontinent, and denying any physical
problems. He was abusive and demeaning to his wife, as if to forestall
any discussion that might address the real problem.

Mrs. Shiver, fifteen years younger, was totally blind but managing to
keep the household going. What she found intolerable, however, was
having to clean up after her husband, who would hide the proof of his
incontinence in corners throughout the house, forcing his wife to grope
blindly for the discarded feces. The old gentleman was so canny and his
wife so ambivalent about the extent of her obligation to continue and
conceal, that neither the doctor nor relatives had any knowledge of the
situation. Mrs. Shiver kept the secret to herself but became violently
nauseous after each search and cleaning session. It was only when she
began to lose weight dramatically that the doctor was able to get her to
describe the conditions at home.

With such a complex range of emotions and attendant
repercussions it is no wonder that the symptom of incontinence is
one of the most frequent precipitants of the decision to seek institutional care. And the decision to choose a particular institution may
be governed by whether or not it smells of urine. This is probably only
in part because the odor is unpleasant or because its presence
suggests neglect.

Incontinence in an adult evokes such primitive repugnance
that even if it is the reason for seeking institutional care, one would
rather not be reminded of the fact. If an odor is not present, one can
pretend that the symptom does not exist.

A daughter who had been looking at nursing homes for her father
described one of those she had visited in glowing terms. The staff was
caring; the food was good; the residents praised the place; it was
meticulously clean. However, even its cleanliness could not mask the
fact that many of the residents were incontinent. "So," concluded the
daughter, "how could I let my father rot in a place like that?"

The severity of incontinence, however, has wide variation,
ranging from total loss of control to occasional accidents. In its most
severe forms incontinence is very difficult to manage at home
without outside help. The milder, more occasional manifestations
may be controlled by maintenance of a very regular schedule,
reminders, and perhaps the use of adult absorbent underpants. A

visiting nurse may be able to advise on equipment and teach hygiene techniques. With some measure of control regained, the frustration of both patient and caregiver may be reduced to the point where both can tolerate the situation.

If the onset of incontinence is sudden rather than gradual, one should suspect the presence of infection or some other treatable condition and get a thorough medical work-up from a physician who is knowledgeable about age-related illnesses. As geriatric specialization increases, such doctors will become easier to find.

Impact on Environment

As we noted above, much of the distress caused by incontinence lies in the fact that it creates unpleasantness in the environment. Other behaviors that do not originate in a physical symptom may have the same effect.

ODORS AND OTHER NUISANCES

The person who neglects or refuses to bathe or change clothes or the recluse who lives with innumerable cats may produce such disagreeable odors that their families or neighbors find their presence intolerable and demand their removal. Bizarre clothing or grooming may also incite disapproval. On the whole, however, smells are much more powerful than sights in creating disgust and revulsion. One can close one's eyes or look in another direction, but controlling one's nose is not so easy. Odors are pervasive and intrusive. The same is true of sound, but elders are seldom the perpetrators of noise pollution, which is more the province of adolescents. Still, a deaf old person or one who is confused about time may play a radio or television loudly or at odd hours and thus disturb the neighbors.

Some avenues exist for reducing the impact of these nuisances on the environment. The hearing-impaired person may be persuaded to use headphones when listening to music or TV programs. The one who is unable to manage tasks of bathing and grooming may be willing to accept assistance, and the recluse with a lot of pets who is overwhelmed by their care and care of self may welcome intervention that offers relief. But this is not always the case. Headphones may be forgotten or ignored, the nonbather may cling stubbornly to familiar though smelly clothes, and the recluse will more than likely resist all offers of help, so legal action may have to be initiated. This puts the unwilling sharers of the offender's environment into the uncomfortable position of having to decide how much they can stand and when they would be driven to act in their own behalf.

FIRE HAZARDS

An environmental hazard that is frightening rather than disgusting is fire. The careless smoker, especially if a hoarder of newspapers or other inflammables, endangers others as well as himself or herself. Cooking is another activity that can be hazardous if the cook forgets to turn off the stove or cannot see which burner is lit. Many old people are acutely aware that incompetence in this area is a threat to their independence. They know that relatives are likely to be quite frightened when they realize that a fire hazard may exist and that landlords often consider it grounds for eviction. Therefore, if a pot or a dinner is burned, the old person may hide the evidence or, worse yet, stop cooking altogether, avoiding the hazard of fire but risking the hazard of malnutrition. Others seem oblivious to the danger and ignore or deny the evidence of cigarette burns or charred food.

Because the issue is so loaded, families may consider it worthwhile to consult a professional who can help evaluate the facts objectively. For instance, was the burned pot an isolated episode or one in a series? Could the danger be avoided by having prepared food brought in? If the old person is a smoker, are there burns on rugs or furniture that would indicate chronic carelessness or forgetfulness? If there is an accumulation of papers or other inflammable materials, can these be removed? Can the old person cooperate in the evaluation of the problem?

This last question is a crucial one. If the old person is aware of the problem and can help in thinking of ways to alleviate it, the difficulty is probably not insurmountable. Obliviousness, denial, and persistence in hazardous activities, however, may force the offender's associates to act in their own defense, regardless of the old person's wishes.

Socially Disturbing Psychological Changes

The environmental nuisances and hazards discussed above are likely to be the result of impaired judgment or memory loss. Memory loss is dreaded in part because it is believed to foreshadow complete loss of cognitive function. This rarely occurs. The social damage inflicted by memory loss is more dramatic because it affects behavior than because it is a loss in itself. Cognitive losses, whose effects go beyond disturbing the environment, may have a direct impact on the safety of the affected persons. How these may be dealt with will be discussed more fully in Chapter 8.

PARANOID ACCUSATIONS

Cognitive changes may result in a frightening loss of personality. Other changes appear not so much as loss but as unwelcome additions. If a formerly pleasant and cooperative woman accuses her daughter of stealing, the daughter is likely to be hurt and shaken: "How can Mother say such a thing? What has gotten into her?"

It would be more correct to ask "What has gone out of her?" If she has lost the ability to remember where she put things, she may accuse others of stealing them rather than consciously recognize such a shortcoming in herself. A deficit of the mind is a far worse threat to self-esteem than a disability of the body. Thus, the personality defends itself, unconsciously and automatically, against such devastation, just as the eye blinks against an excess of light or the hand pulls away from a hot stove. One means of such unconscious defense is to project the responsibility for the loss onto someone else. So the daughter may be accused of stealing stockings or the nail scissors or the favorite kitchen knife; or, as a once competent homemaker, the mother may so resent the fact that she can no longer do the tasks she used to handle easily that she accuses her housekeeper of stealing her pots and pans, which symbolically represent her former role. What the mother has had taken from her is the ability to care for her own home; the daughter or other helpers are handy culprits when the only other alternative is acknowledging her own deterioration. It must, however, be reemphasized that the mother's reactions are not deliberate; they are unconsciously spawned and unwittingly delivered.

The distinction between self-protective and dysfunctional paranoia is the extent to which the defense interferes with necessary routines and important relationships. If the mother only mutters about how things disappear, understanding and a sense of humor on the part of family or staff can keep the situation livable. If, however, the mother barricades herself in her room or refuses to have any contact with her "thieving" relatives, she may endanger herself as well as distress them. The purpose served by the defense is the same; it is the degree of pervasiveness that makes a defense functional or dysfunctional.

Sometimes, loss of control is the most painful issue. The whole family or one particular member (usually the chief provider of assistance) may be accused of having designs on the old person's money, which represents control of one's life. (There may be truth in the accusation, but that is another story.) Such accusations, of course, make it more difficult to help the person who is making them. How can a family deal with such behavior, and how can a professional practitioner support and guide the process?

It may be useful to underscore that the accusations are symbolic rather than factual and to try to help the old person compensate for the loss without getting into arguments about the validity of the accusation. "Let's see if we can find them" may be a way of coping with the distress over misplaced stockings or other household effects. But the very fact of constant misplacement is also a source of aggravation to the affected person's family or associates. It is a strain on one's patience and good humor, and it is often difficult not to believe that the loser-accuser is not doing it on purpose. There may be some truth in this perception also. Impaired people, like everyone else, can easily sense resentment in others and find ways to retaliate.

For these reasons alternative caregivers such as part-time companions or day-care center staff may have less troubles with behavior that is difficult for the family because they are less invested in the relationship.

Mrs. Durham, who was at her wits' end because her husband kept hiding things, was astonished to learn that the staff of the nursing home where he was placed experienced no trouble at all. They found him charming and cooperative, though forgetful. Mrs. Durham was so shocked by this discovery that she insisted on taking her husband home, where the trouble started all over again.

As in this example, family members may feel threatened by alternative caregivers because the success of strangers seems to imply failure on the part of the family. How can outsiders tolerate what they cannot? If they can understand that the alternative caregivers succeed precisely because, being unrelated, they are less invested, they may be able to allow themselves some respite and still maintain their relationship with the impaired person. With less pressure the relationship may become deintensified and more gratifying, or at least less aggravating.

Sometimes, however, paranoid accusations do not stop at the verbal level. They are acted out to a degree that is unmanageable even with assistance.

Mrs. Porter had suffered some mental and physical deterioration. She became convinced that her retired husband was having affairs with other women. This agitated her so that she spent most of each night pacing through their apartment, hunting with a broom handle for the mistresses. This put an intolerable strain on her husband, who was recovering from a coronary attack.

Their family finally had to resort to psychiatric hospitalization. Mrs. Porter improved somewhat but not enough to manage at home with help only from her husband. A nurse-companion, hired to relieve the situation, only intensified the wife's suspicions and original delusion. This left no alternative to nursing home placement. The woman's institutionalization was the result not only of the severity of her symptoms as such but also of the strain and jeopardy to her husband and the fact that no available help was acceptable.

Nonetheless, one must wonder if the threat to Mrs. Porter might not have been removed had it been possible to find a male companion for the household, thus keeping the couple together and preventing or at least postponing institutionalization. It is, of course, also possible that under such circumstances Mrs. Porter might have developed a new set of irrational reactions to replace the sexual insults she had been imagining.

Late-life paranoia, as in Mrs. Porter's case, often represents a marked personality change. It may be the result of a dementing illness or appear as a reaction to loss. But why this particular reaction occurs in some people and not in others is not fully known. Projection of one's own feelings onto others is a very common defense, but paranoid projection in the elderly may appear in people who have never resorted to that defense before. They may have appeared to be quite the opposite: self-effacing, self-blaming, sub-servient to the wishes of others. Much of their self-esteem may have been gained vicariously through giving pleasure to others. Many people with this type of personality become depressed in reaction to loss. Why some others react with paranoid projections is one of the mysteries of human uniqueness.

Paranoid behavior in isolated elders. For some people, however, suspiciousness and projection of blame have been lifelong person-ality traits. They have always been somewhat withdrawn and iso-lated, edging their way through life, avoiding intimate relationships. Often, they are extremely competent workers. Retirement is there-fore likely to be a major trauma because they have had few sources of satisfaction other than their work. Decreasing independence and increasing need for help come into conflict with the lifelong fear of intimacy. Such people are likely, in old age, to become isolated, perhaps leading a marginal existence in some dilapidated rooming house or apartment hotel. They may come to the attention of helping organizations when landlords report that they are quarreling with their neighbors over imaginary slights or when they are actually evicted for disruptive behavior.

Staff of helping organizations often perceive these people as socially deprived and try to help them by offering increased access to social interaction or a one-on-one counseling relationship. Usually, neither approach works. Isolated persons cannot handle close inter-personal relationships, and having them thrust upon them only results in an increase of paranoia. A more cautious approach, with emphasis on concrete services, may be more successful. If the counselor or case manager comes in only when the client requests an interview and then is prepared to deal only with the service request, the helping relationship may be perceived as sufficiently nonthreatening to be acceptable. The object is to offer real support and act in an enabling rather than treatment-focused role, while maintaining an acceptable distance.

> *Mrs. Santini, an isolated seventy-three-year-old, had been threatened with eviction because she had been disturbing neighbors by banging on the walls of her apartment (chasing invisible invaders). She stopped this behavior when service from Meals on Wheels was established. Her health had deteriorated to the point where she could not shop for herself, but she was unwilling to ask for help from neighbors. The agency that provided the meals had first tried sending a shopper to get her groceries. But Mrs. Santini was too forgetful to assemble a list without assistance, and the shopper's questions about what she wanted only increased her suspiciousness and agitation.*
>
> *The Meals on Wheels volunteer who replaced the shopper, on the other hand, was required only to deliver the meals with a pleasant but undemanding greeting. This Mrs. Santini could handle. Assured of a regular source of food and an available but nonintrusive helper, she managed to live independently for several more years.*

If acceptable distance is maintained, the behavior of the hard-core isolated elderly may be easier to deal with than the behavior of elderly persons whose distrust and accusations emerge in family disputes.

VERBAL AND PHYSICAL ABUSE

Paranoid accusations may feel, to the recipients, like verbal abuse, but not all verbal abuse is paranoid. It may range from accusations such as "You never do anything right" to epithets and name-calling. These are usually directed at primary caregivers. In some people such behavior represents a change in personality; in others it is a continuation of a lifelong pattern. Occasionally, verbal abuse erupts into physical abuse; although much has been written, with truth, about the abuse of the elderly by their children or other caregivers, what may have been overlooked is that the elderly can themselves be abusers.

Sometimes, perhaps more often than not, abuse is the result of mutual provocation and mutual reprisal.

Mr. Garrison, a wheelchairbound stroke victim, exhibited bruises, as did his wife. It was ascertained that he had managed to deliver some heavy blows with his one good arm and she had retaliated "to make him shut up."

Asked why, she said that, while she did everything for her husband, he never uttered a word of appreciation. Whenever she left the house, he accused her of being a whore and trying to get rid of him so she could sleep with younger men. "I should have the energy," said Mrs. Garrison wryly. She was trying to manage the care of her husband and the maintenance of their home in addition to a part-time job. Then she added, with classic understatement, "I know it's part of his illness, but sometimes it gets to me."

For many people physical abuse marks the point of no return, the last straw that requires the removal of the offender to an institution. Mrs. Garrison did not want to resort to that solution, partly for economic reasons and partly from conviction that an institution would have less tolerance for her husband's disagreeable ways than she did. In this she was probably right. Unlike some patients who are cooperative with everyone except their caregivers, Mr. Garrison was unpleasant to everybody.

In such situations a possible solution might be to engage some part-time help. If the helpers do not have to deal with the difficult persons for more than a few hours at a time, they are more likely to tolerate ugly behavior, and the principal caregivers gain some much needed respite.

There are many ways of obtaining respite from intolerable behavior. The specific solution preferred by a family is less important than the recognition that everyone's tolerance has a limit and that exceeding that limit is likely to result in disaster. The human interpersonal system resembles an electrical system in that it will blow a fuse if the circuit is consistently overloaded.

EXTREME DEPENDENCY

The interpersonal system is likely to break down when there is extreme dependency on one side without corresponding gratification on the other. Abusive behavior is one manifestation of dependency; the abuser simultaneously tries to get more from the caregiving system, punish it for its shortcomings, and express rage at being dependent in the first place. There are many other manifestations: constant demands for help, whether needed or not; frequent or interminable telephone calls, if the involved others are not under the same roof; and endless complaints, to name a few. All of them have the effect of making the caregiver feel smothered and helpless, like the mother of a colicky baby whom she cannot satisfy no matter what she does.

When this kind of insatiable dependency is part of the relationship between the aged and their children or other relatives, it creates a much more complicated situation than that of adults and infants, difficult as that can be. The aged and their caregivers are adults, with adult needs, rights, and expectations. Both parties dread dependency, and even when the old person desires care, such yearning is seen as regression to an infantile state. The adult children are put off, in part, by the unwelcome additional responsibility coming at a time when they thought they were through with taking care of others. A more profound source of distress is that those who need care are their parents, who are supposed to be the providers rather than the recipients of care. The parents feel the same conflict. They need help, but how can they put themselves in an infantile position vis-à-vis their own children? Much of the irrationality of the demands and counterdemands stems from this conflict.

"One mother can take care of twelve children but twelve children can't take care of one mother" is a folk saying of dubious validity. It implies that mothers are generous and capable, whereas children are selfish and/or incompetent. If this were true, the human race would have died out in one generation. While children often do find the care of aged parents difficult, what the folk saying overlooks is that it is much harder, emotionally, physically, and financially, to care for a deteriorating adult than it is to care for healthy children who are on their way to self-sufficiency. Young parents can look forward to the fact that their children will eventually grow up and be on their own, whereas deterioration of the aged is not likely to reverse itself.

Dependency can be tolerable to the caregivers only if they recognize their limitations and stay within them. Otherwise, guilt may drive them to such overextension that the only remedy they can see is precipitous withdrawal. Frequently, this takes the form of institutional placement, which may not meet the needs of the old person but serves to reduce the anxiety of the caregiver. Or the caregiver may move to another part of the country, leaving someone else—other relatives, neighbors, or helping organizations—to pick up the pieces. This may appear negligent on the part of the caregivers, but it may be the only way they can see to gain relief from responsibility that feels so total and so overwhelming. Others, feeling that institutionalization is a mark of failure, try to maintain their aged relatives at home long past the point where the care they can provide is adequate. Such an unsatisfactory arrangement may be clung to with single-minded stubbornness and terminated only by the illness or disability of the caregiver.

How, then, can relatives deal with dependency without becoming overwhelmed or irresponsibly negligent? And how, if they find themselves in such a bind, can they get out of it?

The first step is to take stock of the real needs, not merely the requests, of the aged person. Old people, like young ones, need nourishment, shelter, safety, recognition, and some degree of social stimulation. The extent of this latter need varies among individuals, some of whom place a much higher value on privacy and non-interference than they do on social interaction. Families often mistakenly think that joining a social group or attending a senior center will cure such relatives' depression, withdrawal, or constant complaints, when in fact they may have been loners all their lives and have very few social skills. Setting these people in the midst of more sociable people may lead only to their being treated as scapegoats, ostracized, or ignored, which then gives them more reason to complain.

The next step is to determine which needs can be met by the family on an ongoing basis, not merely during a crisis but day in and day out. For instance, a woman who has a full-time job may be able to see that her mother has groceries in the house when she comes home from the hospital, or she may prepare meals for mother on weekends; but she would not be likely to cook and bring food every day. It may be possible to involve other relatives who have not heretofore taken an active role in helping the old person. This in itself can help the primary caregiver feel less overwhelmed. Often, in overcoming the reluctance to ask for help, the overextended caregiver is surprised by the availability and willingness of the others in the old persons' network. It is noteworthy that in a study of Alzheimer's disease patients living at home, the degree of pressure felt by the caregivers was related not to the length of the illness or the severity of the symptoms but to the number of visits by other relatives. When the caregivers felt supported, they could cope (Zarit, Reever, and Bach-Peterson, 1980).

Whatever is beyond the extended family's capability may be sought from helping organizations and other community resources. In this respect society gives a double message. Programs for the elderly exist, and their availability is expanding; but sometimes families feel that they are abdicating their responsibilities if they take advantage of them. Families caring for children have the supports of tax breaks and public education. There is no such clear-cut public policy with regard to care for the aged, although one might be developed more quickly if families were to feel entitled to demand it.

Once the rest of the family is clear about who can do what, it is important to discuss this with the aged person. Sometimes, families are reluctant to do so for fear that the old person will be offended if they cannot fulfill all his or her needs and requests. And indeed, some old people are very adept at engendering guilt. For them it has been a lifelong pattern, and their children and other relatives have become accustomed to dancing to that tune. Professional assistance can help break such a vicious circle, though the intervention may not have to be extensive or long-term. It may only be necessary to point out to the family members what they are already doing that is successful and to help them feel that they have permission to just continue doing that.

A distraught daughter called a family service agency for help in finding a more protected living arrangement for her father. He had had a hip fracture and was unable or unwilling to do anything for himself. The daughter, Mrs. Henkin, had hired companions to assist him, but he treated them so rudely that they kept quitting. Mrs. Henkin was afraid that her father's real wish was to move in with her, which she was sure would not work out.

In further discussion Mrs. Henkin revealed that she had delivered an ultimatum to her father: Either he cooperated with the companions, or he would have to go to a nursing home. Father had behaved "like a lamb" ever since, but the daughter was very ashamed that she had lost her temper and "yelled." The agency worker pointed out that what the daughter had done had, in fact, been quite effective. It might not have been necessary to yell, but it was important to make clear what she

could and could not do. This she had done, and it had worked. Mrs.
Henkin expressed surprise and relief at discovering that she had actually
solved her own problem.

Issuing an ultimatum is, of course, not always necessary. It can often suffice to define the limits of available help and in such limit setting communicate that needs and realities exist on both sides. Naturally, this approach would not be effective with a person who cannot remember what has been said. The point is that the family itself must be clear about its abilities and priorities and may need help in sorting them out.

One issue that often distresses families is the feeling that if their elderly relatives are unhappy, it is up to them to do something about it. This is an impossible task. Care and support can be provided, but no one can assume responsibility for someone else's happiness. Unfulfilled dreams and disappointing relationships cannot be compensated by the efforts of others, however devoted they may be. Sometimes, the implied demand is, "Because I am unhappy, you owe me more attention and time." This is a devil's bargain that can result in nothing but misery for all the parties to it. It is like trying to fill a bottomless pit. The one who attempts it will have nothing left, and the pit will still be empty. The capacity for happiness is self-generated, not grafted from the outside. Attempting the impossible is what makes families so frustrated that they abandon both the effort and the person. Paradoxically, attempting less results in more actual support.

It is clear that impairments and age-related as well as long-standing behavioral abnormalities affect the quality of life of the elderly not only by their actual severity but also by their impact on the support system. Families and others close to and involved with older persons can determine what is appropriate and adequate support if they understand the nature of the impairment, can assess their own limitations and communicate them, and are able to obtain a measure of gratification from their involvement. They may need, and certainly deserve, professional help in so doing.

CHAPTER 8

Personality Change, Continuity, and Cognitive Loss

Maintaining a coherent self-identity is a primary concern for people at all ages. This does not change in old age. Older people continue to see themselves as the same individuals they have always been, despite social losses and physical deficits (Tobin, 1987; Lieberman and Tobin, 1983). This self-image persists despite the lessening of opportunities for validation through interaction with others. When validation from the current social environment is lacking, it may be found in memories of the past.

Maintaining Continuity of the Self

Recollection of past accomplishments can shore up self-esteem when the present seems dominated by social losses and physical weakness. That is probably why older persons applying for some kind of assistance often begin interviews by describing their careers.

- "I was a master carpenter. My furniture brought the highest prices in the city. Here, look at this desk . . . you can't buy anything like that today."

177

- "During the Depression, I always managed so that the children had enough to eat. They all went to college too. My son is a doctor."
- "I taught school for fifty years and never missed a day. My pupils still write to me . . . all these Christmas cards are from them."

Statements like these are not social chitchat. They are reminders, to both the speaker and the interviewer, that the applicant is a person of consequence, despite the facade of illness, poverty, or misfortune. These incidentals are only a disguise of the real person being presented.

REMINISCENCE

Older people often like to reminisce about the accomplishments of their younger days. Indeed, this is not a trait peculiar to the old. Who does not enjoy bragging, whether it is about a bargain, a touchdown, a sales contract, or "the big one that got away"? The only difference between reminiscence and ordinary bragging is that for the old the events that are remembered proudly are further removed in time.

Many therapists use reminiscence systematically as a method of promoting self-esteem. They draw on the past to make the present more understandable and encourage clients to describe their lives in detail, from earliest memories to the present, using the happier times as a source of strength. The pleasure in reminiscence can be formalized by using a tape recorder or transcript so that a permanent record of the story is available to the person who lived it. This is a procedure that often appeals to people who are articulate and who feel that they have a lot to tell. The interest of the interviewer, the prospect of hearing the tapes over again once they are recorded, and the possibility of creating a legacy for grandchildren are all potential sources of self-esteem.

"Life review" (Butler, 1963), the therapeutic use of reminiscence, can be a very effective method of helping persons discover and affirm the value of their lives. The process also allows persons who are creating reviews to rework and perhaps resolve old disappointments that may be intensifying the pain of current losses and to gain perspective on their life course. But although it has many potential advantages, life review as a technique must be used selectively. For those who have always functioned marginally, it may intensify their lack of self-esteem and lead to obsessive preoccupation with failure. Others who are not particularly articulate or introspective may feel it burdensome and unproductive to talk about the past. Furthermore, reminiscence per se does not resolve conflict. Rather, it affirms a concept of self-continuity, which is a major task of later life. Although life review is considered a therapeutic technique, it is not the technique but the clients' ways of using the therapist that restores a sense of their past to those who reminisce in the presence of others.

Reminiscences may not be objectively accurate; indeed, they may be highly fictionalized reconstructions in the view of others who had experienced the same events. Cohler (1982) maintains that memories are reviewed and reconstructed throughout the life span, not only in old age. The resulting myth, or personal view of the self, becomes the link between continuity and change. The accuracy of a memory is not the important thing in the story; what is important is its contribution to the sense of self.

RECONSTRUCTION OF REALITY

Some old people react to their lack of actual autonomy by reconstructing not only their own pasts but also social reality. A man with few social skills, for example, may explain the avoidance of others by saying they are afraid of his terrible reputation as a fistfighter; they stay away from him for fear of a beating. Another person may justify her presence in a nursing home by explaining that she very cleverly escaped from a conspiracy of evil scientists who were planning to kidnap her and cut her up for research. Such fantasies do no harm in an institutional setting if the staff accepts them as efforts by the residents to bolster their battered self-esteem. Some therapists encourage grandiosity as an effective antidote to feelings of helplessness and depletion (Goldfarb, 1959). David Gutmann (1964) coined the phrase "magical mastery" to describe feelings of ability to manage a situation that is, in fact, unmanageable.

Magical mastery may work very well in a setting that is, in fact, structured and protected. For people living independently in the community, however, it may provide emotional comfort at the cost of real danger. The man who believes he is "more powerful than a locomotive" will probably not make it across a busy street. A tenant who refuses to pay rent because she believes she owns the building is courting eviction. If she cannot come to terms with reality, she is likely to be removed to an institution, where her fantasy may, perhaps, be better tolerated.

DEALING WITH DANGEROUS FANTASIES

People who exhibit grandiose or paranoid ideas may be persuaded to limit their expression.

Mrs. Betts, who was convinced that a fellow tenant was spreading rumors about her, was persuaded not to denounce the other woman to the Tenants' Council. They wouldn't understand, she was told by her counselor, and might retaliate. Instead, the counselor encouraged Mrs. Betts to confide the nasty stories only to her, and she then praised her client for her fortitude in putting up with such difficult neighbors.

This strategy left Mrs. Betts in possession of her delusion, which she needed in order to justify her social discomfort and lack of friends, as well as her fear of intimacy. It also provided her with a real social support, the praise of her counselor, while protecting her from the antagonism that would have resulted from unrestricted expression of her accusations.

EXPANDING AREAS OF CONTROL

Sometimes older people appear very finicky about details that seem unimportant to others. Whether a housekeeper comes at ten o'clock or eleven o'clock may be the subject of a lengthy discussion. Or a woman may complain that the housekeeper did the bathroom before the kitchen when she wanted the kitchen done first. These may be minor matters to those who exercise freedom of choice in many areas, but to those whose autonomy has been severely curtailed, they loom large. Offering a choice whenever possible is one way of expanding the client's autonomy. "Would you rather go at nine in the morning or at one in the afternoon?" "What are the most important tasks for the housekeeper?" "Shall I see you next week or would you rather wait until the week after?" These are examples of choices that may be used to protect the decision-making capabilities of clients within their current reality. If a client is more interested in having the blinds dusted than in having the rug vacuumed — well, the saying is that "a man's home is his castle." Even in institutional settings, where the loss of autonomy is significantly greater than it is for those still living in their own homes, expansion of available options can be introduced quite easily. For example, in order to lessen the feeling of regimentation, some institutions offer alternatives on a menu or a variety of activities taking place at the same time.

Conflicting Needs of Elders and Families

Argumentativeness, anger, and paranoid accusations are known to have survival value to elders, but these behaviors are very difficult for other family members to tolerate, especially if they are engaged in a caregiving role. Being told that nothing they do is right or that they have designs on the old person's money is very painful for those who may be expending a lot of energy and time without any payoff in appreciation. This has some resemblance to dealing with contentious adolescents; in fact, the rebellious behaviors serve some of the same purposes. The adolescent argues and contradicts in order to establish a separate identity. The old person complains and accuses in order to shore up a sense of identity that is under siege. The difference is that parents can look forward to the time when their impossible teenagers will become adults. On the other hand, old people, whatever their frailties, are coping as well as they can with the erosions of time and circumstance, but they are not likely to outgrow their current behaviors. Caring for them is thus likely to be a more lengthy and less predictable task than parenting children and adolescents.

Adult children, in particular, may have a difficult time with elders who make them feel like naughty children; "six years old, with dirty fingernails," is how one discouraged daughter expressed it.

Sons and daughters may need help in perceiving their parents as *adults* who need care, concern, and dignity but no longer as *parents* who are sources of support and approval or disapproval (Blenker, 1965; Williamson, 1981). Often, such help can best be offered in a group of caregivers who are dealing with the same kinds of behaviors and emotional reactions. The purpose is to assist the caregivers to develop their own coping strategies for dealing with the coping behaviors their impaired elderly are manifesting. Some of the ways the younger adults are helped to react may include detached amusement ("Well, Mama's still up to her old tricks"), distraction rather than argument, and learning to offer help instead of tears or counteraccusations. Because abrasive behaviors are difficult to deal with, caregivers need the support of their peers as well as education and interpretation from professionals.

The Loss of Selfhood

Memory, judgment, and the ability to carry out one's accustomed responsibilities are at the very core of selfhood, and to lose them is to stop being oneself. Popularly known as senility, and more correctly labeled senile dementia, the loss of personality while the body continues to function is dreaded more than death itself; and the fear that this ultimate disaster is an inevitable consequence of long life is a major contributor to the perpetuation of myths about old age.

ALZHEIMER'S DISEASE AND OTHER DEMENTIAS

It is estimated that approximately two million Americans are affected by Alzheimer's disease, the most common form of dementing illness, and this number is expected to triple in the next half century as the elderly population increases (Cohen and Eisdorfer, 1986). Alzheimer's disease is a degenerative brain disorder whose cause is unknown thus far and for which no cure has yet been found. However, not everyone who exhibits memory loss is actually suffering from Alzheimer's. Cohen and Eisdorfer state that in as many as one-third of the patients referred to them because of memory dysfunction, the cause was a reversible treatable condition. Depression, reactions to medication, and many physical illnesses can mimic the signs of dementia. For this reason it is extremely important that anyone exhibiting such symptoms receive a thorough medical workup. Alzheimer's and other progressive dementias cannot be diagnosed in a casual encounter or by telephone. Therefore, if a client or family states that the old person is "senile" (or "has Alzheimer's," "hardening of the arteries," or "chronic organic brain syndrome"), the first step is to find out how the diagnosis was established.

The elements of diagnostic work-up. So that the exact nature of the illness can be determined, a thorough evaluation should be done, including a careful medical history, physical and neurological examinations, a complete accounting of the use of both prescription and nonprescription drugs, and alcohol intake information. Laboratory tests of blood and urine help pinpoint specific diseases that may appear as confusion. A psychiatric examination helps distinguish dementia from depression. CT (computerized tomography) or MRI (magnetic resonance imaging) scans can show areas of damage in the brain that do not show up on X rays. A mental status questionnaire helps determine the extent of memory loss (Mace and Rabins, 1981; Cohen and Eisdorfer, 1986), and psychological tests can differentiate between cognitive deficits and psychological disturbances.

A series of such tests is important for anyone who is exhibiting significant loss of memory, judgment, or ability to reason and meet customary responsibilities. It is particularly crucial if the symptoms are of recent or sudden onset. A comprehensive work-up is time-consuming and can be quite expensive. Medicare covers more of the cost if the patient is hospitalized. However, it is preferable, if at all possible, to have the evaluation done on an outpatient basis. Hospitalization is a stress-producing experience and may cause the patient to appear more confused and dysfunctional than is actually the case.

INVOLVING THE PATIENT IN THE DIAGNOSIS . Long before any doctor is consulted, family members as well as the affected person generally realize that something is wrong. Changes in functioning may be ascribed to normal processes of aging; to stresses such as pressures of work, recent bereavement, or physical illness; or to a variety of other difficulties. The affected person may cover the symptoms very effectively for a time. Usually, routine activities can be managed; it is new learning or unexpected decisions that are difficult for the person experiencing memory loss. Names of people or objects may be forgotten, though the ability to carry on a conversation remains. Because of the dread of progressive deterioration and eventual loss of selfhood, the affected person may vigorously deny that anything is wrong. Therefore, family members are usually the first to consult a physician or other professional on behalf of the impaired person, and they may need to do a great deal of coaxing and confronting before the potential patient agrees to see the doctor. However, the patient can often be involved in arranging for an evaluation once he or she agrees it needs to be done. In any event the patient should be included in discussions of the outcome of the diagnostic work-up and encouraged to ask questions and react to answers. If the outcome and recommendations are available in a written summary, both the patient and other family members can study and react to them.

REACTION TO DIAGNOSIS. If the evaluation reveals a treatable condition, the diagnosis and plan can bring relief and hope. However, if an irreversible dementia is found, the doctor and/or professional team must allow enough time for clarification, questions, and the development of a plan. When cure of the condition is not possible, the focus of planning switches to management, the need for caregiving or other auxiliary services, and the maintenance of physical and mental health. However, patient and family will probably not be able to deal with such concerns immediately. Initial reactions are likely to be shock, denial, fear, and hopelessness. Early questions may focus on how fast the disease will progress and whether institutional care will be needed. Denial may take the form of trying to talk the patient out of the condition. Because the person often looks physically healthy, it can be hard for family members to believe that forgetfulness, repetition, irritability, or unreasonable accusations are not deliberate and spiteful. This is even more likely if the patient, before dementing illness set in, was devious, demanding, manipulative, or otherwise difficult to live with.

It is not unusual for patients and families to shift back and forth between accepting and rejecting the diagnosis. An example of this is found in the situation of Mrs. Sexton and her son.

Catherine Sexton, eighty-three, had always prided herself on managing her own affairs without interference from others. When she began to suffer from memory loss, she covered her lapses by becoming aggressive. If she couldn't find her glasses or forgot to order milk, she accused her maid of stealing the glasses and drinking the milk herself. Or if the maid came on Tuesdays and Mrs. Sexton thought it was Wednesday, she

would send her away, telling her to be more careful about sticking to her schedule. She sometimes refused to pay for household help, saying that she had already paid or that the price was exorbitant. Not surprisingly, Mrs. Sexton experienced a high rate of turnover among her employees.

When Mrs. Sexton's son, John, became aware of her difficulties, he first tried to talk her into being more reasonable. As her poor management became more obvious, he talked to the agency that supplied the maid service and was persuaded to have his mother undergo a thorough medical work-up at a geriatric evaluation center. The result was a diagnosis of early dementia, probably Alzheimer's disease. There were still many things that Mrs. Sexton could do with appropriate help. The evaluation team referred the Sextons to a social service agency that could provide a supportive homemaker service several times a week.

Mrs. Sexton liked the homemaker but refused to pay her. Son John left money in the apartment for this purpose, but Mrs. Sexton mislaid it, forgot it, said she had already paid, or that the homemaker wasn't worth such outrageous wages, depending on her mood. John wanted her to have the greatest possible autonomy, so he responded to her behavior by saying that she must make up her own mind about having the homemaker. It was hard for him to recognize his mother's real limitations because in many ways she was still the same person she had always been—quick-tempered, changeable, and determined to have her own way.

The agency social worker had to spend many hours with Mrs. Sexton and her son, together and separately, before he became convinced that the mother would only get the help she needed if he took over the payments completely. As long as the vexing question of money was not brought to Mrs. Sexton's attention, she had no further trouble accepting the homemaker—at least nothing that couldn't be handled on a day-to-day basis.

The Sextons' story illustrates the difficulties family members often have accepting and dealing with the altered functioning of their impaired elders. At the same time it illustrates the ability of impaired persons to respond to trained and sympathetic assistance. The homemaker who helped Mrs. Sexton did not argue with her when she made accusations of theft or complained it was the wrong day. Instead, she offered assistance ("I'll help you look for it"), distraction ("Let's sit down and have a cup of tea together"), or reassurance ("John sent me to help you this morning").

MEMORY LOSS AND THE ABILITY TO PROCESS INFORMATION. People suffering from severe memory loss have great difficulty dealing with any unfamiliar demand. This is because the specific damage caused by a dementing illness affects the brain's ability to process new information. For instance, an affected person may manage comfortably in his or her own apartment or neighborhood but become disoriented when away from a familiar setting.

Mrs. Shaughnessy knew every house on the street where she lived but became bewildered on a trip downtown. She asked her daughter over and over where they were going. Was it the dentist or the doctor? What was the exact address? What time was their appointment? The daughter became impatient after she had provided this information several times. Mrs. Shaughnessy began to cry and became so agitated that they had to abandon the trip and go back home. The daughter thought Mrs. Shaughnessy was just being difficult because she didn't want to see the doctor. After all, she remembered her own address perfectly well. Why couldn't she pay attention to what she was told?

Forgetfulness and the resulting constant repetition are often very irritating to family members. Perhaps it evokes the three-year-old's everlasting "Why?" However, the child and the impaired elder are in totally different situations. The child is learning to process information and also to carry on a conversation. In the impaired adult the processing machinery has broken down. This results in a world almost devoid of landmarks. How can you know where you are if you can't remember where you've been? Mrs. Shaughnessy would probably have been satisfied if her daughter had been able to say, calmly, "Don't worry; I know where it is," or "I'll see that you get there safely." It was the scolding impatience that upset Mrs. Shaughnessy. She couldn't understand why the daughter was angry, and that made the unfamiliar situation even more threatening.

Helping an impaired person cope with daily routines. The key to helping a cognitively impaired person cope with daily tasks is to keep them as simple as possible. Mace and Rabins (1981) give many suggestions for simplification, most of which are derived from the experience of family caregivers. Some examples are laying clothes out in the order that they will be put on, guiding by touch instead of calling out instructions, using pictures when the ability to comprehend the written word has been lost, and, above all, maintaining an atmosphere of calmness. People who have lost much of their ability to process information are easily panicked by shouting, tugging, or sudden movements. The result is likely to be a vehement emotional response, perhaps involving screams, trying to run away, or hitting out at the person who is perceived as threatening. Such "catastrophic reactions," as Mace and Rabins refer to them, are much easier to prevent than to deal with after they have developed.

WANDERING. A person who is disoriented to time and place may leave home and be unable to find the way back or go out at night and risk being mugged or robbed. Disorientation creates uncertainty and unpredictability of behavior and thus is frightening to families and others involved with the wanderer. It is also frightening to the afflicted person, who may respond to the fear of getting lost by refusing to leave home or by denying that any problem exists.

Sometimes, families also resort to denial as an alternative to recognizing a distressing condition.

Mrs. Garcia, seventy-eight, had been socially active and independent throughout her life. At seventy-six her memory and other abilities began to deteriorate. Her family moved her into a senior citizens' building that included a social center with a receptionist on duty during daytime office hours. They also enrolled her in a day-care program that provided supervised activities, lunch, and transportation to and from her home. This package of services worked well for several months, but then Mrs. Garcia began to leave the apartment building early in the morning and often missed the day-care bus. The receptionist in the social center spent a great deal of time talking with Mrs. Garcia so that she would stay there until the bus came. This usually worked but was not part of the receptionist's regular duties. When distracted by other responsibilities, Mrs. Garcia continued to wander away.

Her children were notified of the problem, but they were reluctant to interfere with her independence, they said. The situation worsened. Mrs. Garcia begged money from other tenants, even though her family kept her well supplied; and she constantly mislaid her keys, so the janitor had to be located to let her in to her apartment.

The situation came to a head one day when Mrs. Garcia tried to go downtown, fell, and injured herself. The police picked her up and, because she was wearing an identification bracelet, eventually returned her to the day care site. She was disheveled, bleeding from a cut on her knee, and famished, since she had not eaten all day. Her family was notified and advised that they must remove Mrs. Garcia to a safer environment. They did so but were very angry about the social center and day-care center staff's "pressure" and "interference."

Mrs. Garcia's story illustrates how a support network, in this case the day-care center, can be pushed beyond the limits of its capacity. In this instance the family used the day-care program as a defense against recognizing their mother's deterioration. In another situation, were the family and not an outside organization the support system, the same kind of episode might have precipitated a much earlier decision to resort to institutional care. In either case the event that convinces everyone that something different has to be done is probably not an isolated incident but one in a long series of near misses.

The follow-up to Mrs. Garcia's placement in a nursing home was that she walked out and tried to return to her old apartment, thus illustrating that institutions may also have difficulty controlling wanderers.

The means of dealing with older persons who have the tendency to go off aimlessly and irrationally on their own are similar for both families and institutions. In an institution wanderers may be assigned one or more employees to stay with and observe them. Or they may be housed on higher floors where it is difficult to gain access to the street. The local police may be given descriptions of those likely to wander, and identification bracelets help in their being returned promptly. In a day-care center that was all on one floor, a bell rang if the outside door was opened; the workers were thus warned that someone might be leaving the building.

Aside from these practical precautions, it is always necessary to try to ascertain the reasons for the wandering behavior. In combination with cognitive deficits they can be the result of boredom or overstimulation, a response to a change in environment, or simply the need or desire to exercise. Calm, reassuring responses by others and efforts at distraction are more effective than scolding, cajoling, or attempts to reason. Because the tendency to wander is usually indicative of cognitive impairment, logic will most likely not be understood, and restraints and physical force will only increase the wanderer's agitation.

For a wanderer living at home, protection may be provided by relatives taking turns staying in or by hiring a companion. For small families of limited means this may not be practical. In addition, because wandering often occurs at night, thus disrupting the sleep and well-being of the caregiver, it is advisable to keep the wanderer active and involved during the day. Daytime naps should also be avoided. Constant daytime activity can be very draining for caregivers, however. Day-care programs, if available, may offer them much needed respite and may meet the need for daytime activity for the wanderer. Such programs may also enable those who work during the day to take an elderly relative into their home or maintain one who is already living with them but has begun to deteriorate. Such an arrangement might have worked for Mrs. Garcia. What made her situation unmanageable was that she was living alone, and the question of living together was something her family did not and could not consider. Living together is not for everyone and depends not only on practical circumstances but also on the nature of the relationships that existed among the members of the family in the past.

In recent years more programs of foster care and home sharing have been developed as alternatives to institutionalization. These help to reduce the pressure on families, who are trying to provide care to a deteriorating family member.

BIZARRE SPEECH. As with excessive mobility such as wandering, an equally disturbing behavior is incomprehensible speech. The old persons may respond to questions in words that seem to have no reference to what was asked. They may appear to be living in a private world, preoccupied with concerns that no one else can share; or perhaps as a result of a stroke, speech may be a jumble of words that make no grammatical sense, even though the affected persons are obviously trying to communicate something. Such behaviors are often ascribed to "senility," and the assumption is made that since the listeners cannot understand the meaning of what is said, there is no meaning.

This assumption is incorrect and may be a defense against the anxiety precipitated by incoherent speech in an adult. How else can one explain the patience with which a parent will try to interpret a baby's sounds or first words and the impatience with which the same person may brush aside the mumbling of a stroke victim? It is joyous to identify with the growth symbolized by the baby; it is frightening to identify with deterioration or disability.

Incomprehensible speech may have a variety of causes, and knowing the cause may make the effort at communication easier to understand. The old persons, aware that they have a problem, may try to conceal the deficit by making replies that sound plausible even if they are unresponsive to the questions. Such actions may be a cover for failing memory, hearing loss, or the inability to make cognitive connections. Attempts to respond that misfire are sometimes called "confabulation." Furthermore, trying to answer specific questions may make such persons so anxious that they release a torrent of angry and agitated speech. This phenomenon is known as "flooding" and provides a diagnostic clue to cognitive loss. Whether the information gained is worth the distress it causes the persons is, however, a question that professionals must consider before they risk exposing their clients or patients to it. The tension produced when old persons are being asked everyday questions that they cannot seem to manage easily may result in an impression of greater deficits than actually exist. In that way the old are no different from students who freeze when taking exams, appearing to know less than they actually do.

Unresponsive answers may also be caused by hearing loss. Hard-of-hearing persons, reluctant to reveal their handicap by asking speakers to repeat, may answer to what was misheard rather than what was said. If hearing loss is the problem, the speakers may compensate by repeating the questions in different words or speaking more slowly. As we suggested in Chapter 2, facing the hearing-impaired person and making sure that one's mouth is seen can also be helpful, even if the afflicted person has never formally learned lipreading. Sometimes varying the pitch of one's voice makes a difference, since some people experience hearing loss in the higher registers and others in the lower. Also, although there is a natural tendency to speak more loudly to persons with hearing loss, the primary disabling feature of this loss in the aged population is the distortion of consonants. Gestures and pointing to the objects being discussed are more effective in enhancing understanding than is shouting. Most important, and this bears repeating, such efforts convey that one wants to understand. This in itself is a great facilitator of communication. The impaired person will invest much more in the attempt to hear and be understood if it is clear that someone is really listening. Again, the crucial factor is hope.

In addition to forgetfulness and hearing loss, there may be a neurological basis for bizarre speech. One of the residuals of a stroke may be an expressive aphasia that results in slurred speech or the jumble known as "word salad," in which the individual words are clear but make no sense. This condition is highly embarrassing and frustrating to the affected person as well as confusing to the family and other associates.

In "word salad" there is usually some kind of pattern. The words that come out may be the opposite of those intended or similar in sound but not in meaning. A skilled speech therapist may help discern the pattern and, while engaging the patient in retraining, may help the family understand what the patient is trying to express.

Patients or clients who seem to be living in a world of their own may do so for a variety of reasons: physical illness, mental impairment, or severe psychological stress. Whatever the precipitant, the person has lost, at least temporarily, the ability to distinguish between inner and outer reality. Thought fragments are spoken aloud as one might relate a dream, not realizing that it is a dream. This is similar to what happens to persons under anesthesia. Patients may go further and project their fantasies onto the outer world in the form of hallucinations.

This is distressing to observers for two reasons. One is that if what persons are saying cannot be understood, it is difficult to respond and or predict their subsequent behavior. The other reason is more profound. Incomprehensible speech evokes the fear of "senility," usually equated in the colloquial with total dysfunction of the mind. At bottom this means loss of the observing ego, namely, the self. If it can happen to the older generation, then it can eventually happen to all. For many people fear of such annihilation of the self is greater even than the fear of death.

This is why family members may argue with or scold persons who are exhibiting such symptoms, trying to talk them out of their "craziness." Or they may ignore the behavior as if it did not exist.

Either way, they are likely to start thinking about institutional care, fearing that the symptom is proof of a problem beyond their coping capacity.

The symptoms of bizarre speech may or may not affect the general functioning of the person. Great-aunt Mary may talk to her television set or describe midnight visitors from Mars and still handle her daily affairs quite competently. On the other hand, if the speech disturbance is associated with behaviors such as agitation, abusiveness, or wandering, professional intervention may be needed to assess both the degree of jeopardy to the person and the pressures on the support system. Sometimes, an outsider can discern a pattern in the apparently bizarre communications and relate them to some event in the person's interpersonal context, such as a recent bereavement or an anniversary reaction to an earlier trauma. A professional may relieve everyone's anxiety by offering suggestions for the management of difficult or dangerous behavior—such as not overburdening the patient with instructions, questions, or responsibility—or simply by advising, and practicing, the need to communicate compassion, patience, tolerance, and acceptance. In some instances suggesting to the afflicted person what he or she is thinking, thus carrying on both sides of the conversation, may evoke positive response while again affirming a caring attitude and giving reassurance. Touch and a smile are valuable tools and important aids in the treatment of problems in communication and their effects on behavior.

INABILITY TO RECOGNIZE OTHERS. Nonrecognition of someone who should be familiar is frightening to the observer for much the same reasons as bizarre speech. It indicates significant loss of self and a fundamental change in personality and interpersonal relationships. If such a permanent deficit does occur, it is usually found in persons who are in the later stages of cognitive deterioration owing to a specific disease process. On the other hand, in the earlier stages of cognitive loss even the patients who do not know where they are or what day it is are still able to recognize close associates, though they may sometimes blur the distinction between son and husband, daughter and sister, grandchild and child. What they do know is that they have some relationship and connection to the persons around them.

Failure to recognize persons is usually referred to as disorientation to person, as opposed to disorientation to time and place.

When it occurs suddenly, without previous warning episodes, it is likely to be the result of an acute situation unrelated to other symptoms, and thus almost always temporary and reversible. What is called for when such a deficit develops is an immediate medical work-up. Infection, a tumor, side effects of medication, malnutrition, or overwhelming psychological stress could be responsible. It therefore cannot be repeated too often that dysfunctions in the elderly are not necessarily due to the aging process as such. They may be the result of treatable illnesses, and this possibility should always be checked out.

WHEN FAMILY CAREGIVERS ARE OVERWHELMED

Guiding a memory-impaired person through daily routines requires immense patience, ingenuity, and emotional stability. Many family caregivers have these qualities and have themselves developed much of what is known about the management of progressive dementia. However, not all caregivers are so fortunately endowed. It is those who have serious trouble dealing with their impaired relatives who are most likely to come to the attention of professionals. Their reactions are quite various. They may deny that any dysfunction exists, perhaps even to the extent of ignoring or neglecting gross problems such as incontinence, bedsores, wandering, malnutrition, and housing without heat or basic sanitation. They may be overprotective to the point of allowing the impaired persons to do nothing for themselves, even when capable. Out of shame or fear they may permit no one outside the family to do anything for the impaired person. They may be punitive or even abusive in their efforts to control and manage the behavior of the impaired persons. Most of all, they are simply ambivalent. To some extent, they recognize the existence of an irreversible medical problem but subscribe to simplistic methods of containing it. A new job (when the old job is beyond the patient's capability), a change of scene (when even the familiar has become unrecognizable and unmanageable), setting firm limits to behavior (when instructions cannot be retained for five minutes) are examples of such methods. It is as if they believe that one can "just say no" to dementia.

 Stephen Wysocki requested an evaluation for his seventy-eight-year-old father, Alexander. A comprehensive evaluation indicated that the elder

> *Mr. Wysocki was indeed suffering from a dementing illness. A structured routine was recommended to help him manage more comfortably and safely. Stephen was quite disconcerted by the amount of planning, coordination, personal attention, and expense that leaving his father in his own environment would entail. He seized on the idea of a Sunbelt retirement community as the answer, oblivious to the facts that had been explained to him: his father was not capable of learning to function independently in a new setting and would require regular monitoring of his health and daily activities. The Wysockis had no relatives or other network in Florida, Arizona, or any other Sunbelt area. Nevertheless, the young Wysocki continued to stress the positives of such a move: climate, recreation, the presence of other elders. Despite all evidence to the contrary he clung to the belief that his father would be able to function in a retirement community if he would only dress "properly." He took to lecturing his father about appropriate clothing. "Remember, Dad," he concluded one such lecture, "never wear plaid with plaid."*

In trying to return his father to his predementia functioning, Stephen Wysocki was resorting to the "magical mastery" strategy described earlier. Very old, severely impaired people in institutional settings sometimes resort to magical mastery to make their environment fit their self-image more closely and thus bolster their self-esteem. For those who have few other options, it can be a creative response to a negative situation and an effective survival technique. But for people living in the real world, who are still capable of changing the situations in which they find themselves, it is counterproductive and distracts the magic user from both the real issues and the real possibilities.

Family members like Stephen Wysocki may resort to magical or unrealistic solutions when they feel overwhelmed. They may be able to deal more effectively with the situation if they can be helped to view it in smaller segments—that is, to partialize. Then, they could take corrective action one step at a time.

Variety of options for care. Considering the least intrusive and most acceptable way of shoring up a cognitively impaired person's functioning, several options may be possible. A day-care center might provide structure, interesting activities, and supervision during the day while allowing the client to return home at night. This is a solution often effective for elders who live with relatives who work during the day and even for some who live alone. A part-time companion or housekeeper may be effective if regular meals and household management are the chief areas of difficulty. It is easier for some people to deal with one new person coming into their homes than to shift back and forth from one setting to another. Family members may be able to provide regular monitoring if their presence is augmented by other services, such as Meals on Wheels or chore-housekeeping. These services may be less intrusive than a full-time companion because they involve less time in the impaired person's home. However, any kind of outside service requires supervision by family members or surrogates if it is to be effective.

Caregiving at a distance. When family members live far away, they may employ case or care managers who help locate and coordinate resources where the aged relatives live. Case or care management services typically include evaluation of the older persons' needs, locating and monitoring services, and serving as links between elder clients, family, and service providers. These services may be provided by social service agencies, if available, or by private geriatric case managers. They are usually listed in the yellow pages of local telephone directories under Social Services, Social Workers, Geriatric Services, Aging Services, Home Health Agencies, or Senior Citizens. There are several nationwide case manager referral sources that can link families and elders living in different parts of the country and some national professional associations that publish directories of practitioners by geographic areas and specialization. Information about them can usually be obtained from local or state agencies on aging, which are also listed in telephone directories.

When in-home services are not enough. For a cognitively impaired person even the most extensive array of services may eventually prove insufficient. It may become too difficult for the impaired person to deal with a variety of helpers, times, and/or settings.

Hilda Koophuis, age seventy-two, lived in her own apartment in a busy urban neighborhood. She had recently had to retire from a longtime job as a salesperson because she got lost going to and from work. Losing her job deprived her of the structure and purpose that had shaped her life, and she became uncharacteristically gloomy. Her daughter, Jean Tredwell, also noted that she was often not dressed or groomed appropriately. One day when she met Jean for a trip to the dentist, she was not completely dressed. Her blouse, sweater, shoes, and stockings had been put on in their correct order, but instead of a skirt, she was wearing only her slip.

A comprehensive diagnostic evaluation determined that although Mrs. Koophuis was somewhat depressed, her chief problem was a mid-stage dementia. Since she was a sociable person who had enjoyed her work contacts, the family decided to enroll her in a day-care program. They employed a part-time companion to help her get through her morning routines and be ready to meet the bus. This plan worked well for a time. However, as her illness progressed, she became more confused about when the companion was coming and on which days she was supposed to meet the bus. As her confusion increased, so did her agitation. One day, she fell while trying to board the bus. She was so distressed and shaken that the companion called Jean. Mrs. Koophuis was hospitalized for observation. She had sustained no fractures or other serious injuries but was thoroughly disoriented, incoherent, and tearful.

Reluctantly, her family decided that Mrs. Koophuis could no longer live alone. Since both Jean and Sam Tredwell worked full-time, there would be no advantage in having Mrs. Koophuis move in with them unless they hired a full-time companion, which was financially out of the question. For Jean to quit her job would also mean financial hardship, since the Tredwells had a son and a daughter in college. The only feasible solution appeared to be a nursing home. Ironically, although the nursing home was the most costly form of care, it was also the most affordable. The state provided a subsidy for nursing home placement but not for home care.

Jean and her family wept over the necessity for nursing home care and were sure Mrs. Koophuis would hate it. To their great surprise, she did not. She enjoyed her roommate, charmed the staff, and seemed unaware that she was not in her own home.

Institutional care is not always a disaster. In many situations it may be the best available option, as it was for Mrs. Koophuis and her family. Mrs. Koophuis was relieved of the worry about where she was supposed to be, who was supposed to be with her, and when her daughter was coming. She was no longer able to keep track of any of these things, and the constant shifting of place and persons had made her frantic. The Tredwells were relieved of their anxiety about their mother's safety and comfort and also of a significant financial burden.

The risk of abuse when family members are also impaired. The memory-impaired elder may not be the only member of the family suffering from cognitive or emotional deficits. In fact, the elder may have been caring for a younger disabled person until progressive memory loss made doing so impossible. When this happens, the younger family member may be incapable of assuming the caregiver role and uninformed or fearful of seeking outside help.

Sons, daughters, or other relatives who are retarded, mentally ill, or alcoholic may fit into such a category. Typically, the older persons, although impaired, feel great concern and responsibility as well as attachment to the younger persons for whom they have been caregivers for so long. Despite their deficits the younger people symbolize continuity for the old. The older persons are not likely to seek intervention, and the younger ones may be fearful of doing so. Such families frequently come to the attention of professionals through reports from others in the community who are aware of their situations.

 A caller to an Area Agency on Aging stated, "I'm the butcher on Grand Avenue, and I'm worried about one of my customers." He went on to explain that eighty-year-old Mrs. Magnuson had always come to his store on Fridays, accompanied by her fifty-year-old retarded son, Jack. Lately, Mrs. Magnuson seemed to have trouble remembering what she wanted to buy. Jack would remind his mother of her usual purchases, and she would eventually get her order together. Today, however, she had been unable to figure out the correct amount to pay. Jack, who had never handled money, didn't know either, and both were very upset. The butcher had to go through Mrs. Magnuson's purse and make change for her, which made him uncomfortable. He called the Area Agency on Aging because he had seen a flyer about their services.

Here is another example:

A building manager called a home health agency, concerned because one of her tenants, Miss Ravenna, had not been able to pay her rent that month. She had bruises on her face for which she could not account, and she seemed fearful and upset. The manager called this agency because she knew one of their nurses visited another of her tenants.

As in both of these examples, callers from the community are apt to contact helping organizations on the basis of casual information or previous experience with them. The organizations called may or may not be appropriate for the problems presented, but they can often provide a linkage. In the case of the Magnusons a worker from the Area Agency on Aging was able to make an assessment visit and refer them to a family counseling agency that provided both immediate services and ongoing planning. Mrs. Magnuson and her son were receptive — indeed, reassured — by the interest of the counseling worker and the homemaker she was able to obtain for them. Miss Ravenna's situation was more complicated.

Marian Ravenna's only relative was a niece, a chronic alcoholic who frequently made financial demands on Miss Ravenna and beat her when she did not comply. Miss Ravenna was terrified of her niece but almost equally terrified of offending her and losing that precarious connection.

The home health nurse contacted the Protective Services outreach unit of the state's Mental Health Department. After a number of visits by the social worker, in which the client was offered reassurance, practical help in securing meals, and financial arrangements for dealing with a rent crisis, Miss Ravenna began to gain confidence in her new helpers. She eventually agreed to sign a peace bond, which excluded the abusive niece from her apartment. For this she had the help of the local Police Department. Thereafter, the focus shifted to helping her secure proper medical care, helping her find a more supportive living arrangement, and appointing a permanent guardian to handle her financial affairs.

All these accomplishments required the coordinated efforts of the social worker, the police, visiting nurses, a clinic physician, and the Office of the State Guardian. The chief obstacle to getting Miss Ravenna the help she needed was her reluctance to bring charges against her niece for fear of precipitating further violence and/or alienating her only relative. She consented to do so only after a supportive and reliable network had been built up around her, making her feel safe enough to permit action in her behalf.

Community Efforts in Behalf of the Isolated and Impaired

As the above examples illustrate, dealing with cognitively impaired elderly who lack a natural support network is difficult because they are not easy to locate, will seldom seek formal help themselves, and will often not permit intervention until they begin to trust their helpers. This is true whether the old person is suffering from self-neglect and lack of a caregiver, as in the Magnuson situation, or is a victim of actual abuse, as is Miss Ravenna.

In some communities organized efforts are being made to identify isolated and impaired elders. Postal employees, gas company meter readers, and others who have routine contacts with the elderly may be trained as observers or "gatekeepers." When, in the course of their rounds, they perceive signs of neglect, confusion, or abuse, they report their observations to a designated community agency, which can make an assessment visit and appropriate referrals. This makes the information gained through ordinary community contacts available to professionals who can take action, without placing the burden of decision on laypersons who have not been trained for such responsibilities. It is then up to the professionals to make outreach visits, identify the problem, determine what action might be helpful, engage the potential client, and make a referral, if indicated. In these, as in any other interventions, professionals are obligated to protect the confidentiality and autonomy of those they hope to serve.

Financial Issues in Caregiving

The cost of care for impaired persons, whether at home or in institutions, can be very high. Family caregivers often need help from professionals in assessing these costs and in understanding the options available for meeting them.

Cost of care may include doctor bills, medications, special equipment, services brought into the home, and environmental modifications. Less visible costs may be loss of income, if the caregiver has to give up employment in order to provide care, and the cost of respite for the caregiver (Horne, 1985). Another, often unanticipated financial burden is the impoverishment of the caregiving spouse if the care recipient needs a nursing home (Sommers and Shields, 1987). In the case of the Tredwells and Mrs. Koophuis, nursing home care turned out to be the most affordable option. However, if Mrs. Koophuis' caregiver had been her husband rather than her daughter, the picture might have been very different.

In most states children are not held legally liable for the support of their parents. This means, in practice, that the income of children is not included in the resources of a parent when the parent's eligibility for government-supported programs is being determined. But husbands and wives are legally liable for each other's care, and their joint income and assets are regarded as one entity. If institutional care or extensive home care is needed, a couple with substantial assets can exhaust them in a very short time. Once that happens, nursing home care for the impaired spouse will probably be subsidized through Medicaid, but the less-impaired spouse may be left with such a tiny income that living in the community becomes a severe hardship. Nursing home care may become the only economically viable alternative to substandard housing, inadequate food, and limited medical care.

It therefore behooves the professionals who work with the impaired and their families to be informed about financial hazards aging families may face and understand the resources that may be helpful in dealing with them. For instance, some states permit an arrangement for separation of assets, which allows the caregiving spouse to retain half of the marital property. However, this does not happen automatically. It requires legal advice and knowledge of the particular regulations of the state or locality.

Medicare, the major health coverage for those over sixty-five, partially covers many hospital expenses and may cover some outpatient medical expenses, including a limited amount of home health care. Medicaid, a state-administered welfare program, covers medical expenses, including some medications, once eligibility has been determined and requirements for "spend-down" satisfied. Spend-down refers to the amount of medical expense that an individual is expected to pay out of pocket before Medicaid can be tapped. These requirements vary from state to state. Health Maintenance Organizations (HMOs) cover both inpatient and outpatient expenses, sometimes including medications, on payment of a monthly premium or membership fee. The size of the fee and the extent of the coverage is determined by the particular HMO. Private insurance plans can supplement Medicare, but they rarely cover nursing home care.

Insurance for long-term care (institutional and community-based) has become a major legislative issue as more and more Americans are affected by the need for it. Legislation passed in 1988 includes some provisions against spousal impoverishment. How these will be implemented in practice is yet to be determined. Professionals will need to follow the debates and concerns about these issues and keep abreast of changes in health care legislation in order to be helpful to their clients.

Legal Issues in Care of the Impaired

Most states have laws allowing for guardianship of adults unable to care for themselves or manage their property because of mental or physical impairment. The terms *guardianship* and *conservatorship* are more or less interchangeable. Sometimes, conservatorship refers only to the management of property and financial affairs; guardianship covers the management of the person and such decisions as living arrangements and provision of medical and other care. However, both functions may be subsumed under either term. For purposes of this discussion, the term *guardianship* is used to include both.

Guardianship requires a legal finding of incompetency, followed by court appointment of a legal guardian or conservator. This person is then accountable to the court or its designate for the management of the incompetent person's affairs. Incompetency is not uniformly defined but generally includes inability to comprehend or remember the nature and consequences of one's actions, lack of judgment, and lack of capacity for self-care.

Guardianship is sometimes the only method available to provide proper care to the impaired person and legal safeguards to both the impaired person and the guardian. However, it is cumbersome, is time-consuming to invoke, and involves massive loss of civil rights by the impaired person. In many situations there are less radical and less intrusive methods that may serve the purpose adequately. Legal advice on which is best to use should be obtained by the family. Professionals in other disciplines can help by being informed about the options and suggesting possibilities to be explored by their clients but should not attempt to offer legal advice.

TRUSTS

If a client's estate is substantial, setting up a trust to attend to expenses and investments may be a useful instrument. A bank or other financial institution generally administers trusts. Although banks have no responsibility beyond the management of funds, it is not unusual for bank personnel charged with a particular trust to seek other professional counsel when the situation appears to require more than financial expertise. For instance, a bank trustee for a single woman living in a nursing home called upon a social agency for help in making an assessment when the woman, after an accident, became quite paranoid, insisting that the home had caused the death of her sister and demanding a change of placement herself. The agency was able to help the trustee and the woman's lawyer put the accusations in perspective and avoid a precipitous transfer.

POWER OF ATTORNEY

People who are physically impaired but mentally intact may sign a power of attorney enabling an agent of their choice to pay bills, sign checks, and carry out other business as specified. An ordinary power of attorney can be revoked at any time by the person who signed it. Even if not revoked, it is automatically invalidated if the signer becomes incompetent or is believed to be incompetent. It is therefore of restricted usefulness for someone who is undergoing mental deterioration.

DURABLE POWER OF ATTORNEY

The Durable Power of Attorney does not become invalid if the signer loses competence. For instance, it would enable a wife to sell a house to which both she and her husband hold title, even if he were no longer capable of signing the necessary papers. Without it or a formally established guardianship, it would not be possible to dispose of the property at all.

A Durable Power of Attorney for Health Care, described in Chapter 6, also enables the designated agent to make health care decisions. In most cases both kinds of durable power would be held by the same person, but in some circumstances they might not be. For instance, a son who had been primarily involved in managing his mother's financial affairs might hold Durable Power of Attorney for that purpose but a daughter who was more closely involved in her mother's day-to-day care might be designated as the one to make health care decisions. Clear understanding and agreement between the two about the responsibilities of each would be essential to make such an agreement work.

PROTECTIVE PAYEE

If the impaired person's only source of income is Social Security or Supplementary Security Income (SSI), a protective payee, usually a spouse or other caregiving relative, may be designated to receive checks in behalf of the beneficiary. This is done through the Social Security Administration and needs no court appointment.

JOINT ACCOUNT

Caregivers sometimes manage an impaired person's expenses by having themselves added to the person's checking or savings accounts. This provides a convenient method of handling expenses during periods of temporary incapacity or hospitalization but lacks legal safeguards and may increase the liability of the caregiver.

The above list provides a thumbnail sketch of methods that assist in managing the affairs of impaired persons. It is meant only to suggest possible avenues of approach. Human service professionals should encourage families facing specific situations to seek knowledgeable legal advice. If no family members are available or able to assume the management of the impaired relative's affairs, some agencies will assume some of these responsibilities. Durable Power of Attorney and ordinary power of attorney agents are not restricted to family members; anyone can be chosen by the person signing the documents.

Professional and home care personnel may find themselves being asked to write checks, pay bills, or otherwise handle money for their clients, especially when there are deficits that prevent the clients from handling these matters themselves. Doing so is hazardous for the professionals, especially if their clients are manifesting even minimal mental impairment, because they leave themselves open to accusations of dishonest intentions, mismanagement, exploitation, and theft. Unless their organization can provide legal protection for such activities, professionals should encourage even the most trusted in the clients' network to obtain legal sanctions offered by the instruments described above.

Sources of Support for Caregivers

Caregivers of the cognitively impaired need many sources of support — family, peers, and professionals. Visits from family members have been found to be the greatest source of relief from feelings of burden (Zarit, Reever, and Bach-Peterson, 1980). If there are no contacts, or if the only occasion for contact is criticism, caregivers are reinforced in feeling isolated, inadequate, and discouraged in what is, at best, a strenuous and lonely job.

Caregiver groups can provide a major source of support even when family members are active and encouraging. As we discussed in Chapter 5, peers can validate each other's feelings, exchange resource information and management tips, and help in the process of grieving for the person who had been lost even if the body still functions. This is a unique form of bereavement, which perhaps can be shared only by those who have experienced it.

Caregiver support groups are not utilized by all those who might benefit from them. Lack of information, lack of access, and lack of someone to stay with the impaired person are some of the reasons. Another is that caregivers may not see themselves as entitled to such support. In fact, they may not perceive themselves as caregivers at all but simply as spouses or relatives who are trying to do the best they can for the person who needs and is entitled to their help.

Professionals can help families and the impaired in many ways: through education, access to services, counseling, assistance in mobilizing family and community resources, provision of timely and sensitive treatment according to their particular disciplines, and collaboration with each other. Aging families need help tailored to their specific needs, and no one discipline has a monopoly on providing it.

CHAPTER 9

Bereavement and Grief

Old age is regarded as a time of high vulnerability to loss —
though, of course, loss is not experienced solely in old age. However,
the prospect of death, the ultimate loss, is ever-present for the old,
as they anticipate not only the death of loved ones but also their
own. Grief and mourning are necessary responses to loss at any age,
but cultural factors, as well as individual dynamics, often interfere
with the process and may result in abnormal reactions. Paradoxically, longer life has given people more time than was available for
earlier generations to anticipate and examine issues of death, loss,
and bereavement and to understand better the distinction between
normal and pathological adaptation to loss.

Grief, Mourning, and Bereavement

Examination of bereavement is almost always linked with
grief and mourning, and these terms, at least in the English language, are frequently used interchangeably, despite the subtle differences they address. A study of various dictionary definitions
indicates that bereavement is a status resulting from loss, usually
through death; grief is the emotional distress occasioned by loss;

and mourning is the behavior engaged in by a person who has suffered a loss.

In other words, bereavement might be defined as a state in which persons find themselves; it is a situation brought about by external circumstances that are emotionally depriving in their effect. Persons thus deprived consequently enter the process of mourning; they are then in a condition of stress that fundamentally affects their functioning but may not necessarily impinge on their consciousness. Grief, on the other hand, is the overt, behavioral reaction to being bereaved; and although such manifestation is not always conscious, its expression is nevertheless essential if the mourning is eventually to be resolved. An important distinction is that bereavement is a normal life event; mourning and grief, as necessary responses to loss, are the tasks that make possible the transition from experiencing a loss to learning to live with it constructively.

STAGES OF GRIEF

Grief, like other life tasks, is accomplished in stages. Before describing these, we note that the idea of stages of dealing with loss was first enunciated and made popular by Elisabeth Kuebler-Ross (1970) in her studies of patients anticipating death. An important distinction between preparation for death and the process of mourning is that the dying person must cope with a loss that is final and total (as far as we know), whereas the survivor of a loss can hope for eventual rebuilding of his or her life. But whether the grief is in anticipation of one's own death or following the death of a loved one, it consists of a range of emotional reactions.

The first stage of grief is shock, usually followed by intense feelings of sorrow, anger, relief, regret, or all of these. Sometimes, these feelings are so unacceptable or so overwhelming that they are repressed, and the mourner experiences only numbness.

This initial, acute stage is followed by a long period that could be characterized as "grayness," in which the mourner tries to adjust to the loss while continuing with ordinary life tasks. He or she may not feel particularly sad but finds it hard to get or keep going. By this time social supports that concentrated on the bereaved at the time of death and immediately after have usually dissipated. Although the task of coming to terms with the loss continues on an unconscious or preconscious level, it feels to the mourner as if nothing is happening or ever will happen again; life is going no-where. What is most helpful to the mourner during this stage is acknowledgment by others, family and professionals alike, that this is a normal reaction. Instead, however, this is the stage that observers, as well as the mourner, are most likely to confuse with depression because of the similarity of behavioral symptoms.

In "chosen" losses, such as divorce, abortion, or termination of a job or a friendship, the process of mourning is similar, but the order may be different. Relief and anger may be experienced earlier, the sense of failure lasts longer, and the gratifying parts of the relationship are recognized and mourned much later.

In the third stage a sense of replenishment begins to be felt, along with a new sense of selfhood. The process is completed when the lost person has become an integral, enriching part of the survivor's self and can be remembered without acute pain or longing.

THE PROCESS OF MOURNING

The acknowledgment that there are stages of emotional response does not imply that all people will experience the same feelings in the same order and on the same timetable. Neither grief, preparation for death, nor any other mourning process occurs in an orderly progression of phases that follow each other to expected restitution. To resolve any of these emotional upheavals, all persons have their own unique style and internal schedule. There are no blueprints for how often despair will come and go nor for how long it will linger. It is only certain that the process must run its full course and that the reappearance of symptoms will be less frequent and of shorter duration with time. Also, individuals do not have uniform expressions of grief for all their losses, though grieving patterns do appear to be affected by whether a loss has been expected (and the person thus afforded a period of preparatory grief) or whether the loss is a sudden, unexpected one. Older persons in particular usually have a realistic view of normal circumstances, such as the expectation that parents and male spouses are likely to predecease them, and assume that traumatic events that occur suddenly or seem to be out of step are harder to cope with. This applies to non-death-related losses as well. For instance, retirement occurring at a normal time is anticipated and often planned for. But when retirement is forced by illness, disability, or firing, it is experienced as bereavement. At best, however, the degree of anticipation afforded the bereaved is less important than the quality of the relationship that has been lost. This is not defined in terms of social labels (for example, does one mourn a spouse more than a mother?) but, rather, in terms of the degree of connectedness the bereaved had to the lost object and the extent of emotional energy invested in that relationship. The impact of losing a good relationship is obvious, but a poor relationship also contains a high degree of emotional investment, known as cathexis, and may result in a longer, harder-to-bear bereavement process, since the frustration of not having resolved the conflicts and having forever lost the opportunity can leave the bereaved fixated at that point of development.

Nevertheless, the opportunity to work out the meaning of the conflict is still there. Life is ended by death, but relationships can live on; and people may still mend within themselves the impact of unresolved relationships long after the objects of those relationships are gone.

Impact on relationships. Even the most gratifying relationships have elements of restriction. If the lost person was an invalid requiring constant care, a demanding or domineering parent, or even a child whose needs blocked out all other concerns, the death may be an occasion for relief as well as sorrow. Just as there are women who are so dependent and intertwined with their husbands that they lose their identities when the husbands die, so there are widows who blossom and find new meaning in their lives after the husbands' death. Both gains and losses are legitimate parts of grief, as is the fact that the prospect of new experiences may feel very risky. Therefore, it may seem safer and more suitable, in terms of societal expectations, to continue the appearance of mourning and remain in a prolonged state of bereavement.

It is important to note that there are feeling states more primitive than grief, which may interfere with the normal grief process. An infant who experiences abandonment (physical or psychological) does not experience grief, because grief requires a more sophisticated stage of development such as language, conceptual thought, ego boundaries, and so forth. What the infant experiences is preverbal terror. Losses in later life may revive the terror, and as a defense against such total devastation, grief may be closed off prematurely. If enough development and security can occur, the potential for grieving may be reopened.

Ability to express grief. The degree of difficulty a person encounters in relinquishing a lost relationship is to a large extent also determined by the lack of opportunity to grieve. Neither the loss of relationship nor the loss of any other aspect of one's life can be resolved, let alone transcended, without an active mourning process. When a significant relationship is lost, the object itself must be mourned, but so must the image of oneself as no longer that person's love object, which is a serious threat to one's self-image. The mourning process must include, further, the relinquishment not only of the object but also of the fantasy surrounding it — that is, the inner meaning to the mourner — if healthy restitution is to occur.

Such fantasies include not only what the relationship meant but also what it might have become. Loss of a parent may mean having to give up the possibility of achieving approval or the expectation of always being cared for. Death of a contemporary is a reminder of one's own mortality. Death of a spouse means not only loss of one's most consistent support but also loss of the opportunity for sharing the "golden years" together. Loss of a young child is generally felt as a failure in the parental role. Loss of an adult child may mean a diminution of one's support system as well as relinquishment of all that the child might have achieved or become. Death of a grandchild is an even more serious assault on one's own guarantee of immortality and on the fantasy of perpetuity.

To be sure, such shifts in one's self-image are characteristic not only of bereavement but also of life transitions generally. Indeed, it is in this respect that bereavement may be seen as a microcosm of the developmental process.

When active grief does not run its course; is not allowed; or is bypassed, set aside, or interrupted; healthy restitution cannot take place. Active grief as an intrapsychic activity assumes many faces. Tears and dejection are familiar signs of sorrow, but many other specific behaviors and feelings — such as anger, fatigue, restlessness, becoming accident-prone, or having hallucinations or supernatural ideation — are also observable. The most dramatic but very normal symptom of bereavement is resorting to primitive means of self-solace, often referred to in psychological literature as "regression in the service of the ego." For instance, Lily Pincus (1974) describes a widow who wrapped herself in a hot, wet towel in a symbolic return to the protectiveness of the womb. A similar example is a mother who, upon the death of her child, drank a huge amount of alcohol in one sitting, which allowed her to express her need for dependency, nurture, and the most primitive level of care that her drunken state demanded. Such behaviors, which under ordinary circumstances may be considered pathological, need not be so in the bereavement process. In fact, they are not at all unusual in the bereaved, who are wending their very slow way to accepting the reality of their losses and the rebuilding of their inner worlds. The importance of these alien behaviors, which are often unfamiliar and frightening even to the bereaved persons themselves, is not in how they appear on the surface but in that they are reactions that help feelings to emerge into consciousness.

Patterns of grief. The uniqueness of individual grief patterns applies to the aged as much as it does to younger persons. Indeed, it probably applies even more, since those of advanced years have had longer to develop their individuality, though the cultural climate of hopelessness about being old may affect their coping ability adversely. The only age-related difference is that old people are more likely to be coping with several losses at the same time or in rapid succession and may have diminished physical, social, and economic resources for dealing with them.

Physical expression of grief. It is not unusual for old people to be more vulnerable to physical illness after bereavement than they are at other times. Since they may be suffering from physical deficits prior to bereavement, preoccupation with these may become a means both of expressing and of avoiding grief. Such preoccupation with physical ailments is often culturally validated, since most people in our society are more comfortable with illness than they are with grief or with any kind of emotional distress.

It has been pointed out (Parkes, 1972) that the recently bereaved (of any age) are more vulnerable to physical illness, to accidents, and even to premature death; and the medical profession has begun to take this hazard seriously.

Behavioral manifestations of grief. The verbal expression of grief may be intense and prolonged or so inhibited as to appear nonexistent. There may be increased dependency on family and friends or a withdrawal from social interaction and a loss of interest in life that may be interpreted as depression by one's associates. Such withdrawal may, however, be used by the mourner to work through the inner meaning of the loss. At a time of intense grief, responding to the reactions of others may be seen as too overwhelming a task to deal with or as too unimportant to command one's attention. Another variation on this theme is that old persons may postpone the overt expression of grief in order to protect themselves from the concern and anxiety of others or in order to protect those around them. Thus, lowered physical and psychic energy may inhibit the expression of grief, just as it inhibits other strong emotions.

Cultural variations in expression of grief. In some cultures grief is customarily expressed through wailing, breast-beating, screaming, crying, or tearing one's clothes. In our society such excesses are frowned upon. This cultural inhibition may give support to the common practice of using tranquilizers or alcohol as a method of managing grief. Although this may initially release inhibitions and allow the mourner to be dependent and accept nurturing, continued use is more likely to become a means of avoiding grief altogether. Such avoidance may also be encountered in some old people who seem to view their survival with an element of glee, often presented as the competitive pride of a youth-focused society. Although this makes the bereaved appear tougher and less fragile, they may really only be manifesting a form of denial, and their grieving might be expressed more freely after some replenishment or realistic acceptance of self has taken place. Such replenishment can be either physical, emotional, or social.

An early means of replenishment lies in the communal rituals surrounding death that serve to express and validate grief. Whether wake, funeral, memorial service, visitation, or shiva (a Jewish mourning ritual that takes place in the home of the bereaved for seven days after the funeral), these familiar and customary ceremonies help the people involved provide structure for themselves during a time of transition. If the person who died had a share in planning for the ceremonies, carrying out his or her wishes becomes another way in which a family can maintain its sense of continuity and mutual support and thus begin to regenerate its energies (Bumagin and Hirn, 1979).

One result of this process is to help the family define and consolidate itself. Recollections of other times of bereavement can help the newly bereaved deal with the present loss. It is a time when bits of family history that would otherwise be forgotten may be recollected and preserved, and remaining relationships are reaffirmed and fortified.

Ecology of emotional resources. As in the ecology of nature, so in the ecology of the human psyche resources can only be used to the extent they are available. If depleted by one kind of demand, the person may have to wait to deal with other demands until enough emotional energy has been regenerated to deal with them.

 Mrs. Rosen, eighty, was seriously ill in a hospital when her husband died. She appeared to have little reaction to the news until she had made some recovery and returned home. Then, her tears flowed freely. Her relatives worried that grief would bring on a relapse and urged her to take tranquilizers every time she started to cry. "I'm not sick," she tried to reassure them, "it's just that my heart is broken." In effect, once concern about her health lifted, she was able to address some of her other feelings, predominantly her grief.

Use of transitional objects. On the whole, old people are more vulnerable than younger ones to being damaged by loss, because they have diminished narcissistic supplies and less opportunity for restitution. We could suppose that they suppress painful experiences in order to survive. However, those who do not fully grieve may not be acting from choice but from necessity. This may be less the function of a weakened ego than the fact that too often, when the aged do grieve, there is no one to listen. On the other hand, a good support system allows for regression in the service of the ego, which, as illustrated above, must precede genuine restitution. Just as expectation of premature adult behavior in children and adolescents results in developmental deprivation, so the suppression of normal grief results in a diminution of the person. Adults as well as children need support in order to allow themselves the necessary "falling apart."

In the early stages of grief the presence of family and friends may provide a transitional resource. Sharing facilitates the process. Sometimes, the grieving persons feel guilty or resentful about accepting the ministration of friends or family and may need help in understanding that this does not mean the rejection of the original object of one's love. Those attempting to offer comfort may also need help in accepting the fact that they cannot provide a total substitute for the loss and should not attempt to do so. The bereaved person needs to adjust to a view of the lost person from one who was living to one who is dead to learn to live with his or her new status.

This can be an extraordinarily difficult process. As in earlier stages of development, the mourner typically makes use of some part of his or her environment as a transitional object to ease the path from loss to resolution. Such an object may be provided by family, friends, a therapist, a pet, hospital staff, or a service-providing agency, to name a few. The possible sources of nurture include the vicarious nurture of having something or someone to take care of. Sometimes, the transitional object is so effective a substitute that the importance of the original loss is not revealed until something happens to the substitute.

Mrs. Rizzo was proud of the stoic courage she had displayed when her husband died. However, three years later, when her cat died, she became inconsolable. Her grief was not resolved until the tears she shed for the cat released the tears she had never been able to shed for her husband. Fortunately, she received some help in understanding the link. Without it she might have felt that her behavior was inexplicable and "crazy."

Anniversary reactions. As we noted in the case of Mrs. Rizzo, the overt expression of grief may be precipitated by a secondary, seemingly minor loss. It may also be occasioned by the anniversary or other reminder of the original loss. In either case the behavior of the bereaved may or may not include tears or other easily recognized manifestations of sorrow. As in the original grief, it may be characterized by irritability or illness. For instance, one woman managed to get herself hospitalized every year during October, the anniversary of her sister's suicide. Such behavior may not be readily identified as grief or, if it is, may be considered a setback, an unfortunate regression. Nevertheless, it furthers the mourner's efforts to deal with the loss. If the work of grief was not completed at the time of the initial loss—and it frequently is not—anniversaries provide additional chances to get on with it.

Introjection. It is important to remember that the process of separation from a beloved object includes introjection, or incorporation. This has been noted when a survivor develops the physical symptoms of the deceased, a phenomenon that is most likely to occur when the relationship was a conflictual one, containing much suppressed resentment. But the essential process is not any different when the healthier parts of the relationship are incorporated. Finding a way to continue the work or interests of the lost person or simply recognizing in oneself the persistence of his or her influence are among the ways in which introjection takes place.

The process of introjection after the death of a loved one is not essentially different from that taking place during other phases of separation and individuation. The infant who learns to tolerate the mother's absence for brief periods; the child who marches confidently to school; the adolescent who, however much he or she may rail against it, is protected by the parents' value system; and the patient who terminates a therapeutic relationship all exemplify ways in which the beloved object can be relinquished because it is retained within the self. The difference between the earlier separations and the final one is that in death there is no longer an opportunity for refueling—that is, through periodic returns to the actual presence of the beloved. The bereaved must eventually learn to find their refueling elsewhere.

In this, society must play a role. Unfortunately, many of our mores prohibit or inhibit a free expression of grief: persons who do not show pain are being "brave," and well-wishers often rush in with every kind of substitution or distraction, thus denying the opportunity to experience grief in the loving presence of others. If the bereaved can learn to share with the community that has also been affected by the loss, they arrive at reciprocal permission to give feelings a chance to rise. Supports such as dependable neighbors can be of great comfort but should not be available to such an extent that the bereaved become too dependent and are thus undermined in their own ability to cope. To break through social isolation and alienation from their inner selves, persons must seek to establish an atmosphere that supports the importance of expressing feelings, even those at odds with social expectations of rational behavior. Although shared pain is easier to bear, the pain must also be experienced and borne alone if it is to result in growth and a reaffirmation of one's own potential and self-sufficiency.

Mourning and reactive depression. Mourning is often confused with depression, partly because the outward signs are similar and partly because the cultural tendency, as we previously noted, is to suppress expressions of mourning and to regard them as pathological. Thus, an anxious relative may say, "Mother is so depressed since Father died." It would usually be more accurate to say, "Mother is grieving." To be sure, if Father died twenty years ago and Mother is still reacting exactly as she did immediately thereafter, her condition could be characterized as depression rather than grief. The crucial distinction between mourning and depression is that mourning progresses to resolution, whereas depression remains static.

Clinical depression may have many causes, including chemical imbalances and reactions to medication. It may be a lifelong personality pattern that seems unrelated to any specific loss. Frequently, however, depression is also the result of incomplete mourning. This is particularly likely to be true of elderly persons who have not had depressive episodes in earlier years. Their grief may be unresolved because it had no outlet or because so many losses had occurred in such a short time that the mourners' psychic energy was too depleted to deal with them. The so-called reactive depressions, which end in spontaneous recovery, would be better defined as episodes of mourning. In a true depression the mourning process gets stuck and cannot progress to the point of restitution without professional help.

Therapeutic Intervention in the Mourning Process

Ideally, since mourning is a normal transitional task and not a disease, it should not require any professional intervention. However, as with many other life tasks, its course is not always smooth.

Furthermore, society provides so little validation for mourning that the mourner may not get the supports that are usually available for those engaged in other life tasks. Indeed, the mourner who seeks professional help may not even be aware of the grieving process and may present his problem as something else. It then becomes the task of the professional helper to reactivate and facilitate mourning and thus assist recovery.

HELPING THE FAMILY

Frequently, it is not the most immediately bereaved person who seeks help but someone else in the family. If the bereaved is elderly, the family often sees the normal regression of mourning as irreversible depression or deterioration. They are likely, therefore, to request an immediate concrete solution, such as help in securing, for the older family member, an activity program, a more protected living arrangement, or nursing home placement. Seldom is the issue defined as needing assistance with grieving. The professional who is aware that there has been a recent or anticipated bereavement can provide education and reassurance to the family, if family members are able to accept it. The issue is complicated by the fact that family members who are not considered the most immediately bereaved (for example, is the loss greater for the widow than for her children?) are nonetheless reacting to the impact of the loss on themselves and may be postponing their own mourning because of their concern for the elder.

Sometimes, the reaction is not even to the same loss as that experienced by the older person.

A middle-aged son became suddenly concerned about his mother's health. Mrs. Wolverton was in her eighties and had been suffering from extreme weakness after a series of illnesses, possibly compounded by the death of her sister a few months earlier. Her son expressed the conviction that if Mother would just go to her doctor regularly and improve her diet, she could "live another twenty years." In the light of the mother's general health, this attitude seemed inexplicable, until the visiting nurse discovered that the son's wife had recently been diagnosed to have cancer of uncertain prognosis and that his teenage daughter was in traction for a spinal problem. Then, the son's determination to make mother healthy

made more sense. He could cope less easily with his other tragedies and focused on mother instead. Mrs. Wolverton's feelings of weakness could now perhaps also be attributed to the loss of her daughter-in-law's availability and her concern about her grandchild.

In this instance the son's displacement resulted in unrealistic expectations of his mother. Often, the reverse is true, and the family feels that the elderly person's abilities have been permanently lost — when, in fact, they have not been — and that moving to a more protected setting is imperative. Making a precipitous move or change in life-style after a major loss, especially for an old person, is likely to compound the problem rather than resolve it, because the bereaved person then has to deal with the loss of familiar environment as well as the loss of a loved one. This is well known to gerontologists but not to the lay public. Professionals can often be of most help by easing family anxiety and slowing down the process of transition, thus giving the bereaved person more time to work toward a resolution of the primary grief.

The family members who are requesting assistance in behalf of the older person may be relying on this activity to avoid dealing with the pain of their own loss. The nature of their relationship with the deceased and the survivors and feelings of resentment, anger, fear of ensuing obligation, concern, and guilt — in short, reactions to the change of equilibrium in the family structure — are targets for therapeutic intervention and help for the family. The professional called into these situations serves as a model for how the process of family mourning can be facilitated by helping all the bereaved talk to each other about their loss and encouraging them to include their elderly members in such sharing. Many families try to shield their older relatives, as they often do their children, from any talk of death. This well-meant effort is actually depriving in its effect. In contrast, having permission to express grief is relieving and necessary for restitution and recovery.

Group counseling with survivors or families of survivors has been done with some success. As with other kinds of bereavement counseling, the nature of intervention depends a good deal on how far in the past the loss took place. Dealing with initial shock reactions is different from examining a long-past trauma that has never been fully resolved. However, in both instances those who share the trauma may be very helpful to each other in a group setting.

HELPING THE ELDERLY MOURNER

Even when grief is identified with a need for counseling, it is likely to come from someone other than the elderly mourner, as in the following situation.

Mrs. Childs, a seventy-eight-year-old recent widow suffering from diabetes and heart trouble, was referred for counseling by her visiting nurse, who noticed Mrs. Childs' lack of interest in caring for herself and thought it might be due to a grief reaction. Indeed it was, though not quite in the way the counselor imagined when she first met Mrs. Childs.

What emerged in counseling sessions was not preoccupation with the loss of her husband but rage—rage at her husband for being an invalid most of his life, thus forcing her to go to work to support the children; rage at her mother for expecting her to assume the maternal role toward her siblings and for thwarting her wish to get an education; rage at her own disabilities. All the disappointments of her life were reviewed.

It might appear that no real restitution would be possible for someone with so much to regret, such limited options, and so little time. However, this was not the case. As the pent-up feelings were vented, Mrs. Childs began to talk more freely to her children, whom she had always tried to protect from awareness of her distress. Concurrently, one of her sons sought therapy for himself, and their ability to talk to each other about family secrets that had never been shared before created a benign spiral that affected the whole family system. Mrs. Childs developed a closer and more gratifying relationship with her children and grandchildren, took pleasure in sharing her artistic skills with them, and developed a wry and humorous philosophy about living with her various diseases.

In the case of Mrs. Childs, though she had not initiated the counseling request herself, the counselor was able to engage her and to help her complete the mourning process for losses that had begun in her youth, so she could achieve restitution. What makes this possible?

First of all, the counselor's role in a therapeutic relationship is to facilitate grief, not avoid it. Counselors or therapists must help clients break the vicious circle of cultural expectation to be brave.

They must also help foster a sense of entitlement to mourn. In order to do this successfully, the counselors must first break the circle for themselves. This means learning to listen, to bear going over the same ground that often accompanies the search for relief, to be receptive to the clients' feelings, to not rationalize or minimize losses, and to resist the temptation to find something about which both workers and clients can be cheerful. Mourners who sense the discomfort of their helpers are forced into the role of comforters, which is nonproductive as well as infuriating and alienating. The counselor's role is similar to that of a midwife—he or she stands by to give help and encouragement, but the client does the work. It is the counselor's business not to interfere with it.

Noninterference does not mean silence, however. Therapists or counselors can use techniques of interpretation or even confrontation; but to be successful with these, they must be unequivocally on the side of their clients. If they are truly their clients' allies—if the ground rules of acceptance have in fact been established—the therapists can say almost anything, because whatever they say will underscore, not undercut, the clients' humanity. Such a stance might be described as "loyal opposition."

It is easy to say one is on the client's side; it is not so easy to be there. Helping professionals, like everyone else, are subject to cultural expectations, as well as to their own conscious and unconscious fears. It has been said that a successful therapist must have experienced therapy personally. Perhaps it is also true that to be an effective counselor with the bereaved, one must be acquainted with grief. Bereavement, to be sure, is something most people have encountered but perhaps not all have experienced. Therefore, counselors must examine their own feelings about grief before they can be helpful to the bereaved. If they are then able to accept the intensity of feelings expressed by the clients and not be devastated by them, the clients will gain hope that they, too, will be able to withstand pain and grow with and beyond it.

It is important for counselors not to underestimate their own feelings, because witnessing bereavement can be very distressing. Even true, healthy grieving may at times appear irrational or present worrisome symptoms of physical illness. Often, there may be loss of appetite, somatic symptoms, and suspension of the will to behave in a routine fashion. When this is not understood as necessary for eventual restitution, the bereaved persons become confused and may believe that their behavior is inappropriate. In all these instances, however, therapeutic intervention can be appropriate and successful, because with consistent help recovery can and does occur. Accepting the expression of grief and offering reassurance about the normality of these feelings and behavior, as well as allowing for an expression of dependency that must run its course, are necessary components of the therapeutic process, which provoke the client's growth from within. Consequently, termination of the therapeutic relationship recapitulates the loss, but at a higher level of growth. Like other losses, the relinquishment of the therapist can be tolerated if something valuable has transpired in the relationship and has been incorporated by the client.

A RANGE OF REACTIONS

Those who would intervene helpfully with the bereaved must remember that there is a wide range of reactions to bereavement and an equally wide range of recoveries. The people who appear to be the least affected by bereavement may, in fact, have been the most damaged by the loss. The loss may be felt as so devastating and dangerous that it cannot be recognized at all. Earlier, we referred to the state of preverbal terror experienced by an infant who is or feels abandoned, a terror that may be reactivated by losses in later life. The apparently stoic reactions of some persons to major loss may thus be the result not of courage or indifference but of repression. When this is the case, there are likely to be other repercussions, such as prolonged depression, vulnerability to illness or accident, or irrational anger.

Repression may not be the only cause of flattened affect. Those who had a period of anticipatory mourning prior to the loss may be better prepared to deal with the actuality. Furthermore, if the quality of the relationship was ungratifying, the bereaved person's chief reaction may be one of relief, though such feelings are difficult to admit since they do not have social sanction.

As we noted earlier, it is easier to recover from a loss if the relationship was either very good or very bad. Conflicted, ambivalent relationships are the most difficult to mourn successfully, and recovery is likely to take a long time to achieve. Survivors of such relationships are also the most likely to need and benefit from therapeutic intervention.

One of the essential but difficult tasks of resolving grief is expressing and relinquishing anger — both anger about the loss itself and anger with the person whose death is felt as abandonment. This is often the part of grief most difficult to deal with because it feels irrational and unacceptable to the person experiencing it.

This is true, to some extent, regardless of the level of development achieved by the mourner prior to the loss. Lael Tucker Wertenbaker (1957), in her memoir of her husband, commented, "How clean is grief without guilt." She and her husband had been able to mourn his approaching death together and were, by that token, at the upper end of the developmental spectrum. At the lower end are those who cannot express their anguish except in inarticulate howls. In either case their pain commands respect.

After dealing with anger comes the task of rebuilding one's view of self without the presence of the other. This means giving up the object of one's love and also the sense of being the object of the love of another. This can be accomplished fully only if the lost love is somehow incorporated in the self. Then, a new role can be developed that reflects the current reality.

There is no "correct" way to experience bereavement. The task of the therapist is to discern the sufferer's need and help him or her express, reflect, and act on it. In so doing, the therapist should not be intrusive and should not push his or her own version of what recovery ought to include. The therapist must be willing to be present, to listen, to accept tears or protests or even anger and rejection without arguing that the bereaved person "should" feel otherwise. It is not advice but acceptance that promotes healing. Therapists must be aware of their own feelings about loss, death, and separation and be careful that reactions such as reluctance or impatience do not interfere with the therapeutic encounter.

Cumulative Losses

To mourn effectively for one significant relationship is a lengthy process requiring much emotional energy. But what of the person who is reacting to several losses or several kinds of loss at the same time? This is often the situation in old age, when loss of spouse, friends, siblings, or children may coincide with loss of role through retirement and decline in health. What of the one who has no energy to invest in a new relationship, therapeutic or otherwise, who rejects counseling as irrelevant or unnecessary or who expresses his or her distress only in somatic complaints?

Among the elderly who are often suffering multiple losses, many do not consider their distress amenable to counseling. Nevertheless, they do reach out for supportive relationships as well as for practical assistance. The housekeeper who cleans the floor, the homemaker who helps with the bath or the shopping trip, and the volunteer who delivers meals may all be used as confidants. The nurse who checks blood pressure is as likely to hear about a daughter's move to Arizona or the illness of a grandchild as is the counselor.

The experience of service providers who deal with younger people as well as with the elderly appears to bear this out. For instance, hospice programs that offer special care to the terminally ill usually include bereavement counseling for survivors. It is noteworthy that these follow-up contacts are not delegated to a social worker or a psychiatrist but are made by members of the health care team — the nurses and physicians who were involved with the family during the illness preceding the death. In consultation with other professionals on the staff, they help the family, during the period of mourning and recovery, work out a plan that will address their social, financial, and emotional needs.

This suggests that cumulative loss may not be characteristic of old age as much as it is a problem of fragmentation among the helping professions. As social change and family mobility increase, there is need for a more holistic approach to therapeutic intervention. If people can be helped to deal with their losses or other traumas in their own context and as they occur, they may be spared the accumulation and its resulting overwhelming psychological burden. It is good to remember that persons who are bereaved are in a period of disequilibrium during which they are more accessible, so they may more readily accept help not only to deal with the current situation but also to mourn earlier losses.

INTRACTABLE GRIEF

Sometimes, no matter how much help, support, or counseling is given, the clients are unable to recover. Whether this is due to cumulative deficits, a particularly devastating loss, basic ego fragility, or some other reason is not as significant as the fact that the persons remain painfully fixated in the bereavement process. They cannot complete their grieving and recover. Their distress affects not only themselves but also their family and associates. Can anything be done? If they cannot be cured, is any intervention worthwhile?

Medical support is developing for the idea that if a patient is terminally ill and suffering from severe and intractable pain, it may be acceptable to use means of pain control that would be avoided in other situations because of risk of addiction. Perhaps this model can be used profitably in considering how to deal with intractable grief. Rather than press for a cure or withdraw from contact, the professional helper may be able to work toward stabilization for the client and relief for the family.

Mr. Sapperstein was a very angry, agitated man. A stroke victim, he was partially paralyzed, and his speech was difficult to understand. Still, his preoccupation was not with his physical deficits but with his survival of the Holocaust, in which his wife, children, and parents all perished. Perhaps because he was an unpleasant and difficult person, there was speculation that he had been a Nazi collaborator. However, aside from the fact of his survival, there was no evidence of this.

Neither Mr. Sapperstein nor his second wife was willing to accept counseling, but they constantly demanded practical services that, when offered, were usually refused. Mr. Sapperstein spent a good deal of time on the telephone, calling various people in a number of service-providing agencies, asking them to intervene and advocate for him.

Eventually, a program of transportation and bathing assistance was provided and seemed acceptable to the couple. In addition, the case manager, who coordinated and monitored these services, called Mr. Sapperstein weekly, at a regular time, and had frequent telephone contact with the wife.

When this system was put into effect, Mr. Sapperstein stopped making his "emergency" calls for help. His preoccupations remained the same, and his defenses were no less rigid, but he and his wife had apparently experienced some relief, support, and respite in their efforts to cope.

The Sapperstein's situation illustrates a fifteenth-century folk saying that is perhaps no less applicable today. In effect, it states that the purpose of intervention is "to cure sometimes; to relieve often; to comfort always." Even when professionals cannot cure those who are grieving, they need not and should not abandon them.

CHAPTER 10

Depression

D*epression is the most prevalent* of the psychiatric disorders. It is actually a cluster of disorders rather than a single entity and may have organic, intrapsychic, or situational causes. These are not mutually exclusive but are likely to exist in combination.

Old people are particularly vulnerable to depression because of the high prevalence of late-life losses, both psychosocial and physical. For this reason depression is likely to be a component of almost any problem brought to the attention of practitioners dealing with an elderly population. As the causes are multiple, so are the means of intervention. Physiochemical, psychotherapeutic, and environmental strategies may be utilized separately or in combination. Reassurance and support to families of depressed persons may be as important as direct treatment of the afflicted. It is important for gerontological and geriatric practitioners to be aware of and to utilize the expertise of other professionals when confronted with depression in the elderly.

It is estimated that 10 percent of all Americans will suffer from depression at some time in their lives (Resnik, 1980; Stenback, 1980). Most of the twenty-five thousand who commit suicide each year are believed to have been experiencing severe depression prior to their deaths (Resnik, 1980). Among those over age sixty-five, many of whom have never encountered psychological problems earlier in their lives, late-onset depressions are not unusual, and suicide rates climb, especially for men. Twenty-three percent of all American suicides are committed by persons over sixty-five (Resnik, 1980), and among those over eighty-five, male suicides outnumber female suicides by a ratio of 12 to 1 (Wekstein, 1979). These figures are particularly striking in view of the fact that in the aged population as a whole women outnumber men.

What is Depression?

In popular parlance, being depressed could mean feeling sad, demoralized, grief-stricken, discouraged, or disenchanted with the world and with oneself. A college student may feel "depressed" at facing a week of final exams; a housewife at the never-ending recurrence of muddy boots and fractious children; a businessman at the loss of an important sales contract. But these moods are temporary and self-correcting. They are part of the vicissitudes of living.

It is when such moods do not evaporate but, rather, seem to get worse that there is need for clinical concern. The afflicted person experiences increasing feelings of sadness, worthlessness, hopelessness, and anxiety, perhaps expressed as a sense that something terrible is about to happen. Energy level and motivation may decrease to the point where all activities become difficult and meaningless. One may be unable to think clearly or make decisions about even the simplest things or experience any pleasure, a condition known as anhedonia. The depressed person is also likely to feel intensely self-critical. This may seem to others to be the function of a negative or hostile personality, or it may appear as rage that simmers just below the apparent immobility.

One source of self-criticism may be the discovery of feelings or wishes that are unacceptable to the self. For instance, a woman whose husband has just died may become depressed out of anger at having been deserted. She is torn because rationally she knows that he did not invite the illness that felled him, and she is ashamed of reacting to her own needs when she should be grieving for him. Or a man may become depressed when an illness forces him to be bedbound and dependent on others. Although most people have negative reactions to loss of autonomy and having to hand over control of their lives to others, the wish to be cared for and cherished is also powerful, especially at times of increased vulnerability. But dependency in adults is frowned upon, except when one is physically ill. Men in particular seem to have difficulty in accepting such needs in themselves, since they have been conditioned to regard themselves as invulnerable and dependable providers at all times. This may explain why widowers are more likely to withdraw after the death of a spouse than are widows; why men may allow themselves to be cared for only after suffering a heart attack or other major illness; and why men have higher suicide rates than women.

SYMPTOMS OF DEPRESSION

The nightmare of depression is painful to experience and painful to watch. It is particularly difficult because, although the afflicted persons are usually aware of great emotional distress, they often do not realize that they are suffering from depression or that it shows. Part of the explanation for this lies in the fact that depression wears many faces. The manifestations may be psychological or biological; they may be the result of a clearly identifiable precipitant or the function of a deeply seated, heretofore unexpressed emotional deficit; they may be easily diagnosed as symptoms of depression or confused with other conditions.

The diagnosis of depression is particularly difficult in the elderly. Given the still-prevalent negative societal attitudes toward getting old, many depressive reactions are regarded as simply characteristic of old age. For instance, in depression, as in old age, many physical and behavioral reactions, including speech, may slow down. The sufferer may be unable to sleep or may sleep almost constantly. Appetite may be affected, resulting in loss of interest in food or overeating. The effect of this may be that the person's mental capabilities are impaired by malnutrition or prolonged sleep deprivation. Such slowing of reactions and the appearance of confused thinking may be misdiagnosed as organic brain syndrome, Alzheimer's disease, atherosclerosis, or some other form of senile dementia, because depression can mimic the symptoms of dementia in a condition called pseudodementia.

Also frequently misidentified with depression is grief, an emotion familiar to the elderly. The mourning period that follows a significant loss may involve many of the characteristics of depression. The difference is that normal grief will eventually run its course, but grief that is not resolved or is not permitted expression may degenerate into depression.

In some persons the periods of gloom and low energy alternate with periods of high energy, hyperactivity, and unrealistic elation. Impaired judgment, overspending, and feelings of grandiosity are frequently associated with this condition. The alternation of unrealistic dejection and unrealistic elation is characteristic of a manic-depressive or bipolar affective disorder. In persons manifesting such symptoms, the mania represents a mirror image of depression. Manic-depressive disease is less common than depression in the elderly, but when it occurs, it is usually of long standing and can be ascertained by gathering earlier psychiatric history. In other words, late-onset manic-depression is rare, but chronic manic-depressives do get old.

Even when the symptoms of depression do not interfere appreciably with the necessary activities of life, depressed persons experience much emotional distress. In extreme cases they may begin to think of suicide as the only possible escape from misery. Convinced of their own worthlessness and unable to share these feelings, they choose suicide as the ultimate expression of hopelessness. Because their turmoil is internalized, their suicides or suicidal gestures take family and friends by surprise, leaving them in a state of shock and self-blame for having been so unsuspecting.

CAUSES OF DEPRESSION

Depression may be attributed to a variety of causes: physiological and biochemical factors; psychosocial reactions; situational or reactive precipitants; cumulative loss responses; and developmental deficits.

Physiological and biochemical factors. There is an ongoing controversy as to whether the causes of depression are physiologically or biochemically induced or whether social and psychological precipitants are more influential. In both instances age-related changes play a significant role.

Neurotransmitter imbalances in the brain (Lipton and Nemeroff, 1978) and other brain impairments found in elderly depressives (Flor-Henry, 1979) suggest that physiological changes may account for some depressions. There are also findings (Goodwin et al., 1982; Gerner and Jarvick, 1984) that indicate that chemical imbalances that are not present in others often exist in depressed persons and that suggest biochemical causes because the symptoms respond to chemical treatment. It is also true that depression and mania can be artificially induced by medications prescribed for other conditions. This is a possibility that should always be taken into account in working with an older population, because old people are likely to be taking more different kinds of medicine than younger people. They are also more sensitive to dosages that would be tolerated by younger people and are therefore more likely to experience side effects. Depressions and manias that are brought on by medication are termed iatrogenic (or medically induced) and, along with other symptoms caused by mismedication, are a frequent reason for hospitalizations of people over sixty-five. Disorders brought on by mismedication or the interaction of many medications may occur at any time these medications are administered and will disappear when they are withdrawn.

Psychosocial precipitants. In addition to the physiological and biochemical precipitants of depression, there may be a range of emotional and social precipitants. In an elderly population the most commonly observed depressions are those in reaction to change and loss. Enforced retirement (in contrast to planned, anticipated retirement), the death of a spouse, or the loss of a physical function—such as vision, hearing, or the ability to walk unaided—are frequently experienced by older people. Depressive symptoms in such cases are really a form of mourning and may dissipate as the sufferers have the opportunity to talk about these losses and work through the accompanying feelings of deprivation. Such depressions may be prolonged if there are few opportunities to express feelings or if the depressed person is inhibited from doing so. In addition, it is usually easier to focus on specific, observable losses, such as death or physical disability, than it is to understand and express the symbolic meaning of a loss reaction. A depression that sets in without an apparent cause or that seems to stem from a minor or unimportant event is harder to discuss with others, because the

person may feel foolish about sharing something that appears unrelated, irrelevant, or as a sign of weakness.

> *Mr. Meyers, a sixty-seven-year-old businessman, wanted to add a line of*
> *hand-held computers to his radio shop. His fifty-year-old partner objected*
> *strongly to such an expansion, insisting that the economy was too*
> *uncertain and that the hobby shop across the street would prove too*
> *much competition. Mr. Meyers yielded unwillingly to these arguments.*
> *But he began to feel worthless, to question his own ability to make*
> *judgments, and to wonder if he should retire.*
>
> *Such a reaction to losing an argument, especially in a vigorous and*
> *capable person, appeared bizarre. A friend of Mr. Meyers, concerned*
> *about his uncharacteristically morose posture, persuaded him to consult*
> *a preretirement counselor.*
>
> *The counselor was, fortunately, perceptive enough to realize that many*
> *other issues were involved. He referred Mr. Meyers to a therapist, who was*
> *able to help Mr. Meyers recall arguments and dashed hopes of several years*
> *ago. At that time, Mr. Meyers's son had refused the offer of a partnership in*
> *his father's business and had chosen to enter another line of work.*
>
> *This was the real loss; its current manifestation was Mr. Meyers's*
> *feeling that he was losing control, that his partner would eventually*
> *replace him, and that the business (the basis for his self-esteem) would go*
> *out of the family altogether. Hence, he questioned the value of his life's*
> *work and of his very existence.*
>
> *In identifying the link between the past and the present, the therapist*
> *was able to help Mr. Meyers make peace with himself.*

As in the case of Mr. Meyers, symbolic loss reactions cannot
be explained away by addressing external precipitants, which are a
cover for the real, underlying issues: rage, guilt, and anger at
unfulfilled dreams and fantasies. These need to be addressed in
treatment, because seeing oneself as a victim of losses is a defense,
one that uses concrete losses rather than one's inner deficits as a
rationale for the depression. Losses occur at every season of the life-
cycle, and old age does not hold a monopoly. Some losses are more
prevalent in youth; for instance, death is no stranger to young people
in wartime, and some diseases, such as leukemia, are more virulent
in the young. Therefore, what must be ascertained in the understanding of depression is its connection to the reality of external
circumstances or its reflection of internal distress.

Situational or reactive depressions. External reality and the practical, visible losses to which old people are prone are less likely to evoke symbolic reactions than to result in what are known as reactive depressions. In reaction to specific events or traumas such depressions will generally run their course and recede without any professional intervention, provided there is a good enough support network. But among old people losses are likely to occur just when the availability of supports is decreasing. Old friends die or move away, and adult children and other relatives may be inaccessible because of distance or complicating factors in their own lives. It is in such circumstances that those who have suffered losses may turn to professional or paraprofessional helpers. The staffs of senior centers are well accustomed to hearing about losses, large and small, as are housekeepers, repairmen, and many others employed by older persons. The visiting nurse or social worker may hear a long story about what appears to be a minor episode, because a seemingly small loss is sometimes easier to talk about. Therefore, one must always be sensitive to the possibility that it may actually be symbolic of a greater loss experienced earlier and perhaps never resolved.

Those who have had the fewest resources for dealing with reactive depressions are persons who are isolated even from casual contacts with others. This may be due to physical immobility or a long-standing tendency to avoid human contact. Such persons may have invested only in their work and, when deprived of this activity, may be unable to utilize any other way of meeting their needs for recognition and a sense of significance. Deterioration in persons who have always been marginal in their coping capacities may be quite precipitous when the one thing they depended on is no longer available. The ability to diversify is not likely to be developed late in life if it was not cultivated earlier.

Symptoms of depression may even occur when the change experienced is not perceived as a loss but rather as an improvement, such as a move to a "better" neighborhood. Loss of a familiar setting is still experienced as loss, and regret may be compounded by feelings of shame over such "foolishness." It is not the sorrowful feelings themselves that create the problem so much as the sense of obligation to feel otherwise and the resulting self-criticism.

Cumulative loss. Another kind of reactive depression may set in when a series of losses occurs with little opportunity for integrating one before another strikes. It is not uncommon for bereavement to be followed, within a few months, by a major illness or injury. But bereavement may not be the first event in the chain.

Mr. Yaseen, who was approaching retirement age, was laid off from his job and despite consistent effort was unable to find another. Two years later, a routine physical examination revealed the presence of lung cancer. Mr. Yaseen gave up cigarettes—a significant loss in itself—and began a course of chemotherapy. After five treatments, he suffered a stroke. Although it did not affect his speech, he stopped talking, slept most of the time, and refused to eat.

In such a situation it may be difficult to distinguish the physical effects of the stroke from the psychological effects of the depression. The person who has been buffeted by a series of traumas may feel so depleted that it seems useless to struggle any longer against fate; or he or she may become so enraged that the only outlet is lashing out at others. If the others withdraw as a result of the behavior, the person sustains still another loss.

Not all cumulative losses are as dramatic or as obvious as the one just mentioned. Perhaps a friend's departure for the Sunbelt is followed by a broken pipe, resulting in water damage to rugs and furniture, and this in turn is followed by the death of a pet canary. None of these events is in itself a major disaster, but in combination or serial succession the events could be devastating to a vulnerable personality.

Another complication of cumulative loss may be that the persons who have suffered one painful experience subconsciously feel that they have "paid their dues" and should be immune from further pain. If more losses occur, they may feel rage at the unfairness of life and become embittered. Turning this rage inward, they become depressed.

The intensity of any reactive depression results from a combination of the real or symbolic losses with the degree of psychic vulnerability of the person who experiences them. For instance, Mr. Meyers might have reacted very differently to the argument with his partner if it had happened ten years earlier. But with retirement approaching, the threat of loss of role and the prospect of eventually being replaced by another created a major crisis. Daniel Levinson et al. (1977) described the mid-life crisis as a state of mind resulting from some event that makes the inevitability of death real rather than abstract. It is a time when one begins to think of the future in terms of time left to live. Although referred to as a mid-life phenomenon, such a realization can happen at any time and probably happens more than once in the lives of most people.

Developmental depressions. The majority of depressions whose onset occurs for the first time in late life are probably reactive in nature. However, there are people who have suffered from some degree of depression throughout their lives or who have had periods of depression from time to time. These chronically or recurrently depressed people also get old. In them depression is more a personality characteristic than it is a reaction to loss, though it may be exacerbated by loss. Chronically depressed people tolerate the changes of aging less well than do those whose affect has been more normal in earlier stages of their lives.

One explanation of chronic depression, as we previously noted, is that it results from a chemical imbalance that has a genetic basis. Another is that it develops as a defense against rage. Melanie Klein (1975) describes a stage of early development in which the infant becomes aware that he or she is separate from the mother and cannot control her actions. When the infant's needs or wishes are not fulfilled, rage and disappointment are turned inward against the self because at that stage of development the infant is totally dependent on the mother and cannot risk alienating her. As more autonomy develops, the young child experiments with saying "no" and opposing the mother's wishes in order to express his or her own. If all goes well, the child eventually masters the ability to be assertive about his or her own needs while understanding and accepting the needs of others. But in some people this socialization process remains uncompleted. The normal response to frustration is anger, but an anger that is self-limiting and appropriate to its cause. Those who have gotten stuck in the process of socialization and have not achieved mastery over their infantile impulses are unable to express normal anger openly because it feels too dangerous — too much like the original infantile rage. Instead, it is turned inward so as not to risk alienating the significant others who might then reject and abandon the offender. Instead, the person appears depressed but also covertly hostile. Such depressed hostility may become a life-style and may not even be felt as depression by the person exhibiting it. Thus, the depressed person may express surprise when confronted with the observation that the depression shows.

In other persons the depression/anger syndrome may appear only at times of special vulnerability, intense disappointment, or the realization that a cherished fantasy is unfulfillable. Anger and disappointment are important, though often unrecognized, components of grief. If these feelings are expressed and accepted at the time of bereavement, they run their course; but if unresolved, they may harden into a chronic life stance.

In this culture most people have some degree of difficulty dealing with anger because it is considered socially unacceptable and is therefore inhibited in childhood. Those who are depressed to a degree that warrants clinical concern are thus exhibiting the intensification of an almost universal reaction. The seriousness of the depression is a matter of degree of its intensity, duration, and the amount of functional disability that results.

IMPACT OF DEPRESSION ON OTHERS

For a full understanding of the complexities of depression, what must be addressed is the effect of the depressed person's condition on family and friends, as well as on those who would intervene professionally.

Depressed persons' feelings of hopelessness often make those around them feel helpless. Trying to break through the shell of withdrawal, families may urge the sufferer to "pull yourself together," "snap out of it," or "take some interest in life—do something!" This is just what the depressed person cannot do, and such advice only increases the already pressing feelings of hopelessness, worthlessness, and discouragement. Professional helpers, too, are likely to be told: "You can't help me"; "You wouldn't understand"; "I'm not worth helping"; "You have more important things to do"; or, "Go away, don't bother me." The professional who feels his or her competence threatened or the helping person whose generous impulses are being rejected may feel all the more obligated to remove the symptom and helpless when not able to do so. The feeling of helplessness produces anger at the unresponsive person and guilt over the anger.

Rather than being withdrawn, the depressed person may beg constantly for companionship and assistance. These demands become wearing, especially if the person seems physically capable of managing on his or her own. Such behavior may be seen as manipulative, which also evokes anger. And the depressed person's own underlying anger, whether openly or subtly expressed, brings on angry responses from others. The feelings of those who are trying to deal with a depressed person are usually a mixture of helplessness and anger, which mirror the depressed person's own feelings.

The first and most difficult step in helping a depressed person may be recognizing and dealing with one's own feelings about the condition. It helps to remember that healing proceeds from within and that the process can be assisted but never imposed. The depressed person will relinquish the depressed behavior when ready — that is, when it is no longer needed in his or her psychic ecology. Realizing that one need not and cannot remove a symptom by force results in a more relaxed and patient attitude, less anger toward the sufferer, and less feeling of discouragement at one's seeming lack of success. The professional helper who can do this also provides an excellent role model for the family and friends of the depressed person and can help them deal better with their feelings of frustration and helplessness.

Diagnosis of Depression

How does the professional practitioner recognize the presence of depression, evaluate its seriousness, determine its cause, and develop a plan of intervention?

SIGNS AND SYMPTOMS

Assessment, as always, is the first step in treatment. Some symptoms of depression are easily identified, such as flatness of affect, expressions of feeling worthless and hopeless, appetite and sleep disturbances, lethargy, and extreme slowness of motor reactions and speech. Less obvious but often telling clues to the presence of depression are self-neglect, inability to manage daily activities, agitation, confusion, and hostility. It is particularly important to look for signs of depression in persons who appear confused, because in older people confusion is often assumed to be the result of senile deterioration alone. Tears and expressions of sorrow over recent loss are part of normal mourning and should not be considered pathological. A man whose wife has recently died and who weeps at every mention of her name is not depressed; he is grieving. On the other hand, a woman whose husband has been dead for a year and who still sits immobilized in her undusted house, wearing the same clothes day after day, indifferent to food and unable to plan for the future, is clearly depressed.

HISTORY

The next step in determining the cause of the depressive symptoms is to look at the person's history. How long have the symptoms been present? Is there a recent loss or a series of losses that may account for them? How did the person cope with stress before the recent trauma? What is the health history? What medication is the person taking? If there are several physicians involved, are they aware of each other's prescriptions? It is particularly important to investigate health history when there is no obvious socioemotional precipitant of the depression, and the possibility of complicating medical factors should always be taken into account.

SYMBOLIC MEANING

One should not assume too quickly that all causes of depression are accounted for. The meaning of an event to an individual is even more important than the event itself. Perhaps a seemingly minor mishap triggers memory of a far more significant trauma in the past. One should also be alert to the possibility of anniversary reactions. The season of the year when a beloved person died may bring on a melancholy that seems unrelated to any current event, and tracing the reaction historically can be very relieving, especially because of the therapeutic value of reminiscence in the reworking of old issues.

DISTINGUISHING CHRONIC FROM SITUATIONAL
DEPRESSION

With or without recent losses the depressed person may have
a history of depressive episodes throughout life, perhaps involving
hospitalization. Even without clearly defined episodes of depression,
the person may always have been somewhat self-focused and dependent, unresponsive to the needs of others. Observations of family
members can provide a picture of what the person was like in earlier
years, and it is important to draw on these, if available and if the
client consents. When family members are the ones asking for help
in dealing with a depressed relative, such information is easy to
obtain; if the elderly person is alienated from family or refuses to
permit contact, it is more difficult to get a sense of the earlier
functioning. Observing the person's interaction with peers and with
service personnel can provide some useful clues. One who is quar-
relsome and suspicious, or passive and withdrawn, critical of all
services, or fearful of displeasing anybody, probably did not become
that way overnight. What may emerge from such a study is a picture
of someone who has always depended on external factors for getting
his or her needs met and who has few inner resources. As such a
person's support network shrinks and physical capabilities wane,
the inner emptiness is revealed. The person exhibits symptoms of
depression, but it is a depression qualitatively different from that of
a formerly well-functioning person who has lost a cherished loved
one, an object, a role, or a physical and/or cognitive capacity. This
type of depression is harder to resolve because there is less to work
with. In the capable person who has suffered a loss, on the other
hand, the mourning process may be intense, but the chances of
resolution are much better. In other words, the prognosis for depressions resulting from reaction to recent loss or to displeasing
changes in self-image is better than for those that are chronic or
characterological. Two case examples may illustrate this difference.

*After her husband died, Mrs. Abrams moved to the Sunbelt and spent
many years in a retirement complex, where she was sustained by
services, activities, and many available friends. But her arthritis became
worse, and her best friend moved to Ohio to be near her children.*

Mrs. Abrams decided to return to the city where her son and his family were living. Her expectation was that they would make her the focus of their lives and meet her needs as fully as the retirement complex had done. This proved to be unrealistic. When it became apparent that her family members were not willing to spend all their free time with her and include her in all their social activities, Mrs. Abrams began to slip. She showed no interest in shopping unless her son took her and would go without food rather than go on her own to the shopping center a block away. She refused to seek out any social opportunities on her own but complained bitterly of being lonely. Some days, she did not even bother to get dressed unless her son came to visit.

Her son was at his wits' end, for his mother's demands, explicit and implicit, were cutting into his social and professional life and putting a strain on his marriage. He consulted an agency serving the elderly.

With professional help, the son and his wife were able to assess Mrs. Abrams's capabilities more realistically, decide what they were willing and able to do, set limits accordingly, and stick to them. The son decreased his daily visits to one weekly shopping trip and one weekly trip to the community center, which Mrs. Abrams enjoyed but would not visit on her own. She had dinner with the family one night a week, and her son checked in with her by telephone every day that he did not see her in person.

To many people, this would seem a very high level of involvement. To Mrs. Abrams, it was skimpy in comparison with her wishes, but as the family remained consistent in the plan and behavior, she gradually resigned herself to the inevitable rather than risk her family's further withdrawal.

A second example illustrates another case of depression.

Mrs. Montero, a capable and active woman, became depressed after her retirement. She began to notice signs of memory loss and feared that she was developing Alzheimer's disease and would become totally incapacitated. She began to make frequent calls to her daughter in another state, expressing her feelings of misery and helplessness and begging for direction.

Her daughter became frantic, since there was not much she could do at such a distance. She made a hasty visit to her mother during which she urged her to "pull yourself together" and reminded her how competent she had always been. This, of course, made Mrs. Montero, who was terrified of losing her competence, feel even worse.

Her daughter then contacted an agency servicing the elderly for help in planning. The worker who met with the two women suggested an evaluation to determine what was really happening to Mrs. Montero. She also related to Mrs. Montero's distress and offered her an opportunity to talk with a professional counselor about her fears and feelings of misery. Mrs. Montero brightened at the prospect, and her daughter expressed relief at the opportunity to share the responsibility for determining and meeting her mother's needs with professionals who would remain available after she returned home.

These two situations appear superficially similar but are actually very different. In both cases concerned family members wanted to do "the right thing" but were not sure what was appropriate. In both cases, assessment of the older person's actual capabilities was essential. However, the emotional resources and reactions of the two women were very different. Mrs. Abrams had no interest in understanding the causes of her distress or how she contributed to the disappointing interactions. She only wanted to be cared for. In contrast, Mrs. Montero was greatly concerned about the perceived changes in herself and wanted someone to help her deal with them. The possibility that she could regain more control of her life was extremely welcome to her. Mrs. Abrams really preferred to have other people structure her life and only did it herself when she had no alternative. The assessment of emotional resources is as important to differential diagnosis as is the assessment of physical and cognitive capacity.

ASSESSING COPING STRATEGIES

How does the depressed person deal with misery?

People have many methods of dealing with or distracting themselves from unpleasant feelings. Some have been described above as symptoms of depression, although they are also adaptive behaviors, whether consciously or unconsciously arrived at. Thus, some persons withdraw into sleep or stare at the TV set; others maintain a frenetic level of activity or indulge in spending binges. In the elderly, the latter two may have become impossible because of physical limitations or lowered income. What then?

Some old people attempt to fill the void by making increased demands on their children, siblings, or friends. This is likely to result in conflict. Or, so as not to risk losing contact with relatives, the old may content themselves with complaining to their peers about the indifference of their families. Such indifference may be real or may represent the gap between felt need and what is available. In the absence of family, or if they fear alienating close relatives, some older people will turn to formal sources of support, seeking personal contacts with agency personnel under the pretext of needing concrete services. In all honesty, they may also believe that services — particularly those that symbolize nurture, such as meals or personal care — will replenish the emotional void and thus provide comfort.

Another means of self-solace may be a preoccupation with physical symptoms and frequent visits to doctors in search of some pill or potion that will dissipate the emotional pain. Even though no such pill is available, the doctor's attention helps. And there is some comfort in the ability to focus on physical pain, because it is more acceptable than psychic pain.

The search for a pain-relieving substance may result in reliance on tranquilizers or alcohol. These may be regarded as self-administered anti-depressants. Although soothing in their immediate effect, such home remedies are actually physiologically depressing and so compound the problem they are meant to solve.

Alcohol may also serve to release aggressive feelings, thus providing a temporary prop to wounded self-esteem and feelings of inadequacy. In the later stages of a drinking binge the drinker may become quite helpless and have to be taken home and put to bed, which allows for the fulfillment of forbidden dependency wishes. Alcohol may thus serve to provide expression to two sets of unacceptable feelings because "it wasn't me, it was the booze." In contrast, tranquilizers serve mainly as sedatives, with no preliminary "high." However, if tranquilizers are used in conjunction with alcohol, the combined depressive effect on the central nervous system can be lethal.

The above-mentioned strategies for coping with depression range from unsatisfactory to self-destructive. It is when unsuccessful coping methods are used that the individual is likely to come to the attention of professionals. Those who are able to devise more successful means of dealing with their feelings usually do not seek out helping organizations. However, underlying depressions may become evident at the point when the older persons begin to need some form of concrete, practical assistance with daily tasks.

ASSESSING THE SUPPORT STRUCTURE

What supports are available to the depressed person may be as important as the etiology of the depression itself. In the two case examples just cited, there were concerned family members — overwhelmed, perhaps, but involved and available. This is not always the case. There may be no relatives; or they may be geographically unavailable, in conflict with the older person or each other, or preoccupied with problems of their own, such as the care of a seriously ill spouse or disabled child. A crisis generally brings family members together but may also reveal long-standing conflicts that make it difficult for them to work together in behalf of the older person.

A daughter complained bitterly about the amount of responsibility she was forced to take in planning for her father but refused to allow anyone to contact her brother, though he lived in the same city as the father and she did not. Further exploration indicated that the daughter, who was the older child, had always been protective of her brother and also envious of his position as the only son. Because of her own need to return to her home in another state, she was eventually persuaded to allow her brother to become involved and to relinquish some of her jealously guarded responsibility.

This does not always prove possible, but it is always worthwhile to make the attempt. The first refusal should not be taken at face value.

Aside from children, it may be possible to involve other relatives, friends, neighbors, and membership organizations such as churches and synagogues. Assessment of the support system includes not only what is already available but also what might be made available. Because dealing with a depressed person can be so draining to the caregivers, the more extensive the support network that can be mobilized, the better for all concerned. Otherwise, caregivers may become so overwhelmed that they withdraw, leaving the old person in greater jeopardy. It is important to assess not only who is providing what but also at what emotional, financial, and physical cost and with what opportunities for respite. The best way to help a person suffering from acute or chronic depression may be to afford the caregivers some relief and help them permit themselves to accept it. The case of Mrs. Abrams's son, cited above, is a prime example. It was not the services he provided but the guilt engendered in him that created havoc in the family. The focus of professional help was to give him permission to relinquish some of the guilt while acknowledging his continuing responsible behavior.

ASSESSING THE DEGREE OF JEOPARDY

Another important factor in evaluating a depressive disorder is the degree to which it may be life-threatening. Whether one is making a formal assessment as a social or health professional or observing changes in behavior as a staff member of a senior center or some other setting, it is important to consider the extent to which the depressed person may be at risk.

Statistics about American suicides, which indicate that 23 percent of these are of persons over sixty-five (Resnick, 1980), reflect only the reported suicides and do not include those who died as a result of prolonged self-neglect. Deaths from malnutrition, dehydration, alcoholism, or failure to take medications would not be reported as suicides, yet they are sometimes the result of indifference brought on by depression. Functionally, these might be considered "passive suicides," but the statistics refer to those who ended their lives by more overt and aggressive means.

It is important to assess the risk to life that may result from self-neglect, but it is equally important to consider the risk of active suicide. Any statement an elderly person (or any person) makes to the effect that he or she wants or intends to die should be taken very seriously and explored further. It is important to determine whether the person has a plan and a means of implementing it. Human service workers are often reluctant to mention the possibility of suicide, fearing to insult the client or, perhaps, to put ideas into his or her head. They need not worry. No one commits suicide at the suggestion of someone else. And the person who has been thinking about suicide but fearing to mention it will be relieved, not insulted, if someone helps speak of the unspeakable. The very act of speaking may serve to lessen the preoccupation and therefore the risk.

*In the course of a routine health evaluation a nurse asked her patient
if she ever thought about dying. The patient's reaction startled the
nurse. "I though you'd never ask," she said. Then, she proceeded to
outline a very specific plan for ending her life. She was diabetic and took
insulin on a daily basis. If "things got too bad," she would just take an
overdose.*

*The nurse was concerned, and rightly so. Returning to her office, she
conferred with her supervisor, who asked the social worker attached to
their home health agency to visit the patient to find out what was
going on. The social worker did so and had a long discussion with the
patient about her fears and frustrations. In the course of their
conversation the patient stated that she did not wish to kill herself. Her
plan was a fantasy escape hatch, "just in case." But she was greatly
relieved to be able to tell someone about it.*

Most people have had passing thoughts of suicide at one
time or another. These usually remain unspoken because of the legal
and social stigmas attached to even the suggestions of suicide. Those
for whom the thought of suicide becomes a real possibility, even an
obsession, may not speak of it unless helped to do so. On the other
hand, they may voice the wish in the desperate hope that someone
will prevent them from carrying it out. Tragically, those to whom
they speak may not take them seriously. There is a folk myth that
those who talk of committing suicide never act it out. This is not
true. The person who speaks of suicide and is not believed may be
confirmed in the conviction that no one cares whether he or she lives
or dies; that the world would be just as well off, if not better, without
him or her; and that life is not worth the pain involved in maintaining it.

Besides the spoken word, there are other clues to the seriousness of a depression that may end in suicide. One is the absence
of any sense of future. A person who makes no provision for next
month's rent or tomorrow's groceries may not expect to be around
much longer. Such a person may respond to questions about plans
for self-care or intentions about tomorrow with "I don't know" or
"It doesn't matter." Such a pervasive sense of hopelessness may
result in an active suicide attempt. Even if it does not, it may make
the person more vulnerable to physical illness, such as a massive
stroke or heart attack. Sometimes, it appears almost as if the illness

provides a physiological solution to the socioemotional impasse in which the sufferer finds himself or herself. Mind and body are not separate entities but impact on each other continuously.

Another and more ominous clue to the potential for active suicide is a sudden appearance of cheerfulness after a prolonged period of depression. This is often misinterpreted by observers as a lifting of the depression and therefore as an improvement. However, real improvement comes about gradually, not suddenly. An apparently instantaneous change in affect is more likely to mean that the depressed person has finally reached a decision not to struggle any longer with the agony but to end it by ending life. After such a suicide friends and relatives may comment that the person "was so cheerful yesterday."

Suicide may occur not only as the result of a decision long wrestled with by the person but also at the genuine beginning of recovery, when the depression has lifted just enough to allow the patient access to sufficient energy to act on the wish to die. The beginning of recovery is probably the greatest danger point in deep depression. Even in hospitals, patients may succeed in killing themselves despite the best efforts of staff to protect them.

Suicide gestures, especially when not completed, are usually regarded as cries for help. While it is true that desperation and depletion may drive one to seek attention in irrational ways, suicidal gestures must be taken very seriously. Even if the action is one of desperation rather than a consciously arrived at plan and is one that the patient is enacting on impulse, it may result not in help and understanding but in death. The response to gestures therefore requires intensive treatment to prevent their recurrence and potential finality. It must also be considered that persons who are suffering from some degree of dementia or psychosis, whether or not they are depressed, may make suicide attempts because of their poor impulse control. The risk of suicide is therefore not limited to the clinically depressed.

The question has been raised of whether it is right to interfere with a person's decision to die. This is a legal and philosophical issue more than a clinical one. The clinical defense of such interference with individual self-determination is that a person in a profound depression is not capable of rational decision making and/or that such a decision, once acted upon, is irrevocable.

Treatment of Depression

Much of the work in dealing with depression, as in dealing with cognitive loss, lies in enabling the families of the afflicted older person to understand the disorder, to cope with their own feelings and reactions, and to obtain appropriate help. This is because the depressed persons, as well as the cognitively impaired, may not be able to respond to interventions. While the demented may lack the comprehension, the depressed may either deny that anything is wrong or feel too hopeless or lacking in energy to seek help in their own behalf. Professionals can play an important role in acknowledging and validating such feelings and, by gaining the depressed persons' trust, encourage them to avail themselves of the treatment modalities that deal directly with their condition.

There are three major approaches to the treatment of depression: physiochemical, psychotherapeutic, and supportive/environmental. They are not mutually exclusive but are frequently used in combination. Ideally, the treatment of choice should be determined by the etiology of the depression. In practice, however, it is more likely to be determined by the skills of the practitioner who has been consulted by or about the depressed person. It is therefore important for any professional helpers, regardless of the discipline to which they belong, to know as much as possible about the various methods in order to make appropriate referrals as needed.

PHYSIOCHEMICAL APPROACHES TO DEPRESSION

Physiochemical treatment presupposes that depression is the result of chemical imbalance that can be corrected by appropriate medication. There are a large number of antidepressant medications on the market, all requiring doctors' prescriptions. Like other drugs, antidepressants have side effects, and a doctor may have to try several before finding one that is both effective and well tolerated by the patient.

In an older population, because of increased sensitivity to medication and the probability that other medications are also being taken, it is very important to monitor the use of such prescriptions closely. If possible, the family or patient should seek out a geriatric physician or psychiatrist who is aware of the effects of and combination of drugs and who is willing to follow the patient after the prescription has been written. In all cases the patient and concerned others should get to know the specifics of each medication and ask how each one works, what side effects may be expected, and what indications there may be for or against their use.

Antidepressants are widely used. Sometimes, they are prescribed in conjunction with sedatives, tranquilizers, or antipsychotic medications. The range and combination of medications are so great that informed consumerism is essential to ensure the most effective and least harmful treatment for the patient.

Another form of organic intervention is electroconvulsive, or shock, therapy, commonly known as ECT. It can sometimes reverse deep depressions that have responded to nothing else. Basically, the method consists of inducing a convulsion in the patient by means of a mild electric current. The technique of administering ECT has become more sophisticated since the early days of its use. Sedation and muscle relaxants make the procedure less terrifying to the patient and reduce the risk of fracture. Sometimes, the improvement is dramatic. But nobody knows exactly why or how the method works. In this case, the state of the art is probably similar to the knowledge of nutrition before the discovery of vitamins. That is, it was known that those who ate citrus fruit did not get scurvy and that those who ate unhusked rather than white grain products did not get beriberi. But nobody knew why. Thus, the use of ECT remains mysterious and controversial. It cannot be used without the consent of the patient and/or the family. When ECT has been recommended to them, they should find out as much as they can about how it will be administered, what results are anticipated, and the risks that may be involved, both in using it and in not using it. In the case of a suicidal patient for whom other treatments have been ineffective, the risk of not trying ECT may be greater than the risk of possible side effects. A good doctor will take the time to explain all this to the patient and family and help them weigh the alternatives.

PSYCHOTHERAPEUTIC TREATMENT OF DEPRESSION

Psychotherapeutic treatment of depression is based on a diagnosis that the depression is the result of reaction to loss or to intrapsychic conflict and that the person will get better when the significance of the loss has been integrated or the conflict resolved. Late-onset depressions, as we noted above, are frequently reactive in nature and respond very well to the opportunity to talk about and work through the loss with a sympathetic listener. To resolve long-standing problems is more difficult; but if the person is sufficiently motivated and the therapist both skilled and hopeful, age is not a barrier to psychotherapeutic treatment.

Effective psychotherapy depends much more on the therapist's attitude than on technique. The most important components of attitude are respect for the client's reality, internal and external; willingness to permit expression of feeling without being overwhelmed by it; hopefulness based on perception of the client's strengths and on a genuine belief in human growth potential; and security in one's ability to be of help so as not to require such assurance or validation from the client.

These attitudes, easier to describe than to implement, are important in any psychotherapy, but they are crucial in treatment of depression. The depressed person has probably been subjected to family demands to "pull yourself together" or to "feel better" so that they can stop worrying. This only reinforces the victim's hopelessness. When the therapist conveys an attitude of interest without intrusiveness and is able to separate external stresses from their inner meanings, he or she can work with depressive reactions in a hopeful fashion and lead the client to new growth and relinquishment of the depressive symptoms.

Facilitating the expression of feeling. If the depression appears to be reactive to one or several losses, the depressed person can be encouraged to describe the sorrow being experienced as well as express anger with the situation. To suppress anger requires a great deal of effort, even though the effort may be unconscious; but anger expressed becomes a source of energy. This is a fact that must be experienced to be believed, for almost everyone thinks the opposite is true. An analogy may be helpful to clarify this.

In the days before anyone actually circumnavigated the globe, most people believed that the earth was flat. After all, it looked flat. Obviously, anyone who got too close to the edge would fall off. In a similar way, people who have been conditioned from early childhood to believe that anger is dangerous will automatically try to avoid the danger. They may be able to experience it only in small doses, about matters that seem relatively unimportant, or in the presence of those who are permissive about its expression. Therapists can be role models for the acceptance of angry feelings but must guard against two dangers.

One such danger is that if clients are pushed to express feelings with which they are not yet comfortable, they may become frightened and withdraw or simply decide that the therapists don't understand. This could be a correct perception, because therapists who are pushing for something of which the clients are not aware are not attuned to or respectful of the clients' reality.

The other and opposite danger is that if the clients become verbally abusive, the therapists may allow themselves to become doormats in the interest of facilitating the expression of anger. This is not helpful to either clients or therapists. It is likely to undermine the clients' confidence or to promote feelings of grandiosity. Therapists provide better role models by defining the limits of acceptable behavior; for instance, what might be more helpful is saying, "I understand that you are angry, but I can't hear you when you scream"; or "Name-calling isn't necessary to get your point across, and I won't allow it."

Protecting themselves from unacceptable behavior not only makes therapists feel less vulnerable but also gives clients the basically reassuring message that their anger will be kept within bounds and not allowed to become destructive. It also helps clients distinguish between *feeling* and *acting* and to begin to understand that all feelings are acceptable but not all behavior is permissible.

Use of life review. As indicated in Chapter 8, the past may be utilized to make the present more understandable and, perhaps, even more tolerable. Questions such as "Have you ever felt like this before?" may elicit memories that throw light on the current loss or trauma. Especially for depressed persons, another use of the past is to draw upon happier times as a source of strength and self-esteem.

However, it must be noted that because severely depressed persons may tend to remember only negative events, use of reminiscence may be counterproductive unless conducted by skilled therapists who can use the material as a basis for interpretation, clarification, and potential confrontation. And those who are most deeply depressed can probably not summon the energy to engage in life review. Even if they could, the present depression would color and distort the past so as to deprive it of any healing power. But for articulate people who are experiencing mild to moderate reactive depressions and who have histories of good coping capacity in earlier years, life review can be a very useful tool.

Dealing therapeutically with depression when it is a defense. Sometimes, depression is not a reaction so much to loss itself as to feelings evoked by loss that the person experiencing them finds unacceptable. For instance, a wife who is caring for a sick husband may feel natural anger at the restrictions his care places on her yet feel so ashamed of being angry at a helpless person that she turns the anger against herself and becomes depressed. The husband, on the other hand, may be depressed not only by the loss of physical function imposed by the illness by also by the loss of his self-image as an invulnerable and competent human being who can manage most situations. Even deeper may be his shame in wanting to be cared for by his wife. The professional who concentrates solely on the reality of the stressful situation and does not take into account its impact on the self-esteem of those who are experiencing it may miss a very significant element in the cause and potential treatment of depression.

In a lecture in 1979 David Gutmann defined a therapist as "one who brings news about the self." News about the underlying anger or dependent wishes may be initially shocking to the client but ultimately relieving. But how is the news to be conveyed if the feelings are so unacceptable to the person experiencing them?

The setting in which help is offered may determine this. In a mental health clinic, for instance, it may be relatively easy to bring such underlying feelings to the attention of clients, because they have come with the mind-set that there is some disorder in their emotional lives that requires treatment. In a service-providing agency, where emphasis is on offering practical help, the suggestion that anger and frustration are present may be viewed as an accusation or as an irrelevant observation.

Some organizations that provide care for frail elderly also offer support groups for those who work with or are caring for older persons. These have proven to be very effective means of conveying the news that anger and frustration are not unique and shameful reactions to chronic illness or personality change, either in the clients or in those who care for them. Rather, they are universal and natural responses to difficult and demanding situations.

SUPPORTIVE AND ENVIRONMENTAL APPROACHES TO DEPRESSION

The supportive and environmental, or external, approach to depression is based on the belief that a person who has experienced a loss can learn to accept substitute gratifications and/or that improving the overall quality of life will help the person deal more effectively with the loss. This is the commonsense approach taken by, for instance, friends of a new widow when they visit and offer practical help, invite her to lunch, or include her in their social activities. These attentions are usually helpful in the mourning process, as long as the friends recognize that nothing they can do is an adequate replacement for the lost spouse and that it is their continued interest and concern, rather than any specific activity, that provides comfort. It is also essential that they respect the widow's own timetable and priorities and do not feel rejected if she turns down invitations or suggestions because she is in a depressed mood.

This model is a useful one for those who would attempt to help a depressed elderly person by modifying the environment or offering concrete services to offset the emotional reaction to loss. Although the lost person cannot be replaced, a combination of human compassion and practical assistance can provide a measure of comfort.

This has been demonstrated by organizations that provide homemaker services. Homemakers are trained not only to provide assistance with household tasks or personal care but also to develop a relationship with their clients. One agency's study of client satisfaction illustrated quite vividly how clients perceive this service. Client satisfaction with homemakers, whom they saw as "friends," was consistently high, in contrast to their low satisfaction with housekeepers who only provided housecleaning or laundry service (Zweibel, 1980). The reason for this is quite clear: A housekeeper's performance is never as satisfactory as was the client's own performance in earlier years, and needing to have someone else do the household tasks only underscores the client's feelings of inadequacy and loss. On the other hand, although homemakers also give services that the clients had once provided for themselves, the fact that they hold conversations during the bath or after the shopping trip, ask about the grandchildren, and sympathize with aches and pains makes their practical assistance not only acceptable but also comforting. This indicates the great contribution that paraprofessionals can make to the emotional as well as the physical well-being of their clients.

There may be a potential danger in this approach if the clients or the service providers imagine that the service can or should provide an adequate substitute for what has been lost. Nothing in the professionals' or other helpers' bag of tricks is going to replace a lost relationship, function, or self-image, and to suppose otherwise will only lead to disappointment and frustration. This probably accounts for many refusals of services that seem suitable to the old persons' situations. Housekeeping, Meals on Wheels, shopping assistance, volunteer visiting—all may be turned down or tried for a brief period and discontinued, because they did not fill the emotional void or ease the underlying ache. On the other hand, the depressed person may request one service after another, finding something wrong with each and complaining constantly about matters that seem trivial. These kinds of clients are similar in dynamic to the hypochondriacs who attempt to meet their emotional needs by seeking treatment for nebulous physical complaints. Both the service refuser and the service abuser are trying to deal with an emptiness that is emotional rather than physical: One rejects services that may be realistically needed because they do not offer emotional support; the other demands services that may not be needed in a vain but persistent effort to find something "out there" that will ease the inner agony.

Changing the environment is another frequently proposed solution to emotional distress. Families and practitioners often hope that a better apartment, a location providing easier access to socialization opportunities, or a more protective setting may ameliorate complaints of loneliness and prevent further withdrawal. And, in fact, such changes may improve the person's quality of life—but only when the old person is willing and able to make use of them. Otherwise, the offer is likely to be rejected or sabotaged; or if agreed to initially, it may fail in its anticipated goal. In fact, the depression may deepen in reaction to the change.

These are the pitfalls of trying to offer a concrete service to meet an emotional rather than a practical need. Yet such offers continue to be made, either because the clients will not accept any other kind of intervention or because the organizations to which they apply do not provide any psychological or counseling treatment.

Practitioner Values versus Client Values

Trying to modify a client's situation according to the professional's perceptions and values usually does not work very well. It is essential that clients participate in the planning in their own behalf. Thus, if clients can be helped to implement plans that originated with them, they may benefit considerably, because this approach restores a measure of control over their lives and thus reduces feelings of helplessness.

To stimulate depressed persons' confidence in regaining control requires skill and patience. Depressed people are likely to feel unable ever to control anything again or to believe that life circumstances can be improved. The first step in helping is to get them to acknowledge the misery and then to ask, in as many ways as possible, how things could be made better. The first answer is likely to be that nothing will help. The dead spouse cannot come back to life, the estranged child will not be reconciled, the failing eyesight or hearing cannot be reversed. Substitutes are not readily accepted; yet the sustained and caring interest of the helping person, the spoken or unspoken confidence that improvement is possible, may be incorporated by the client. In time the seeds of hope may begin to grow.

Mrs. Ramos's husband had suffered a stroke and required not only physical care but also decision making about the course of treatment. He had always been the decision maker, and Mrs. Ramos felt inadequate to assume this task. Their son, who had been very supportive, had moved to another city and so was less available to his parents. His wife was not sympathetic to having him spend time with them and was totally opposed to having them move to their city. Mrs. Ramos felt that without

her son's help she could not function and that permanent separation from him and from the grandchildren made life not worth living. She was seriously depressed.

Several intervention strategies were used with the Ramoses. Mr. Ramos was enrolled in a day-care center where he could get physical therapy as well as social stimulation. Some household assistance was provided for Mrs. Ramos and she also joined a caregiver support group. A social worker from the agency providing these services also saw Mrs. Ramos on a regular basis. However, when it appeared that Mrs. Ramos felt burdened by regular appointments, the worker offered to let her decide when she needed to come in to talk so that she could be in control of at least that little bit of her life. This was an acceptable arrangement.

Gradually, Mrs. Ramos's voice took on a stronger quality, her facial expression became more mobile, and she moved freely. Sometimes, she even laughed spontaneously and joked about her situation. She also dealt more competently with various aspects of her husband's care. These changes were observed by the worker, the group leader, the housekeeper, and Mrs. Ramos's son. To some extent, they were even acknowledged by Mrs. Ramos herself, but she continued to say that the task was too much for her and that she could not continue. Nevertheless, she did continue to do an adequate job by the standards of others, if not her own.

The case of the Ramoses is an example of the multiple approaches that may be used in dealing with depression, especially depression associated with handicaps or losses. It is also an example of the fact that others may see improvement before the depressed person experiences or perceives any changes. Professional helpers must attend to clues given by body language and general functioning and not pay attention only to words.

PART THREE

End Phase of Intervention

CHAPTER 11

Terminating Treatment

Termination is the last phase of intervention. Knowing when to stop requires the same skills in dynamic assessment as knowing where to begin and how to continue. Yet termination as a professional process has received relatively little attention in the literature of intervention.

Perhaps this lack of attention masks discomfort. Termination implies separation, which always involves a degree of loss and sadness. Even triumphant, long-anticipated terminations such as graduation have overtones of regret at parting from friends and classmates, a familiar way of life, and an accustomed status.

Termination of professional intervention implies not only separation but also recognition that nothing further can be or needs to be accomplished. If, from the point of view of the professional, the intervention has been successful, completing it gives rise to feelings of satisfaction and accomplishment. But it is the rare intervention that achieves everything that the professional or the client hoped for. So termination also represents the acknowledgment of finiteness — the gap between hope and actuality.

Specific Issues in Termination with the Old

There are dimensions to termination with the old that are somewhat different from those of termination with other populations. The old are (at least statistically) closer to death; for some older clients the risk of death is imminent. Old age, in and of itself, evokes our society's death phobia, which is shared to some extent even by professionals. Reminders of mortality provoke a variety of reactions, which may include avoidance, denial, or intensified so-called rescue fantasies. The sense of responsibility and accountability felt by professionals may insidiously produce the feeling, not necessarily conscious or articulate, that they can and should prevent death and/or that their continued presence in the lives of older clients will have this result. These rescue fantasies become a source of frustration and disappointment because they cannot be realistically achieved.

For most persons who work with the elderly, frailty alone does not create as much anxiety as frailty combined with isolation. Many old people live alone, and their expressions of loneliness, of pleasure in the attention of professional helpers, and of reluctance to relinquish it add a seductive and thus complicating factor to termination and make the withdrawal of help, if required, very difficult to accomplish. Terminating contact with the elderly may seem like abandoning a vulnerable population to the forces of death.

Some professionals, rather than try at all costs to prevent the inevitable or wrestle with the need for separation, may encase themselves in apathy. Their attitude might be, "They're going to die anyway, so what difference does it make?" This is a rationale that makes withdrawal easier than standing by and observing the last stages of life played out before their eyes.

Of course, all persons, whether lay or professional, intellectually know that death cannot be prevented. Even the most avid devotees of health and fitness regimens succumb in the end. But a serene acceptance of death is easier to describe than to achieve; in their mature wisdom the old themselves may come closest to this goal. Most older people fear death less than pain, disability, and loneliness, and many hold that life is precious though fleeting, that they wish to be nurtured but not smothered, and that separations, even from life, are part of the flow.

Termination with those closest to death is the most difficult and not only is often impossible to achieve but may also be inadvisable. Professionals who have been in ongoing relationships with the old can play a significant role at the end of their clients' lives in the resolution of old conflicts and the completion of unfinished business, both emotional and practical. This is particularly necessary for those who have no family. But even if they have devoted families, their overall social network is likely to be smaller than it was in their earlier years. As the clients become increasingly more frail, in unstable health and prone to sudden crises, they welcome the presence of those in whom they can confide, to whom they can express their fears, and on whom they can count to arrange practical help. Most significantly, they can often speak more freely with outsiders about their impending death and their need to put their lives and, perhaps, their family relationships in order before they die. Since they still exercise the parental prerogative of shielding their children from emotional pain, they often rely on the more objective professional helpers in an effort to protect their family members. The professionals thus become part of the support system.

In addition to planned terminations, there are many that are involuntary. The older clients may die or leave the area where particular helping organizations or professional helpers can serve them. Sometimes, this happens when deterioration forces the old persons to move to institutional settings or to leave one kind of residential setting, such as a retirement home, for another kind that can provide more care, such as a nursing home.

Other involuntary terminations are caused by the departure of professionals from their service organizations. This is particularly true of students in practicum training or fellows in temporary placements, but it is also a frequent feature of professional advancement. Career ladders do not lend themselves to staying in one place.

Another cause of involuntary terminations is the instability of grant money or other funding sources that frequently make possible the provision of practical services and counseling help. Agencies dependent on private or public funds are often in jeopardy of having to eliminate or cut back programs, the jobs that were developed to implement them, and the services on which elderly clients have learned to rely. Although clients and/or families can now purchase more and more services that are being developed by the private sector, their financial situations may not be able to sustain the high costs of such care, forcing involuntary terminations, self-denial of needed help, or settling for less than adequate care.

These factors—voluntary and involuntary, mandated by circumstances, the conditions of the clients, and professional and fiscal considerations—affect terminations with the old. Each of these requires thoughtful response from professional helpers. Basically, the issues of termination are these: have the original goals of intervention been met? What remains to be done? Who should do it?

EVALUATING READINESS FOR TERMINATION

In considering whether a particular client is ready to relinquish the professional helping presence, one may begin by reviewing the initial goals of intervention and their subsequent modifications. Have the goals been achieved? If so, what need is there for continued professional contact, and whose need is it? If the goals have not been met, what has prevented this? Are they still feasible, or would it be more realistic to change or abandon them?

The process of review should be mutual, not unilateral. Goals and achievements should be evaluated as a regular part of contacts between clients and professionals. If this is done consistently, on an ongoing basis, there is less likelihood that the goals of clients and professionals will become divergent or, perhaps, even contrary to each other.

Congruent goals. An example of goal achievement and successful termination is that of Mrs. Walker and her family.

Millie Walker, seventy-two, called a family service agency saying she wanted a better relationship with her grandchildren. She met with a counselor weekly for three months. They discussed each of the grandchildren and how Mrs. Walker might initiate contacts with them. She tried some of the suggestions and was gratified when they worked out.

As the sessions progressed, it became apparent that Mrs. Walker had a somewhat conflicted relationship with the grandchildren's mother, her daughter-in-law. However, she did not want to try to change this. She was satisfied to have achieved more frequent and more gratifying visits with the grandchildren.

The counselor also suggested that Mrs. Walker might wish to join a grandparents' group in which grandparenting issues were discussed. Mrs. Walker was not interested in that either. She said she had plenty of friends of her own, most of whom had grandchildren. She did not wish to invest time and energy in meeting with a group of strangers. Consequently, after three months she terminated her contract with the agency.

Mrs. Walker and her counselor had congruent though not identical goals. They agreed on the objective of a better relationship with the grandchildren, but the counselor would have liked to see Mrs. Walker also work toward a more gratifying relationship with her daughter-in-law, either through continued individual counseling or as a result of group process. Mrs. Walker did not see the need for this and did not wish to pursue it. She had gotten what she came for.

Divergent goals. Developing congruent goals is relatively easy when clients are clear about what they want and direct in expressing their objectives. However, the request and the underlying agenda do not always match. The resulting muddle may lead to the insidious development of divergent goals, as illustrated by the case of Florence Appleton.

Mrs. Appleton, age seventy-five, lived alone in a second-floor apartment. Because of a childhood bout of polio, her right leg was shorter than her left, which caused difficulty in walking. She got around indoors with a cane but used a wheelchair outside her apartment. She had one daughter living nearby, with whom she was in frequent but conflictual contact.

Mrs. Appleton called a social agency serving the elderly and asked for help in dealing with her landlord. She wanted him to replace her carpeting because it was torn. The landlord claimed he was not responsible because she had damaged it herself. The agency social worker met with both and persuaded them to share the cost of replacement.

At this meeting Mrs. Appleton presented herself as very needy because of her physical disability and her estrangement from her daughter. The social worker suggested counseling to her to develop a more satisfactory life-style, and Mrs. Appleton agreed. However, the plan did not work out as the counselor anticipated.

Mrs. Appleton was eager to tell her life story and emphasized the times she had been exploited and misunderstood. When the counselor tried to engage her in considering what she might have herself contributed to these relationships and their ruptures, Mrs. Appleton backed off. She didn't want a psychiatrist, she said, only a friend—someone who would understand her. After any session in which some confrontation had been attempted, she usually canceled the next appointment. Yet she insisted she did not want to terminate her contacts with the counselor. She considered her a "lovely girl" and very kind, even though she didn't always understand Mrs. Appleton's special needs.

Frustrated by this yes-no approach, the counselor kept trying, but nothing happened. When she discussed the case in supervision, the underlying pattern began to emerge.

The counselor had been aware that Mrs. Appleton, with her dramatic self-disclosures and her long practice in making others feel guilty, contributed substantially to the cooling of friendships and to the conflict with her daughter. Because the client was articulate and eager for contact, the counselor was seduced into believing that she could develop insight and, more importantly, that she wanted to change. Mrs. Appleton stated, repeatedly and emphatically, that she wanted no such thing. She saw no reason to try to change her style of relating to people. After all, *they* were wrong, not she. The counselor, being young and unsure of herself, felt that she must be doing something wrong. She kept trying to engage and reassure Mrs. Appleton, but nothing happened. What had begun as a counseling contract had turned into a cat-and-mouse game.

The counselor's supervisor helped her see that Mrs. Appleton's pattern of inviting and then rejecting the counselor duplicated her ways of relating to her friends and daughter. She begged for their help, then reproached them because it did not take the form she wanted. To an observer, this did not make for satisfactory relationships, but it did give Mrs. Appleton a permanent sense of injured superiority to those around her. Perhaps she had developed such a defense in childhood as a means of dealing with her disability; in any case it was firmly entrenched and she had no motivation to change it.

The counselor told Mrs. Appleton that, as a counselor, she couldn't act as a substitute friend. Since Mrs. Appleton had no counseling issues she wished to work on, the visits from the counselor would have to end. If Mrs. Appleton wanted social visits, the agency could arrange for a volunteer.

Mrs. Appleton was outraged. "How could you pull the rug out from under me like that!" she protested. (The counselor thought, wryly, that here they were back to square one. It had all started with a rug.) Mrs. Appleton also dismissed the idea of a volunteer visitor. She wanted a "real" counselor, not some suburban lady who thought she knew everything and wanted to do good.

Mrs. Appleton's rejection of the volunteer reflected her pattern of discounting the capabilities of those around her, thus maintaining her own sense of superiority. She felt that having a professionally trained person visiting enhanced her status. She may also have had some secret recognition that a volunteer might not accept her view of herself, just as, eventually, her friends and daughter did not.

Still the visits were terminated. Mrs. Appleton continued to function much as she had before, seeking, partially utilizing, and ultimately rejecting various resources for meeting her needs. She was a difficult person to deal with but, nonetheless, a survivor.

Counselors are not the only professionals who must deal with double (contradictory) messages from clients. Mrs. White, a visiting nurse, had a similar experience with her client Mrs. Norris.

Mrs. Norris, eighty-four, was hospitalized for a hip fracture. She made a good recovery and was discharged to her home with a plan for receiving services through the Visiting Nurses Association. Until she regained her mobility, she was to receive bathing and walking assistance provided by a nurse's aide, Meals on Wheels, and regular visits from a nurse to monitor the course of her convalescence and need for services.

Mrs. Norris was delighted to see the nurse, related her whole health history, and described as many details of her circumstances as the nurse could stay to hear. As her mobility improved and the nursing services approached their end, Mrs. Norris began to make other requests. She wanted the nurse to continue regular visits to check her blood pressure.

The nurse suggested that she go to the senior center, two blocks away, where blood pressure screenings were available on Tuesdays. The exercise would be good for Mrs. Norris, and the aide who had been assisting her could go with her the first time to make sure she could manage the distance. Mrs. Norris protested that she didn't want her neighbors at the center to see her with a walker or in the company of an aide. She complained that the nurse was unsympathetic. Besides, she argued, if she needed meals brought in, she was surely also entitled to have medical services delivered.

The nurse insisted that Mrs. Norris's condition did not warrant home visits to check her blood pressure. The doctor would not authorize it, and Medicare would not pay for it. Mrs. Norris was disappointed but said she was not surprised. Everyone knew, she said, how inadequate Medicare was.

Like many relatively housebound people, Mrs. Norris had come to rely on her home service workers for social contact as well as assistance. The nurse, perceived as part of the medical establishment, also gave her a sense of security about her health. She was reluctant to give up what had become familiar in order to try something new. Having her neighbors see her as disabled and needing help was another unwelcome idea. All of these reactions were perfectly natural, but they had no bearing on Mrs. Norris's need for the Medicare-reimbursed services of a professional nurse. For Mrs. Norris, making Medicare the scapegoat for termination of service was easier than acknowledging her own dependency.

It may be worth noting that the nurse had an easier time terminating with Mrs. Norris than the counselor had in terminating with Mrs. Appleton. This was primarily because the nurse's mandate was narrower and more specific. Having made her assessment and recommendation and completed the approved number of visits, she had fulfilled her task. Those who engage in ongoing work without a built-in time limit have a more nebulous assignment and must make frequent reassessments to determine whether they are indeed doing what they set out to do.

Noncompliance and risk. Mrs. Appleton's style of relating to people subjected her to frequent disappointments, but she was not at risk as far as her safety and health were concerned. Mrs. Norris felt socially deprived by the departure of the visiting nurse, but her physical recovery was progressing very well. Other clients who must relinquish services or who reject professional recommendations may be in real danger. Mr. Durnwald was one of them.

Henry Durnwald, at age eighty, was a widower and living alone. His son and family lived in the same city. They kept in touch but did not meet frequently. Mr. Durnwald's chief sources of social activity were the senior center, which he visited almost daily, and his friend Fritzi, with whom he regularly had lunch in the restaurant across the street.

When the center staff noticed that Mr. Durnwald was neglecting his appearance and seemed to be losing weight, they became concerned. The center's social worker made several attempts to see him, but he did not keep appointments. It was hard to tell whether he forgot them or was trying to avoid intrusion.

The social worker then attempted to engage him by joining him and Fritzi at the restaurant. They were pleasant but wary. Mr. Durnwald insisted he didn't need to see a doctor because he wasn't sick. Fritzi said she was looking after him and everything would be fine. However, the staff sometimes saw Mr. Durnwald on the street without a coat in cold weather. Neighbors reported that he sometimes went to the center at night when it was closed. When he found it locked, he pounded on the door, shouting angrily. As he became more confused and disoriented, Fritzi backed off and spent less time with him.

The director of the center contacted Mr. Durnwald's son and reported their observations. The son said that the family was also concerned but that Mr. Durnwald had always been a stubborn man and did exactly as he pleased. Efforts by the family to persuade him to accept help were no more effective than the staff's had been.

Eventually, Mr. Durnwald had a heart attack, for which he was hospitalized. From the hospital he was placed in a nursing home. He was indignant but did not have the physical strength to leave.

Mr. Durnwald successfully eluded both professional and family efforts to protect him from his deterioration. Although his behavior placed him at risk, he was not committable, since he was not suicidal and had not injured or threatened to injure anyone else. A court hearing, needed to have anyone declared incompetent, might or might not have found him so, depending on his behavior at the hearing and the attitude of the judge. If the family had attempted to institutionalize him prior to his heart attack, he would probably have walked out. The center staff felt they could not abandon him because of his vulnerability, but there was nothing they could do to protect him effectively. Eventually he succumbed, not to persuasion but to physical disability.

Mr. Durnwald's termination with the center came about involuntarily. In one sense it was not a termination at all, because in Mr. Durnwald's view there had never been a beginning. To him, the center was a place where he dropped in to read the paper or have a cup of coffee with his cronies. He had never asked it for help. His goals and those of the center staff were totally at odds. He saw professional intervention as an attempt to interfere with his own management of his life. The possibility of greater security and comfort, if he could have grasped and retained the concept, did not appeal to him enough to provide any redeeming features.

In a situation such as Mr. Durnwald's, professionals may be unable to do anything until a crisis occurs. Rather than terminate with the client or family, they may maintain an interested but nonintrusive stance. For someone like Mr. Durnwald, this might mean brief conversations in the senior center or during chance encounters in the neighborhood. Thus, staff might be familiar and unthreatening enough to be in a position to intervene if the occasion arose. They may also act as consultants to family and associates who are frustrated by an elder's risky behavior and unwillingness to accept help. Often, these people put pressure on the professionals to "do something," in desperation endowing them with a magical competence to accomplish the impossible. Assurance of willingness to act as soon as circumstances permit may help them contain their anxiety and avoid discouragement and withdrawal from involvement with the impaired person. In this way there is a plan for potential or eventual intervention and a process that might lead, in time, to a more satisfactory termination for all concerned.

Risky situations that do not permit intervention often create anxiety in observers and conflict among professionals. The feeling that "somebody should be able to do something" may lead to mutual criticism and blame for not having done it. Such finger pointing creates the hazard of making cooperative intervention difficult when the opportunity to become actively involved does arise.

The hazards of attachment. Without a therapeutic alliance between professional and client, little can be accomplished in treatment. This is a truism of the psychosocial therapies, but it also applies to the more technical forms of treatment such as medicine, nursing, and physical and occupational therapies. The patient's or client's confidence in the physician or other therapist is often a critical factor in the success of the treatment. But confidence creates attachment. Conversely, the investment of the therapist in the client's or patient's progress also creates attachment. When treatment is completed, the attachment may remain and may complicate the process of termination. The paradox of the therapeutic relationship is that it is essential to treatment, but it makes termination difficult.

The hazards for client and professional in a service-providing or practical help-providing situation are somewhat different. If successful, the professional may be tempted to continue the relationship in the hope of accomplishing more, even when the established goals have been achieved and the client is capable of continuing without further help. If unsuccessful, the temptation is to keep trying in the hope of finding something that works.

For the client, on the other hand, the attention and interest of the professional helper are experienced not only as helpful but also as socially gratifying. Terminating the relationship may feel like losing a friend. This may be a significant bereavement, especially for someone whose social network has been depleted by earlier losses. Clients who have come to depend on professionals for help in the management of day-to-day living may be less capable of dealing with problems on their own once the relationship terminates.

A more subtle hazard is suggested by the research on learned helplessness. In one study nursing home residents who had visits from students during the study returned to their depressed condition after the students stopped visiting (Schultz and Hanusa, 1978). In another study residents in a nursing home were each given a plant to care for. For them, the sense of control persisted after the study ended (Langer and Rodin, 1976). Although these studies were not measuring the effects of terminating a professional relationship, the findings are suggestive. The implication seems to be that prolonged dependency, without reciprocity or responsibility, reinforces feelings of helplessness and depression.

Preparing for separation. The social side effects of therapeutic alliance can be minimized if both parties are aware that their relationship is temporary and instrumental. Such awareness can be built into the relationship from the beginning. A definite time frame for completing an assessment or working on a specific problem helps reinforce the message that the helping relationship is time-limited. Sometimes, there is an arbitrary time frame imposed by agency policy or funding sources. If so, it can be used as a reminder that whatever the client and helper accomplish together must be completed by a certain time. This approach can be used whether the client is an older individual, a caregiver, or several family members trying to work out a plan. As we noted in Chapter 5, it can also be used with groups.

Expanding the network. A frequent obstacle to termination is the clients' unwillingness to give up the persons who have brought new social dimensions into their lives, as in the case of Mrs. Norris described above. The professional helpers may also feel guilty about withdrawing from those whose social networks are extremely limited. One way of dealing with this is to make expansion of the network a part of the tasks to be worked on during the intervention.

There are many ways in which a shrunken social network can be enhanced. One obvious but frequently overlooked possibility is mobilizing family members to visit. Adult children are usually the most regular visitors, but grandchildren, siblings, and other relatives are often available, if they know that their presence is desired. A relative or neighbor with a car may be able to facilitate visits to friends who live at a distance. The sibling relationship has been shown to be of particular importance in old age (Gold, 1987), but face-to-face contact may be restricted because of physical immobility.

Often, the old person does not ask for such excursions, not wishing to "be a burden" or assuming that family members know what is needed without being asked. Discussion, encouragement, and perhaps rehearsal may be needed to enable clients to make their wishes known. If an old person is too impaired to initiate such a request, the professional may take it up with family members directly. While one must be cautious about contacting others without the client's knowledge, it is probable that if the older person is significantly impaired, the family will have initiated contact with the professional and therefore already be involved. Discussion of visiting can easily be incorporated into the agenda of other concerns to be addressed. It is important to assure family members that they are not being criticized but that the professional may be able to help them think of ways to increase socialization without unduly burdening any one individual. Such discussions may also provide a means to address division of labor and limit-setting, which are often difficult issues for families of impaired persons.

Another avenue of socialization, in addition to or instead of increasing family contact, is through visits by volunteers. Many agencies recruit, train, and place volunteers either as their principal activity or as an adjunct to other services. Elders who are basically sociable may welcome the possibility of thus making new friends. Visits from members of a client's church or synagogue may be more welcome than visits by total strangers. It is worthwhile to explore whether the client has a religious connection that is a potential source of visits or other social activities. Some congregations provide other volunteer services besides visiting their elderly members as well as others in the community, but often need to be informed when and by whom such help is needed.

Not everyone welcomes the prospect of visitors. Some find the idea intrusive or burdensome. Those who appear most isolated do not necessarily object to being alone. If they have been loners during their whole lives, they are not likely to welcome the presence of strangers in their old age. Socialization may be seen as desirable by the professional or the family, but that value is not necessarily shared by the client. Family members, in particular, often press for social activity as a solution to whatever relationship problems their older relative presents, and they must be helped to reflect on the person's earlier patterns to ensure that their solution is consistent with the individual's personality.

For those interested in social contact who are somewhat mobile or for whom transportation can be arranged, a group setting may be most congenial. Senior centers, nutrition sites, Golden Age clubs, and religious institutions and organizations provide a locus of activity and opportunity to broaden social horizons.

Those who are reluctant to engage in social or recreational visits may welcome more instrumental contacts. Housebound elders who receive in-home services often become attached to their household helpers. Regular but brief contacts from Meals on Wheels volunteers may be seen as an important part of the service—perhaps as important as the food itself. The hazard of relying on service personnel for social contacts, however, is that if and when the service is no longer needed, the client may be reluctant to give up the social connection, as we noted above.

In rural areas postal carriers and other service personnel may provide a welcome diversion for elders living alone and also a means of observation and message relay if someone is in difficulty (Buckwalter, 1988). As we noted in Chapter 8, some communities, both rural and urban, have organized utility meter readers, mail carriers, and others into an observation network for the elderly. This is a potentially valuable resource for isolated or lonely persons.

In the absence of such community networks creative professionals may be able to organize mini-networks for isolated individuals. In addition to the interests and involvement of neighbors, landlords, local shopkeepers, or others may be mobilized to check in on housebound persons and report concerns to family or appropriate service organizations. Such networks may provide more frequent and therefore more comprehensive observations than the occasional visits by busy professionals could perhaps achieve. Cultivating such networks may also help locate friends and relatives whose existence had been unknown.

 Mrs. Washington, an eighty-five-year-old black woman, lived alone in a large, ramshackle house. Utilities had been turned off for nonpayment, and Mrs. Washington would not or could not give any information about how she managed. Her house was across the street from the local fire station; and when the social worker who had been sent to do an assessment stopped there to use the telephone, she learned that Mrs. Washington had a sister who lived out of town but who visited every two weeks. She cleaned, shopped, and cooked for Mrs. Washington and carried enough water from the fire station to make basic sanitation possible until her next visit.

Following this lead, the social worker was able to locate the sister, who was extremely glad to have professional assistance in planning for Mrs. Washington. She had not known what agency to contact, and since she visited only on weekends, nothing was open to enable her to make inquiries. The fire station provided the vital link.

Locating and mobilizing a network may enable professionals to complete intervention more effectively and leave the clients, at termination, with more resources than were previously available.

The Process of Termination

Whether termination is planned or arbitrary, it should be discussed well in advance. For a planned termination discussion should focus on what has been accomplished in the view of both client and counselor. How does this compare with what was hoped for originally? Does the client see the situation differently as a result of counseling? How so? What does the client see as next steps? If the client can gain a clearer idea of what has been achieved, plans for the future will probably emerge naturally.

What the client believes to be significant about the counseling process and what he or she wants to do next may not be what the counselor anticipated. However, the client's own perceptions and plans should be supported, unless they are clearly damaging or dangerous to the client or others.

WHEN THE PROFESSIONAL RESIGNS

It often happens that a counselor or other human service professional leaves the service organization before the planned work with clients has been concluded. How should this be dealt with?

Much, of course, depends on the circumstances of the clients. Those who require ongoing practical help will need to continue and learn to take comfort in the fact that it is the agency, not any one particular individual within it, that is the source of support and assistance. If the help is essential, the clients soon accept the change in staffing, though the incoming person may hear some reactions. However, these are usually benign and nonrejecting; a dependent client cannot afford to alienate a much-needed helper. Automatic transfers must also be made in situations in which agencies have assumed major responsibility or actual guardianship for impaired clients. In such cases, of course, the responsibility cannot be unilaterally abandoned.

On the other hand, clients who were involved in a therapeutic or counseling alliance are in a different position, because their involvement was largely voluntary. When a professional's departure from the helping organization results in termination, the clients need plenty of time to absorb and integrate this loss. The longer the relationship has continued, the more time is likely to be needed. In many agencies professionals are required to give a month's notice when leaving the job. Clients need at least this much time and will benefit if more can be made available.

Sometimes, clients take the news of impending termination very casually when they first hear it. The professional may be lulled into thinking that termination is not an important issue. Later, however, feelings of grief, anger, and hopelessness may emerge. Discussions of the change should address the meaning of the loss to both client and professional but must also, as in planned terminations, focus on what has been accomplished and what may be hoped for. The question of transfer and the client's feelings about it will arise naturally in this context. When the counselor leaves, should the case be transferred to another worker?

There are arguments for and against automatic transfers. On the positive side, transfers, if possible, give clients assurance of continuity. The agency is still there despite personnel shifts. On the negative side, clients may become so angry at losing a departing counselor that they may sabotage the efforts of the replacement. If the counselor who receives a transferred case does not allow sufficient time and empathy for the client to work through what is essentially a mourning process or finds the anger too difficult to deal with, the transfer will probably not take.

It is also often true that transfer cases are added to already heavy caseloads. Receiving professionals may not have the same investment in the new additions as they did in cases they developed from their inception. It is not uncommon for new counselors to conclude that the transferred clients do not need or are not motivated to engage in further work. Whether this reflects impatience on the part of the new counselor or unrealistic concern on the part of the previous one is a moot point. It is certainly true that departing professionals often feel uncomfortable about their unfinished business with their clients and want to make it up to them by providing a replacement.

A frequently overlooked positive factor in the departure of a human service worker is that it removes the social overlay from the treatment relationship. The clients may conclude that while the relationship with the counselor had been valuable, it is not necessary to have another counselor because the clients are now capable of further growth on their own. Such decisions should, of course, be encouraged. It may be preferable to terminate existing counseling contracts and wait until the clients feel ready to seek renewed connections with the agency. If the subsequent initiative comes from the clients, the resulting work is more likely to be successful. Clients should, of course, be assured that the agency is available to them and that reentry is possible whenever they feel further help is needed. In instances where this would not be possible, other options should be discussed at the time of termination and extensive resource information given.

Because of discomfort about leaving the individual clients with unfinished business, however, the professional may wish to urge the client to accept a transfer to another helper. Nevertheless, it is wiser to let the clients wrestle with the loss before rushing in to provide a replacement. The same principle applies here as in work with the bereaved: Avoid haste in offering a substitute for what has been lost.

If, after thorough exploration, the clients strongly request to be transferred, the professional can begin to address the feelings of loss so that they will not all be dumped on the new counselor. Nevertheless, there will be grief work for the new counselor to deal with; it cannot all be done in anticipation. In preparing for a transfer, the client should be reminded several times that the new relationship will indeed be new; it will not be a repetition of the one that is coming to an end.

The logistics of transfers, if they are to take place, should also be addressed. It is customary in some agencies for the departing professional to personally introduce the new counselor to the clients. In other settings this is not the practice; and in particular situations it may not be feasible. The clients' reactions to the method should be explored and preferences honored if possible.

DEALING WITH DROPOUTS

Not all terminations happen by mutual consent or from external circumstances, such as the departure of the professional helper. Sometimes, the older person or other family members discontinue contact abruptly. They may or may not explain why they are dissatisfied with what is happening. Perhaps the plan takes longer than expected or seems like too much work. Perhaps the deterioration or other problems seem too frightening. Perhaps the intervention turns out to be different from what they had anticipated.

Virginia Hamilton, seventy-five, visited a mental health clinic asking for help because she felt she was "mentally ill." She had seen a notice in her church bulletin stating that help for the mentally ill was available, so she had called at the address given. Mrs. Hamilton believed she was mentally ill because she was experiencing memory loss. Memory is a function of the mind, right? Therefore, if her memory isn't working properly, she must be mentally ill.

Mrs. Hamilton received a comprehensive evaluation at the clinic, including a mental status examination. Her memory loss was significant, but the evaluation team believed that she could be helped to compensate for it. They set up a plan for her to meet regularly with a behavioral therapist to help her modify her routine activities and possibly her living arrangements.

Mrs. Hamilton kept several appointments, but then left angrily, saying that her memory was no better and that the doctors had deceived her. In her view treatment should lead to recovery of the damaged function. If it didn't, what good was it?

Those undergoing psychosocial interventions are not the only ones who may become disappointed and quit. Many people leave hospitals and other health care settings against medical advice. Having done so, they may be reluctant to return, especially if their departure involved a vigorous warning about what would happen to them if they refused the recommended treatment.

It is not surprising that professionals are dismayed when their clients refuse help, especially if their refusal puts them at risk. Even aside from the risk factor, professionals may feel that their time has been wasted and their expertise discounted. Such an experience is ego-deflating and often results in anger and even scolding. This reaction, while understandable, is usually counterproductive. Siegel (1986) points out that patients whose physicians have berated them for not accepting their advice are likely to avoid seeing a doctor from then on, even when they develop new or frightening symptoms. Because of their fear of an angry confrontation, they may die unnecessarily of diseases that could have been treated successfully. On the other hand, if the professional can convey a message of respect and willingness to see the patient or client again, the outcome may be different. "I don't agree with what you are doing, but I wish you well, and I'll be glad to see you again if I can help" conveys a very different message from "How can you be so irresponsible?" A dynamic intervention involves the wholehearted efforts of both clients and professional helpers. The professionals cannot intervene effectively if the clients' feelings of fear, anger, or confusion are disregarded. Even if the clients choose to leave, the door should be left open.

WHEN CLIENTS MOVE AWAY

If termination is about to occur because of a move by the client, perhaps to another community or to a more protective setting, discussion should focus on what this will mean for the client and for other family members. Time for mourning the change in life-style must be allowed before discussion of future plans can be productive. Where there has been an opportunity to mourn, the client and family may be able to evaluate the move more realistically. What will the advantages be and for whom? What disadvantages are anticipated? How can client and family find ways to compensate for them?

If the move is to a nursing home or other residential setting, the counselor may pave the way by alerting the staff of the facility to the client's needs and, if distance and agency policies permit, by making one or more visits after the move. Postmove discussions with staff and family members may also be helpful. Family members, in particular, may feel guilty and apprehensive about the move and can usually benefit from help in working through their feelings. Ideally, they should be linked to staff at the residential facility who can help them do this by answering their questions and reporting on their relative's progress. However, not all institutions have an established orientation process or staff available to help new residents and families deal with this change in their lives. At such transition points peer support groups can be particularly helpful to families. If one doesn't exist, perhaps family members can gain informal support through contacts with other families whose relatives live in the same facility. In any case families should be encouraged to continue to visit regularly. Their presence and interest facilitates better care for the resident and also helps them deal with their own feelings about placement.

WHEN A CLIENT DIES

It is an occupational hazard of work with the old that intervention may be terminated not by plan but by death. In some cases the clients are known to be seriously ill and death is anticipated. In other instances death is sudden and unexpected. In either situation what is the responsibility of the professionals who have been involved?

If the relationship has continued for some time, it is natural and appropriate for professionals to reach out to the survivors, perhaps by attending the funeral, wake, or shiva observance, making a phone call, or writing a note. It is comforting for friends and family to know that their relative was important enough to the professional helpers to warrant that kind of concern. It also helps the professionals put closure on the case. Sometimes, professionals feel that their time was wasted if in the end the client dies. Talking with the important people in the client's life may reveal that the professional's intervention or support was valued, perhaps in unexpected ways. Thus, the formal and informal helping networks can reinforce each other's worth.

Those who have provided concrete services to the client, such as housekeepers, companions, or drivers, often wish to attend the funeral or otherwise share in the mourning rituals. This is also appropriate and underscores the importance of the service and its providers to the quality of life of client and family.

Professionals may also be able to facilitate mourning among the client's peers. For instance, when a member of a senior center dies, other members may wish to attend the funeral together. If the center can arrange for transportation, it not only is a convenience to the individuals involved, but it also reinforces the bond among them.

Their friend was important and they too are important, both in themselves and to each other.

In nursing homes, where death is a frequent occurrence, staff and administration sometimes try to minimize or ignore it, hoping to avoid distressing the other residents. The empty bed is made up without comment, and no announcement is made to explain the vacant place at the table. Such an approach is likely to have the opposite effect to that intended. If no notice is taken, the message received is that residents are not important. They die, and their lives are forgotten like a tale that is written on sand. Those who survive can expect the same treatment when their turns come. Such an expectation does not foster self-esteem. Recognition of death and respect for the dead gives the living reason to believe that they too will be remembered.

PROFESSIONAL FEELINGS ABOUT SEPARATION

What is sometimes overlooked in the termination and transfer process is that professionals also experience feelings of loss. These may range from feelings of regret at giving up a successful and gratifying case, to anxiety about what will happen to the client in the hands of a stranger, to relief at finally closing the books on a difficult and/or unproductive relationship. Intermingled with feelings about particular clients are the professional's feelings about separation from the organization. The separation may be basically friendly, a prelude to career advancement or further education; or it may be hostile, the result of dissatisfaction by the worker or others. It is harder to keep negative reactions from spilling over into client relationships, but it is the mark of a professional to be able to do so. The first step is to be aware of the feelings and then to compartmentalize them when talking to clients. The task is much easier if the professional has confidants with whom feelings can be shared safely, such as a spouse, friends, colleagues outside the organization, or the professional's own therapist.

Termination is not easy, but it is worth working at. Thoughtful and sensitive termination makes it more probable that the gains made during the course of intervention will be lasting.

CHAPTER 12

Evaluation of Practice

*H*ow can professionals know whether their interventions have been helpful?

In recent years a great deal of attention has been devoted to measuring effectiveness and accountability. These concepts are related but not identical. Effectiveness is the extent to which a particular intervention did what it was supposed to do and how successful it was in correcting or alleviating the condition for which it was undertaken. Accountability refers to the question of whether clients received what they were promised or entitled to and whether it was cost-effective. Although in theory professionals are accountable to the people who receive their services, in practice they are often accountable to the organizations that fund those services, such as government bodies, insurance companies, or foundations that provide grants.

Accountability and Cost-Effectiveness

Accountability is generally measured by the extent to which required procedures have been followed. The rationale is that if the procedures that have been developed to standardize the service are adhered to, the service will be effective or at least uniform. There has been no research to measure the relationship between uniformity and effectiveness. However, uniformity of procedures does make it easier to know how many units of service have been delivered and what each cost.

Cost-effectiveness and cost containment are related concepts. The connecting link is that the most economic method of service delivery will provide more service for the same money or will free funds for other purposes.

In an effort to contain rising health care costs, funding bodies have devised various ways of capping the amount of service that will be approved and therefore reimbursed. One of the most widespread in its effects is the use of diagnostic-related groups (DRGs) as a method of predetermining how much Medicare or an insurance company will pay for a specific hospital stay. Each diagnosis is worth a certain number of hospital days. If a patient can be discharged in fewer days, the hospital receives payment for the unused days; if the stay is longer, the hospital is not paid for the excess days unless the case is successfully appealed. This has resulted in earlier discharges and greater use of outpatient treatment, even for procedures such as cataract surgery. The effect on quality of care, in the view of most users, is that patients are discharged "quicker and sicker," with the result that greater pressure is put on community health services and family resources. The end result of an effort to make health care more affordable appears to be a diminution of the quality of care in many individual cases.

Attempting to measure the value of professional services by cost containment methods has both positive and negative implications. On the positive side, since both public and private resources are limited, it is essential that people get the greatest possible value for what they expend for health care and social services. On the negative side, there may be pressure to use only the least expensive methods, without paying sufficient attention to their effectiveness in accomplishing what is needed.

Examining Impact of Intervention

Methods of measuring effectiveness cover a wide range of activities. They include quality control procedures, peer review, follow-up surveys, research on treatment methods, and various systems of evaluating individual practice. In addition to these, supervision, consultation, and continuing education provide opportunities for critiquing and upgrading one's work with clients.

QUALITY CONTROL

Quality control procedures, which are generally used in hospitals and to some extent in clinics and community settings, seek to measure outcomes of patient or client encounters in various ways. These may include consistency and appropriateness of referrals, adherence to recommended procedures, or the extent to which an identified condition has improved. They are useful in determining whether all members of a target population were actually served. For instance, if hospital policy is that all persons over age seventy are automatically referred to Social Service, it is a simple matter to compare patient ages and number of referrals. What may not be so easy to measure is the nature of the activities resulting from referral. How thorough was the exploration of need, and how effective was the resulting plan? Capturing such data might be accomplished through a combination of reading the charts and making follow-up calls to patients or family members to learn how the plan worked out. This is not a matter of simple counting. It involves both judgment and person hours devoted to the activity. Even on a limited basis, however, it may provide a fairly accurate estimate of how patients are serviced and who tends to fall through the cracks. Other measures of quality control may include completeness of recording by all persons charged with that responsibility so as to secure a complete picture of the treatment provided in each case or written explanations of any departures from usual procedure.

PEER REVIEW

Peer review refers to the practice of having treatment reviewed by members of the same discipline as that of the therapist — that is, physician treatment by physicians in the same specialty, nursing by nurses, social work by social workers, and psychiatry by psychiatrists. The intent is to bring state-of-the-art knowledge to bear on the work of individual practitioners. It may be done when questions arise about the handling of particular cases or, more commonly, as a prerequisite to third-party payments by insurance companies or government agencies. In such instances it is more geared to consistency of funding decisions than to excellence of practice.

CONSUMER SURVEYS

Consumer or follow-up surveys are more typical of community agencies than of hospitals. The intent is to find out the opinions of those who received a service as to its effectiveness. The consumer survey may be done in several ways. Clients or clients and professionals may complete an evaluation form at the time of termination. This helps identify whether professional and client agreed or disagreed about the outcome of intervention. Another method is to have a follow-up interview, in person or by telephone, several months or even several years after termination. This highlights what the client remembers about the experience and whether gains have been maintained. This may be particularly enlightening when contrasted with the termination interview, if one was held. Surveys also identify clients' felt needs for other services, which were not provided. This information may lead to the development of new programs.

RESEARCH ON TREATMENT METHODS

Research on various methods of treatment, both medical and psychosocial, is extensive and is regularly reported in professional journals. Keeping abreast of research developments exposes the professional to new ideas that may be tried out in individual practice. It may be particularly valuable for a group of professionals in the same discipline, such as nursing, social work, occupational or physical therapy, or others, to meet and report on articles they have read. Gerontological and geriatric journals cut across all disciplines and may be used as an additional resource. It may also be useful for such groups to consider how research outside the field of aging may be applied to or adapted for an aging client population.

EVALUATION OF INDIVIDUAL PRACTICE

The methods described above are useful in identifying trends and probabilities. But how can a professional measure progress in a particular case? After goals have been established with a client, how can both client and professional estimate how close they are to being reached?

Single-system design research.   Single-system design is a method that lends itself to both research and case monitoring (Bloom and Fisher, 1982). As a research method, it involves measures of validity and reliability, which will not be discussed here. Those who wish to pursue the research aspects should consult the Bloom and Fisher text, which is both detailed and readable. As a method of case monitoring, it involves setting goals, identifying behaviors that indicate progress or lack of progress toward those goals, and systematically recording the behaviors. For instance, a family caregiver of an Alzheimer's patient might have the goal of reducing the patient's catastrophic reactions of screaming, fighting, or uncontrolled weeping. The professional who is working with the family may provide explanations of these behaviors and suggest methods for their reduction, such as simplifying routines, guiding by touch rather than by verbal instructions, and maintaining a calm attitude. The caregiver might then keep a diary of the dates and times when catastrophic reactions occur. This has several advantages. First, a list shows actual occurrence rather than a global impression of frequency and does not depend on the caregiver's mood at the time of the discussion. Second, a documented decrease in the frequency of undesired behaviors reinforces feelings of success and hopefulness. Third, specific episodes can be discussed to determine what may have triggered them. This helps focus the efforts of the professional and client on the areas where further intervention is needed. The diary can and should be simple: for example, "10:00 A.M., Tuesday. Father refused bath, yelled." The diary is used as a memory aid to focus discussion; it is not supposed to be an exhaustive (or exhausting) document.

Single-system design works best when the older client or someone in the family can act as recorder, since this increases client investment in the project. It can also be used with service personnel, such as housekeepers or companions, as an aid to training and as reinforcement of successful intervention.

Perhaps the client lives alone and cannot maintain records or has no interest in doing so. Can single-system design be utilized? It can be, but the professional would have to initiate the recording. Suppose, for instance, the client is severely depressed. The behavior selected to show change in the depressed affect might be the number of times during an interview that the client initiates a comment rather than responding to a question, or the number and duration of crying episodes, or the number of comments indicating interest in some current or future activity, to name some possibilities. The number of times a behavior occurs could be recorded unobtrusively with check marks on a card or a piece of masking tape attached to wrist or briefcase or with an inexpensive golf score counter. If the client agrees to having the interview tape-recorded, the worker can study the tape later. This allows not only a count of the selected behaviors but also a means of exploring what led up to them. Reviewing the tape with a supervisor or a peer group of colleagues may lead to further understanding of the client's style of relating. In some cases playing part or all of the tape for the client brings home a realization of what is being said.

Jean Stroud, a woman in her forties, brought her eighty-one-year-old mother, Maude Whitman, to an agency providing services to the elderly. Her objective was to get her mother to accept some services, such as shopping and transportation. Mrs. Stroud's work schedule did not allow her to do these things as frequently as she felt her mother wanted them done.

Mrs. Whitman, however, insisted she was perfectly willing to wait until her daughter was able to escort her on these errands. Mrs. Stroud felt that her mother was "laying a guilt trip" on her, trying to force more frequent contacts. Mrs. Whitman insisted she was doing no such thing. Besides, she had friends in the building who helped her with errands when necessary.

It became obvious to the social worker who was conducting the interview that the two women were talking past each other and that neither was hearing what the other said. She suggested that they tape the interview and play it back. They agreed. When the tape was played back, both of them were surprised. Mrs. Stroud realized that the guilt trip was more in her head than in her mother's mouth. Mrs. Whitman was relieved to be allowed to manage on her own, without services she considered intrusive and unnecessary. They had finally heard each other.

No matter how the progress of an intervention is being measured, the professional will, of course, be alert to unforeseen changes. If a client suddenly begins talking about suicide, for instance, the new factor must be explored and dealt with. Research must not interfere with the needs of the client. It is also important to take into account changes in affect or in the intensity of a behavior, not only its frequency. In general, however, intervention will be enhanced rather than retarded by having a means of tracking what is going on, as long as the means does not become an end in itself.

In addition to recording behaviors, another means of tracking is by administering a standardized measure, such as a rating scale for contentment or self-esteem, at intervals before, during, and at the conclusion of intervention (Hudson, 1982). Some clients are more amenable to responding to a relatively short questionnaire than to more elaborate recording methods. The professional must exercise judgment as to what seems most suitable to the problem being addressed and to the needs and abilities of the client.

Goal Attainment Scaling. Another method of documenting progress toward established goals is called Goal Attainment Scaling. It was originally developed at the Hennepin County Mental Health Center in Minnesota (Kiresuk and Sherman, 1968). It has since been replicated in a variety of settings. Examples of use with an older population are a study of hospital discharge planning (Spani, Kiresuk, and Lund, 1977) and a companion service and respite care program (McDonald, Mitchell, and Schuerman, 1988).

The principal features of the Goal Attainment Scale are (1) establishing goals, (2) listing obstacles to goal attainment, and (3) indicating what would constitute most favorable, least favorable, and most probable outcomes of intervention.

In the companion study the agreed-upon goal was hiring a part-time companion to assist in the care of Mr. Lapidus, seventy-six, who was limited in his ability to handle daily routines because of severe muscle weakness. Mr. Lapidus and his daughter and son-in-law wanted someone of their own ethnic background, but no such person was available. This constituted an obstacle to achieving the goal. However, the family agreed to interview candidates of different backgrounds. In predicting most favorable, least favorable, and most probable outcomes, staff decided that the best possible scenario would be for the family to interview one companion and hire him or her; the worst would be that they would interview many candidates but not hire any of them; and the most likely would be that after interviewing several, they would agree to hire one on a trial basis. In this case the family did hire the first companion interviewed, so the most favorable outcome was achieved.

Subsequent goals would deal with the match between client and companion: would family and client be well satisfied and retain the companion; would they be somewhat dissatisfied but able to work out the problems involved; or would they be so dissatisfied that the companion would be discharged in a very short time? The work of the professional staff would focus on identifying the problems and helping client, family, and companion work out solutions. If the match proved unworkable, establishing another goal would be discussed with client and family. Possibilities would include finding another companion or considering a totally different method of care.

One advantage of Goal Attainment Scaling is that it gives recognition to partial successes. If, in a situation such as that of Mr. Lapidus, the companion lasted only long enough to enable the daughter and son-in-law to take a brief vacation, that would be a partial success. Because of the first experience, later attempts to hire a companion or other helper might have a more satisfactory outcome.

As in the single-system design method, goals are established with the client or clients, not in spite of them or in their absence. This helps clarify the tasks of both clients and professionals. Because of the structure of Goal Attainment Scaling, goals are partialized and very clearly specified. This enables practitioners, no matter what their professional disciplines, to focus their efforts on one goal at a time.

Goal Attainment Scaling lends itself very readily to an interdisciplinary team approach. Everyone is working toward the same goal, but members of different disciplines have different responsibilities in contributing to it. The structure helps to minimize turf battles and finger pointing and to maximize collaboration and complementarity.

Single-system design and Goal Attainment Scaling are two methods of practice evaluation that can be adapted to a variety of problems and situations. They are not the only ones that might be used or developed. But if practitioners want to gauge the effect of their practice, two characteristics of an effective instrument of practice evaluation to look for are structure and flexibility. Without structure it is difficult to measure progress; without flexibility the measurement system is too limiting. The object is to clarify client situations in order to make them workable, not to encase them in a straitjacket of rules and regulations.

Self-Evaluation of Practice

Even in the absence of a formal evaluation instrument, professionals exercise judgment about the effectiveness of what they are doing. They also rely on supervision, consultation, and continuing-education opportunities to enhance their expertise and measure their accomplishments by their own standards and the objective standards of others.

EVALUATION BY OBSERVATION AND JUDGMENT

A nurse who is teaching self-administration of insulin shots to a patient who has hand tremors in addition to diabetes knows when the patient has succeeded. Furthermore, she or he can identify steps in the learning process as they are mastered. This is based on the nurse's judgment of whether or not progress is taking place.

Similarly, a counselor recognizes significant shifts in a client's attitude, often before the client does.

Jane Meredith had been overwhelmed by fear of being alone since her husband suffered a stroke. When well, he had driven her everywhere, and she had become very dependent on him. In an effort to cope with her

fears of being alone and responsible, she insisted on live-in help and also considered moving to a retirement home, even though she was not satisfied with any companion she hired or with any home that she inspected. When she spontaneously commented that she knew her fearfulness was the problem, not the companion or the homes, the counselor knew she had turned an important corner. That shift permitted the counseling to focus more directly on attitude rather than environment.

Observation may also provide information on the effect of an intervention.

Mr. Verolini, a seventy-eight-year-old, was highly anxious about his health and was also hard of hearing. He frequently called the nurse who saw him at the clinic he attended to ask for advice. If she was not there, he became frantic. As his agitation increased, his hearing got worse. Because of his lack of comprehension, his calls could tie up the switchboard for many minutes at a time, affecting other callers and upsetting the switchboard operator.

The nurse he was trying to call was also assigned to spend two afternoons a week at a neighborhood center near Mr. Verolini's home. She concluded that on each of the days she was there, she would reserve fifteen or twenty minutes to meet with Mr. Verolini in person, since he heard much better face to face than on the phone. As he gained confidence in her availability, the frantic calls to the clinic decreased from three or four a week to one or two per month. The intervention, based on practice judgment, had clearly achieved its objective.

Formal methods of measurement can help the professional avoid aimless or unfocused activity, but they cannot substitute for judgment. As aids to observation they can be very valuable, but they cannot replace it. One must guard against allowing the form to become more important than the substance. To some extent, this is a hazard in learning any new method. But the hazard tends to decrease with familiarity. In the end one still has to rely on observation and judgment—what Professor Wayne Miller, who taught statistics at the University of Chicago, called "the difficult method of inspection."

SUPERVISION AND CONSULTATION

The methods discussed so far are suitable for professionals working individually or as team members. Another means of evaluating practice is by drawing on the expertise of a more experienced member of one's own or another discipline, through supervision or consultation.

Nearly everyone who works for an organization has a supervisor. The nature of the supervision may be purely administrative, but it may also be clinical or practice-oriented. If so, the supervisor can be helpful by enabling the practitioner to examine his or her work more comprehensively and perhaps to gain a different perspective. The description in Chapter 11 of a counselor's use of supervision in clarifying her frustrating work with Mrs. Appleton as being characteristic of the client's personality is a case in point.

A supervisor, not being directly involved with the client, can be more detached and objective in evaluating what is going on. Involvement is necessary for effective intervention, but it makes objectivity more difficult. One's own biases and blind spots may be obscured. The supervisor, being further away from the trees, can often see the forest more clearly. It is not a matter of greater knowledge so much as optimum distance.

As an adjunct to clinical supervision, or in its absence, agencies often bring in consultants. In organizations where psychotherapy and supportive counseling are offered, these consultants are frequently psychiatrists. However, consultants may belong to many other disciplines as well, depending on the needs of the staff and the mission of the organizations that retain them. The purpose of bringing in consultants is twofold: to help the staff gain a deeper knowledge of particular cases or issues and to expose them to principles that will give them a more comprehensive understanding of the field of aging and the situations that occur therein.

One issue that both consultants and supervisors must often address is the feelings of staff about their clients in multigeneration families. Ageism and the dread of being old (despite wanting a long life) is pervasive in society and affects human service workers as it does others. Although it is unlikely that those who dislike and avoid the old will be attracted to work for agencies serving that population, ageism may take less blatant forms. Some professionals act as if they believed all old people were fragile or incompetent and are more protective or paternalistic than is good for their clients. Others who have age-integrated caseloads are less hopeful about their older clients and devote less creative attention to them. A difficulty experienced by some young professionals is that although they have no trouble establishing rapport with old people, they have a hard time relating to the middle-aged sons and daughters of the elderly. The adult children belong to the same age group as the professionals' own parents, and dealing with them can stir up unresolved issues in their own relationships. They may have trouble confronting or challenging the middle generation or may go to the opposite extreme and be unreasonably critical of the adult children's relationship with their elders. A consultant or supervisor can often help staff identify and understand such feelings so that they do not interfere with the work to be done.

If the organization does not provide consultation or clinical supervision, a group of professionals may collectively hire a consultant for themselves. Meeting regularly as a group, they can share the consultant's fee and also learn from each other. Professionals who offer consultation services can be located through professional journals and the newsletters of local professional organizations. Consultation in this format is usually similar to agency consultation in that it combines case discussion with the teaching of principles.

CONTINUING EDUCATION AND EVALUATION OF PRACTICE

For professionals in the field of aging, there are many opportunities for continuing education. Books, periodicals, seminars, conferences, workshops, and courses provide a wide range of information on many subjects. In group education settings, such as conferences, workshops, and seminars, discussion among members of the audience adds to the information provided by speakers or faculty. Time and financial constraints force one to set priorities, since no one can experience everything that might be useful. Agencies usually set a limit on the amount of time and/or financial support they can allow for professional education and in many instances cannot offer such encouragement at all. If they do, they should expect those allowed time for educational opportunities to share what they learned with remaining staff. This may prove a bonus, because reflection and discussion with colleagues helps all of them adapt new ideas to their own practice situations.

Sometimes, professional conferences provide volunteer opportunities for professionals or students who are able to help with registrations or other services in return for free attendance at lectures. This can be both a financial and an educational asset.

For professionals working with the elderly and their families, time devoted to professional education might be divided between gerontology, practice with families, and new learning in one's own discipline. An interdisciplinary approach also requires a degree of familiarity with the new learning being developed in other disciplines. It is not enough to be a competent specialist in one's own corner of the field. Evaluation of practice also means being able to understand the relationship of one's own area of expertise to the contributions of others.

New learning and ongoing evaluation of practice are both essential to professional excellence. Indeed, new learning is an important means of sharpening one's evaluation skills. This applies to evaluation of one's own practice as much as to evaluation of client needs and abilities. Intervention is a dynamic interaction between professional and clients that needs to be continually reexamined to ensure maximum effectiveness. Among the many methods of practice evaluation that are available, it is up to the individual to choose those most likely to be helpful. However, the choice may be considerably enriched by the contributions of colleagues.

In essence, it is the interdisciplinary multigenerational character of gerontological and geriatric work that attracts and stimulates those who are engaged in helping aging families. In the final analysis, the most significant professional evaluation is the one that examines one's work and finds it rewarding, gratifying, and forever challenging.

References

Aging America: Trends and Projections (1987–1988 edition). U.S. Senate Special Committee on Aging, in conjunction with the American Association of Retired Persons, the Federal Council on the Aging, and the United States Administration on Aging. Based on U.S. Census Data.

American Association of Retired Persons (AARP). Prescription Drugs: A Survey of Consumer Use, Attitudes and Behavior. Washington, D.C.: 1984.

Anderson, C., and S. Stewart. *Mastering Resistance: A Practical Guide to Family Therapy.* New York: The Guilford Press, 1983.

American Association of Retired Persons. *A Profile of Older Americans*, 1986. Washington, D.C. Based on data from the U.S. Department of Health and Human Services.

Ascione, F.J., et al. "Seniors and pharmacists: Improving the dialogue." *American Pharmacy*, 5, 1980.

Blenkner, M. "Social work and family relationships, with some thoughts on filial maturity." In E. Shanas and G. Streib (Eds.), *Social Structure and the Family: Generational Relations.* Englewood Cliffs, N.J.: Prentice-Hall, 1965.

Bloom, B. "Prevention of mental disorders: Recent advances in theory and practice." *Community Mental Health Journal*, 15, 1979.

Bloom, M., and J. Fischer. *Evaluating Practice: Guidelines for the Accountable Professional.* Englewood Cliffs, N.J.: Prentice-Hall, 1982.

Blythe, R. *The View in Winter*. New York: Harcourt Brace Jovanovich, 1979.

Boszormenyi-Nagy, I., and G. Spark. *Invisible Loyalties*. New York: Harper and Row, 1973.

Botwinick, J. *Aging and Behavior* (2nd ed.). New York: Springer, 1978.

Bowen, M. *Family Therapy in Clinical Practice*. New York: Jason Aronson, 1978.

Bowlby, J. *Attachment and Loss*. New York: Basic Books. In three volumes: Volume I, *Attachment*, 1969; Volume II, *Separation*, 1973; Volume III, *Loss*, 1980.

Brink, T.L. (Ed.). *Clinical Gerontology: A Guide to Assessment and Intervention*. New York: Haworth Press, 1986.

Brody, E. "Women in the middle and family help to older people." *The Gerontologist*, 25, 1, 1985.

Brody, E. "Parent care as a normative family stress." *The Gerontologist*, 25, 1, 1985.

Buckwalter, K.C. "Overcoming barriers to service delivery for the mentally ill elderly." Paper presented at the American Society on Aging Regional Seminar on Mental Health and Aging; Cleveland, Ohio, September 1988.

Bumagin, V., and K. Hirn. *Aging is a Family Affair*. New York: Crowell, 1979.

Burack-Weiss, A. "Clinical aspects of case management." *Generations*, 12, 5, 1988.

Busse, E. "Old age." In S. Greenspan and G. Pollock (Eds.), *The Course of Life: Psychoanalytic Contributions Toward Understanding Personality Development*. Volume III: *Adulthood and the Aging Process*. Adelphi, Md.: National Institutes of Mental Health, 1980.

Busse, E., and D. Blazer. "Disorders related to biological functioning." In E. Busse and D. Blazer (Eds.), *Handbook of Geriatric Psychiatry*. New York: Van Nostrand Reinhold Company, 1980.

Butler, R.N., and M. Lewis. *Aging and Mental Health* (3rd ed.). St. Louis; C.V. Mosby Company, 1982.

Butler, R.N., and M. Lewis. "Life review therapy: Putting memories to work in individual and group psychotherapy." *Geriatrics*, November 1974.

Butler, R. N., and M. Lewis. *Sex After Sixty: A Guide for Men and Women for Their Later Years*. New York: Harper and Row, 1976.

Butler, R.N. "The life review: An interpretation of reminiscence." *Psychiatry*, 26,65, 1963.

Butler, R.N. *Why Survive? Being Old in America*. New York: Harper and Row, 1975.

Capra, F. *The Tao of Physics*. Boulder, Colo.: Shambhala Publications, 1975.

Carter, E.A., and M. McGoldrick. "The family life cycle and family therapy." In D. Carter and M. McGoldrick (Eds.), *The Family Life Cycle: A Framework for Family Therapy*. New York: Gardner Press, Inc., 1980.

Cohen, D., and C. Eisdorfer. *The Loss of Self.* New York: Norton, 1986.

Cohler, B.J. "Adult development psychology and reconstruction in psycho-analysis." In S.I. Greenspan and G.H. Pollock (Eds.), *The Course of Life, Volume III.* Washington, D.C.: National Institutes of Mental Health, 1982.

Cutler, N.E. "Age variations in the dimensionality of life satisfaction." *Journal of Gerontology,* 34, 573–578, 1979.

Darbyshire, J.D. "The hearing loss epidemic: A challenge to gerontology." *Research on Aging,* 6, 4, 1984.

Diagnostic and Statistical Manual of Mental Disorders III. Washington, D.C.: American Psychiatric Association, 1980.

Edelson, J.S. "The mentally impaired aged: reordering priorities." *Journal of Jewish Communal Service,* 53, 1, 1976.

Erikson, E. *Childhood and Society* (2nd ed.). New York: W.W. Norton, 1963.

Fisher, D.C. "Almera Hawley Canfield." In *A Harvest of Stories.* New York: Harcourt Brace and Company, 1956.

Flarsheim, A. "Treatability." In P.L. Giovacchini (Ed.), *Tactics and Techniques in Psychoanalytic Therapy.* New York: Science House, Inc., 1972.

Flor-Henry, P. "On certain aspects of the localization of the cerebral systems regulating and determining emotion." *Biological Psychiatry,* 14, 1979.

Garfinkel, R. "The reluctant therapist." *The Gerontologist,* 15, 2, 1975.

George, L.K. "Life satisfaction in later life." *Generations,* 10, 3, 1986.

Germain, C.B., and A. Gittelman. *The Life Model of Social Work Practice.* New York: Columbia University Press, 1980.

German, P.S., S. Shapiro, and E.A. Skinner. "Mental health of the elderly: Use of health and mental health services." *Journal of the American Geriatric Society,* 33, 4, 1983.

Gerner, R., and L. Jarvik. "Antidepressant drug treatment in the elderly." In E. Friedman, F. Mann, and S. Gerson (Eds.), *Depression and Antidepressants: Implications for Consideration and Treatment.* New York: Raven Press, 1984.

Gold, D. *Siblings in Old Age: Their Relationships and Roles.* (Monograph.) Chicago: Center for Applied Gerontology, 1987.

Goldfarb, A.I. "Minor maladjustments in the aged." In S. Arieti (Ed.), *American Handbook of Psychiatry,* Volume I. New York: Basic Books, 1959.

Goldfarb, A.I., and J. Sheps. "Psychotherapy of the aged." *Psychosomatic Medicine,* 16, 3, 1954. (Reprinted in S. Steury and M.L. Blank (Eds.), *Readings in Psychotherapy with Older People.* Washington, D.C.: U.S. Department of Health, Education and Welfare-National Institutes of Mental Health, 1977.

Goodwin, F., A. Prange, R. Post, G. Muscettola, and M. Lipton. "Potentiation of antidepressant effects of L-triiodothyronine in tricyclic nonresponders." *American Journal of Psychiatry,* 130, 1, 1982.

Graham, J. *In the Company of Others; Understanding the Human Needs of Cancer Patients.* New York: Harcourt Brace Jovanovich, 1982.

Greene, R. *Social Work with the Aged and Their Families.* Hawthorne, N.Y.: Aldine de Gruyter, 1986.

Gubrium, J. *Living and Dying at Murray Manor.* New York: St. Martin's Press, 1975.

Gutmann, D.L. "An exploration of ego configurations in middle and late life." In B.L. Neugarten and Associates, *Personality in Middle and Late Life,* New York: Atherton Press, 1964.

Gutmann, D.L. Unpublished lecture presented to Society for Life Cycle Psychology and Aging, Northwestern University, 1979.

Gutmann, D. *Reclaimed Powers.* New York: Basic Books, 1987.

Gwyther, L. "Family therapy with older adults." *Generations,* 10, 3, 1986.

Hammarlund, E.R., J.R. Ostrom, and A.J. Kethley. "The effects of drug counseling and other educational strategies on drug utilization of the elderly." *Medical Care,* 23, 2, 1985.

Hayter, J. "Hypothermia and hyperthermia in older persons." *Journal of Gerontological Nursing,* 6, 2, 1980.

Herr, J., and J. Weakland. *Counseling Elders and Their Families.* New York: Springer, 1979.

Horne, J. *Caregiving: Helping an Aging Loved One.* Washington, DC: American Association of Retired Persons; Glenview, Il.: Scott, Foresman, and Company, 1985.

Hudson, W.W. *The Clinical Measurement Package: A Field Manual.* Homewood, Ill: Dorsey Press, 1982.

Kadushin, A. *The Social Work Interview* (2nd ed.). New York: Columbia University Press, 1983.

Kahana, R.J. "Psychoanalysis in later life." *Journal of Geriatric Psychiatry,* 11, 1978.

Kalish, R.A. "Death and dying in a social context." In R.H. Binstock and E. Shanas (Eds.), *Handbook of Aging and the Social Sciences.* New York: Van Nostrand Reinhold, 1976.

Kane, R.A., and R.L. Kane. *Assessing the Elderly: A Practical Guide to Measurement.* Lexington, Mass.: D.C. Heath and Company, 1981.

Kiresuk, T.J., and R.E. Sherman. "Goal attainment scaling: A general method for evaluating comprehensive community mental health programs." *Community Mental Health Journal,* 4, 1968.

Klein, M. "A contribution to the psychogenesis of manic-depressive states." In *Love, Guilt and Reparation and Other Works,* Volume I. London: The Hogarth Press, 1975.

Klein, M. *The Psychoanalysis of Children.* (Originally published by Leonard and Virginia Woolf.) London: The Hogarth Press, 1932.

Korzybski, A. "General semantics, psychiatry, psychotherapy, and prevention." *American Journal of Psychiatry,* 98, 2, 1941.

Kuebler-Ross, E. *On Death and Dying.* New York: Macmillan Publishing Company, 1970.

Kurtz, K.J. "Hypothermia in the elderly: The cold facts." *Geriatrics,* 37, 1, 1982.

Langer, E.J., and J. Rodin. "The effects of choice and enhanced personal responsibility for the aged: A field experiment in an institutional setting." *Journal of Personality and Social Psychology,* 34, 1976.

Lieberman, M.A., and S.S. Tobin. *The Experience of Old Age: Stress, Coping, and Survival.* New York: Basic Books, 1983.

Lesage, J., and M. Zwygart-Stauffacher. "Detection of medication misuse in elders." *Generations,* 12, 4, 1988.

Leventhal, E.A., and T.R. Prohaska. "Age, symptom interpretation, and health behavior." *Journal of the American Geriatrics Society,* 34, 1986.

Levinson, D.J., C.N. Darrow, E.B. Klein, M.H. Levinson, and B. McKee. *The Seasons of a Man's Life.* New York: Alfred A. Knopf, 1977.

Lipton, M.A., and C.B. Nemeroff. "The biology of aging and its role in depression." In G. Usdin and C.K. Hofling (Eds.), *Aging: The Process and the People.* New York: Brunner-Mazel, 1978.

Mace, N.L., and P.V. Rabins. *The 36-Hour Day.* New York: Warner Books (by arrangement with Johns Hopkins University Press), 1981.

Mahler, M., F. Pine, and A. Bergman. *The Psychological Birth of the Human Infant.* New York: Basic Books, 1975.

Mahoney, M.J., and D.B. Arnhoff. "Cognitive and self-control therapies." In S.L. Garfield and A. Bergin (Eds.), *Handbook of Psychotherapy and Behavior Change* (2nd ed.). New York; John Wiley and Sons, 1978.

Maluccio, A.N. (Ed.). *Promoting Competence in Clients.* New York: Free Press, 1981.

McDonald, M., J. Mitchell, and C. Schuerman. "How do I know when I've helped: A look at goal attainment scaling." Paper presented at the 34th Annual Meeting of the American Society on Aging, 1988.

McNight, J. "Professionalized service and disabling help." In I. Illich (Ed.), *Disabling Professions.* London: M. Boyars, 1977.

Montgomery, R.J.V., and J. Prothero (Eds.). *Developing Respite Services for the Elderly.* Seattle, Wash.: University of Washington Press, 1986.

Nahemow, S., and L. Ponsada. *Geriatric Diagnostics: A Case Study Approach.* New York: Springer, 1983.

Neugarten, B.L. "The awareness of middle age." In B.L. Neugarten (Ed.), *Middle Age and Aging.* Chicago: University of Chicago Press, 1968.

Parkes, C.M. *Bereavement.* London: Tavistock, 1972; New York: International Universities Press, 1972.

Parkes, C.M., and R.S. Weiss. *Recovery from Bereavement.* New York: Basic Books, 1983.

Parsons, R., S. Hernandez, and J. Jorgenson. "Integrated practice; Framework for problem solving." *Social Work,* 33, 5, 1988.

Peck, R. "Psychological developments in the second half of life." In B.L. Neugarten (Ed.), *Middle Age and Aging.* Chicago: University of Chicago Press, 1968.

Pfeifer, E. (Ed.). *Multidimensional Functional Assessment: The OARS Methodology, A Manual.* Durham, N.C.: Center for the Study of Aging and Human Development, 1977.

Pincus, L. *Death and the Family.* New York: Vintage Books/Random House, 1974.

Plomp, R., and A.J. Duquesnoy. "Room acoustics for the aged." *Journal of the Acoustical Society of America,* 68, 6, 1980.

Rathbone-McCuan, E. "Promoting help-seeking behaviors among elders with chemical dependencies." *Generations,* 12, 4, 1988.

Resnik, H.L.P. "Suicide." In H.I. Kapman, A.M. Freedman, and B.J. Sadock (Eds.), *Comprehensive Textbook of Psychiatry* (3rd ed.). Baltimore: Williams and Wilkins, 1980.

Ripple, L., E. Alexander, and B. Polemis. *Motivation Capacity and Opportunity: Studies in Casework Theory and Practice.* Social Service Monographs, 2nd series. Chicago: University of Chicago Press, 1964.

Rupp, R.R. "Understanding the problems of presbycusis." *Geriatrics,* 32, 1970.

Ryff, C.D. "Successful aging: A developmental approach." *The Gerontologist,* 22, 2, 1982.

Sandler, A.-M. "Problems in psychoanalysis of an aging narcissistic patient." *Journal of Geriatric Psychiatry,* 11, 1978.

Schaie, K.W., and S.L. Willis. *Adult Development and Aging (2nd ed.).* Boston: Little, Brown and Company, 1986.

Schiff, S.M. "Treatment approaches for older alcoholics." *Generations,* 12, 4, 1988.

Schultz, R., and B.H. Hanusa. "Long-term effects of control and predictability-enhancing interventions: Findings and ethical issues." *Journal of Personality and Social Psychology,* 36, 1978.

Seligman, M.E.P. *Helplessness: On Depression, Development and Death.* San Francisco: Freeman, 1975.

Shanas, E. "The family as a social support system in old age." *The Gerontologist,* 19, 1979.

Siegel, B.S. *Love, Medicine and Miracles.* New York: Harper and Row, 1986.

Silverstone, B., and A. Burack-Weiss. *Social Work Practice with the Frail Elderly and Their Families.* Springfield, Il.: Charles C. Thomas, 1983.

Sommers, T., and L. Shields. *Women Take Care.* Gainsville, Fl.: Triad Publishing Company, 1987.

Spano, R.M., T.J. Kiresuk, and S. Lund. "An operational model to achieve accountability for social work in health care." *Social Work in Health Care,* 3, 1977.

Spirduso, W.W., and P. Clifford. "Replication of age and physical activity effects on reaction and movement time." *Journal of Gerontology,* 33, 1978.

Starr, B., and M. Weiner. *The Starr-Weiner Report on Sexuality in the Mature Years.* New York: McGraw-Hill, 1981.

Stenback, A. "Depression and suicidal behavior in old age." In J. Birren and R.B. Sloan (Eds.), *Handbook of Mental Health and Aging.* Englewood Cliffs, N.J.: Prentice-Hall, 1980.

Stoddard, S. *The Hospice Movement.* New York: Stein and Day, 1978.

Sussman, M.B., and L. Burchinal. "Kin family network: Unheralded structure in current conceptualizations of family functioning." *Marriage and Family Living,* 24, 1962.

Thompson, L.S., and D. Gallegher. "Psychotherapy for late life depression." *Generations,* 10, 3, 1986.

Tobin, S.S. *The Unique Psychology of the Very Old: Implications for Practice.* Chicago, Il: Center for Applied Gerontology, 1987.

Turner, H. "Use of the relationship in casework treatment of aged clients." *Social Casework,* 42, 5–6, 1961.

Wacker, R. "The good die younger: Does combativeness help the old survive?" *Science,* 85, 6, 1985.

Warheit, G.J., S.A. Arey, and E. Swanson. "Patterns of drug use: An epidemiological overview." *Journal of Drug Issues,* 6, 1976.

Weintraub, M. "A different view of patient compliance in the elderly." In R.E. Vestal (Ed.), *Drug Treatment in the Elderly.* Boston: ADIS Health Service Press, 1984.

Wekstein, L. *Handbook of Suicidology: Principles, Problems, and Practice.* New York: Brunner/Mazer, 1979.

Wendley, P.G., and R.J. Schiedt. "Person-environment dialectics: Implications for competent functioning in old age." In L.W. Poon (Ed.), *Aging in the 1980's.* Washington, D.C.: American Psychological Association, 1980.

Wertenbaker, L.T. *Death of a Man.* New York: Bantam Books (by arrangement with Random House), 1957.

Wilensky, H., and J. Barmack. "Interests of doctoral students in clinical psychology in work with older adults." *Journal of Gerontology,* 21, 1966.

Williamson, D. "Personal authority via termination of the intergenerational hierarchial boundary: A 'new' stage in the family life cycle." *Journal of Marital and Family Therapy,* 7, 4, 1981.

Winnicott, D.W. *The Maturational Processes and the Facilitating Environment.* New York: International Universities Press, 1965.

Zarit, S., K. Reever, and J. Bach-Peterson. "Relatives of the impaired elderly: Correlates of feelings of burden." *The Gerontologist,* 20, 6, 1980.

Zweibel, N. Unpublished study conducted at the Council for Jewish Elderly, Chicago, 1980.

Index

About the Authors

Victoria E. Bumagin, M.S.S.W., is Director of the Center for Applied Gerontology and of Professional Social Services with the Council for Jewish Elderly in Chicago. As Educator, supervisor, and clinical practitioner, she has trained human service workers both here and abroad, is currently Associate Professor at the Loyola University School of Social Work and a partner in GeroPsychiatric Associates, a treatment and consultation practice for the aged and their families. For her services on behalf of the elderly, she was elected to the Senior Hall of Fame for the City of Chicago in 1986, and was named Distinguished Chicago Gerontologist by the Association of Gerontology in Higher Education in 1988. She holds many local and national honorary appointments and elected positions, including board memberships with the Metropolitan Chicago Coalition on Aging, the American Society on Aging, the National Council in the Aging, the Columbia University School of Social Work Alumni Association, and the Wilmette, Illinois Senior Resources Commission. A Fellow of the Gerontological Society of America, she is also a member of the editorial board of its journal, *The Gerontologist.* A prolific writer and public speaker, she has authored numerous articles in professional journals and has coauthored several works with Kathryn Hirn.

Kathryn F. Hirn, M.S.W., is a gerontological social worker in private practice providing counseling for the aged and their families. She was a supervisor of social work programs at the Council for Jewish Elderly for 15 years and became a social worker with United Charities of Chicago after receiving her degree from the University of Chicago. She is a member of the board of the Chicago Older Women's League and is active with the National Association of Social Workers, the American Society on Aging, and the Metropolitan Chicago Coalition on Aging. A poet and writer of professional articles, she and Victoria Bumagin have collaborated on two previous works: an article for the *American Journal of Psychoanalysis* entitled "Changing Relationships of Older Married Women" (1982) and an earlier book, *Aging is a Family Affair* (1979).